The Art and Science
of Physician Wellbeing

W0050677

Laura Weiss Roberts
Mickey Trockel
Editors

The Art and Science
of Physician Wellbeing

A Handbook for Physicians
and Trainees

 Springer

Editors
Laura Weiss Roberts, MD, MA
Stanford University School
of Medicine
Palo Alto, CA, USA

Mickey Trockel, MD, PhD
Stanford University School
of Medicine
Palo Alto, CA, USA

ISBN 978-3-319-42134-6   ISBN 978-3-319-42135-3   (eBook)
https://doi.org/10.1007/978-3-319-42135-3

This Springer imprint is published by the registered company Springer Nature Switzerland AG
The registered company address is: Gewerbestrasse 11, 6330 Cham, Switzerland

For my mom, Anne L. Weisskopf, RN, who is always telling me to take better care of myself.
Laura Weiss Roberts, MD, MA

For my wife, Eva Yagues Pascual, whose wisdom inspires me to let go of fear and let love reign.
Mickey Trockel, MD, PhD

Preface

In the past, physicians-in-training worked around the clock, making a few dollars a day. They lived in the hospital and were permitted to return home, briefly, on Sunday afternoons. Fully trained physicians commonly entered solo practice working 24/7, 365 days a year to care for patients in their communities and at the hospital. Doctors made home visits and took care of entire families across generations. The physician as an isolated, tireless, self-sacrificing, and perfect superhero became the cultural ideal. Doctors fulfilled their professional calling by sacrificing their more inclusive identities as complete, healthy, personally fulfilled people for their all-encompassing, all-demanding lives as physicians. The culture of medicine was built on a system of concepts, behaviors, and structures that implicitly and explicitly required physicians to set aside their wellbeing for the privilege of serving others.

Modern medicine is very different. Most physicians work in organizations and serve as team leaders and collaborators rather than solo practitioners. The time devoted to caring for patients has decreased, and the time spent on administrative activities has grown so much that the duties of the present-day physician would be unrecognizable to physicians of the past. Men and women are now entering the profession of medicine in near-equal numbers. Many physicians work part-time. Physicians make more money than in the past, but they have more debt, too. Many physicians focus on health promotion and recovery rather than disease intervention or eradication. Many physicians hold roles where they do not see patients but advance science and improve human health by innovating and partnering with others. Attitudes toward physician wellbeing have evolved as research has shown that exhausted, overburdened physicians are unhappy, make more mistakes, and leave the profession prematurely for other career opportunities or retirement.

The fundamental calling of the physician as a health professional has not changed; doctors are people who acquire specialized knowledge and skills in order to help others and society as a whole. Doctors step forward to use their strengths to do good, to avoid harm, and to serve people in need. Embracing this calling does not require isolation, exhaustion, overwhelming self-sacrifice, or the subordination of the self. In fact, doctors who themselves engage in healthy behaviors are more likely to support the healthy behaviors and illness prevention strategies of their patients. Doctors who are happy and feel a sense of purpose and alignment with the values of the organizations where they work are less likely to become burned out and demoralized.

And, as in the past, humanity continues to have a need for physicians as healers and leaders, scientists and teachers, and advocates and innovators. Though some aspects of the work may have changed, the mission and specialized knowledge and skills of physicians have a vital, impactful role in our world. The meaning has stayed the same. The model has changed.

This book affirms the evolution of the culture of medicine while embracing the fundamental, enduring sense of physicians' calling and affirming the importance of physicians as individuals whose health and wellbeing has intrinsic value and value to others. The book has three parts. The first part focuses on the nature of the health professions and on advancing a culture of wellbeing in medicine, giving particular emphasis to the idea of compassion as the quintessential motivator of physicians' actions to care for others and to care for self. The second part focuses on threats to physician wellbeing, including mistreatment during training, burnout, demands associated with the electronic health record, financial and legal anxieties, and mental illness and substance use disorders among physicians. The third part outlines approaches to strengthening physician resilience, such as the sustenance drawn from healthy relationships, mindfulness approaches, and optimal approaches to exercise, nutrition, and sleep. This book represents guidance from experts in the field of medicine and offers evidence and evidence-informed practices.

The editors and authors of this book have attempted to ensure that all information is accurate at the time of writing and consistent with general medical standards. As medical research and practice continue to advance, however, information and standards may change. No information in this book should be construed as providing treatment recommendations. For these reasons, and because human and mechanical errors sometimes occur, we recommend that readers follow the advice of physicians directly involved in the care of patients. The general principles of medical care in this publication should not be construed as specific, or complete, instructions for individual patients. The editors and authors cannot assume any legal liability for any mistakes or omissions in this book.

The editors wish to express their appreciation to the authors who contributed to this volume and to members of the editorial team whose engagement with the work makes it so much better. We specially thank Ann Tennier and Gabrielle Termuehlen of Stanford University and Richard Lansing, Caitlin Prim, and Diane Lamsback of Springer Publishing.

Palo Alto, CA, USA   Laura Weiss Roberts, MD, MA
             Mickey Trockel, MD, PhD

Contents

Contributors

Chwen-Yuen Angie Chen, MD, FACP, FASAM Stanford University, Department of Primary Care and Population Health, Palo Alto, CA, USA

Erica Frank, MD, MPH Faculty of Medicine, School of Population and Public Health, University of British Columbia, Vancouver, BC, Canada

Jessica A. Gold, MD, MS Washington University in St. Louis, Department of Psychiatry, St. Louis, MO, USA

Maryam Sarah Hamidi, MSc, PhD Stanford Medicine WellMD Center, Department of Psychiatry and Behavioral Sciences, Stanford, CA, USA

Debora R. Holmes, MES NextGenU.org, Clear Lake, WA, USA

Robert Horowitz, MD Stanford University School of Medicine, Stanford Prevention Research Center, Palo Alto, CA, USA

Christina Tara Khan, MD, PhD Stanford Health Care/ Stanford Children's Health/Veterans Affairs Palo Alto Health Care System, Department of Psychiatry and Behavioral Sciences, Stanford, CA, USA

Tiffany I. Leung, MD, MPH, FACP, FAMIA Maastricht University, Maastricht, The Netherlands

Maastricht University Medical Center+, Maastricht, The Netherlands

Nikitha Krishna Menon, BA Stanford University School of Medicine, Department of Psychiatry and Behavioral Sciences, Palo Alto, CA, USA

Jeffrey G. Miller, DNP, APNP, ACRN Medical College of Wisconsin, Department of Psychiatry and Behavioral Medicine, Milwaukee, WI, USA

Caroline Uchechi Okorie, MD, MPH Lucile Packard Children's Hospital and Stanford Children's Health, Department of Pediatrics, Division of Pulmonary, Asthma and Sleep Medicine, Palo Alto, CA, USA

David J. Peterson, MBA FACMPE Medical College of Wisconsin, Department of Psychiatry and Behavioral Medicine, Milwaukee, WI, USA

Jessica Rainey-Clay, MD Stanford University, Department of Emergency Medicine, Stanford, CA, USA

Kristin S. Raj, MD Stanford School of Medicine, Department of Psychiatry and Behavioral Sciences, Palo Alto, CA, USA

Christopher Sharp, MD Stanford Health Care, Stanford University School of Medicine Department of Medicine, Stanford, CA, USA

Rebecca Smith-Coggins, MD Stanford University, Department of Emergency Medicine, Stanford, CA, USA

Lindsay Stevens, MD Lucile Packard Children's Hospital and Stanford University School of Medicine Department of Pediatrics, Palo Alto, CA, USA

Mickey Trockel, MD, PhD Stanford Hospital and Clinics, Department of Psychiatry and Behavior Science, Palo Alto, CA, USA

School of Medicine, Stanford University, Palo Alto, CA, USA

Dana Welle, DO, JD Stanford Hospital, Risk Management, Stanford, CA, USA

Louise Wen Stanford University Hospital, Department of Anesthesiology, Stanford, CA, USA

Part I
Advancing Professional Calling and the Culture of Wellbeing in Medicine

Chapter 1
Calling, Compassionate Self, and Cultural Norms in Medicine

Mickey Trockel

On a fall day in New York City, I walked up a hill toward the location bordering Central Park where I would soon present to a group of physician leaders on strategies to improve physician wellness. As I hurried up the hill, pulling a travel-size suitcase and dressed like a local Manhattan businessperson, I found a man struggling to push himself up the hill in a wheelchair. His left arm was injured. He used his right arm to work the right wheel and used his left leg to push, moving inches at a time up the hill in reverse. I did what I presume most people would do in this situation—I offered to push him up the hill. At first, he declined my offer with a kind, "It's alright; I know you're busy." He looked away and continued his solitary struggle. Heeding his wishes, I started to walk away but then turned back to ask again: "Are you sure? I'm happy to push you up the hill." This time I extended a hand, and he answered

———
M. Trockel (✉)
Stanford Hospital and Clinics, Department of Psychiatry and Behavior Science, Palo Alto, CA, USA

School of Medicine, Stanford University, Palo Alto, CA, USA
e-mail: trockel@stanford.edu

© Springer Nature Switzerland AG 2019
L. Weiss Roberts, M. Trockel (eds.),
The Art and Science of Physician Wellbeing,
https://doi.org/10.1007/978-3-319-42135-3_1

with willingness to receive my help. At the top of the hill, and a short distance more to his bus stop, we said our goodbyes. Without any obvious external indications of my profession that I can recall, he said, "Thank you, doctor." Prior to that moment, I had searched my repertoire of experience in vain for a way to begin my talk to physician leaders searching for answers to the growing disillusionment and wellness needs of physicians. In guessing my profession, this man handed me the opening for my talk and added another line of evidence to the veracity of the words from former Surgeon General Vivek Murthy, "Physicians are people who answer to a calling" (Murthy 2017).

Mounting evidence indicates that physicians themselves suffer collateral damage as they fulfill their calling to alleviate suffering. Healers in training report higher than average mental health before medical school, even while engaged in rigorous study (Brazeau et al. 2014). During training, on average, physicians lose their former mental health advantage over same-age non-physicians (Dyrbye et al. 2014). In particular, compared to other professionals, physicians experience more burnout, which is defined by symptoms of work exhaustion and interpersonal disengagement (Trockel et al. 2017a). Compared to other populations, physicians have similar—not greater—levels of generalized depressive symptoms (Davis et al. 2003). It is work-specific suffering described by burnout that is epidemic among doctors, and worsening, consistent with the hypothesis that physicians are robust people often subjected to immense stress during training and practice of medicine (Shanafelt et al. 2015). A recent self-disclosure of a trauma surgeon's struggle with depression and suicidal ideation provides a compelling example:

> I didn't know it then, but I had long experienced classic signs of burnout: emotional exhaustion, depersonalization, and low perceived personal achievement. But the burnout had been waxing and waning for 22 years; now, I was in the worst episode of major depression of my life. I wanted out, out of work and out of life. I wished I would get hit by a car, and sometimes took steps to increase my risk. I felt trapped in my work and worried that I would expose my shortcomings if I sought a leave or disclosed my feelings (Weinstein 2018).

Medical Cultural Norms

Deferring Personal Needs to Serve Others

Through clerkship (typically years 3 and 4 of medical school) and on into residency, physicians in training typically sacrifice sleep, exercise, dating, and time with friends and family in order to meet training requirements that include long duty hours and intermittent study. When on duty, "patients first" ethos often propels long hours of service with little regard for basic self-care. Although many physicians have greater control over their time after completing residency, the habit of deferring self-care in service to others may persist. There are instances when this is good for patient care—stretching rather than accepting personal limits may lead to peak performance and, in some instances, make the difference needed to save a life. Physicians who stretch far outside of their comfort zone to save a patient's life are also likely to experience significant professional fulfillment.

Constant stretching beyond healthy limits, however, leads to persistent self-neglect, depletion, and less optimal performance over time. The following analogy serves to illustrate the negative effects of the "patient first" ethos: In the instance of an ambulance, we as a society have agreed to give the ambulance driver sirens and permission to drive over the speed limit, as doing so may save someone's life. Nevertheless, in most cases, speeding does not have a favorable risk-benefit ratio. Many people get used to rushing and tend to drive with a high sense of time urgency, despite circumstances that are not pressing. Similarly, there are times when a physician's push past normal healthy limits at work is indicated to save a patient's life and may provide personal/professional fulfillment. There are many other instances, however, when pushing past normal healthy limits at work does not have a favorable risk-benefit ratio. For example, completing electronic health record notes late in the evening instead of sleeping leads to daytime sleep-related impairment and increases risk for burnout. Even persistent extra volunteer work at a community clinic after hours can lead to burnout and difficulty being empathetically present with patients if it results in chronically deferred self-care. The cultural norm of placing nonemergency work in front of self-care is likely to worsen performance.

The relationship between deferred self-care and worse clinical performance is perhaps most obvious with sleep deprivation (Krause et al. 2017). One night of complete sleep deprivation, two nights in a row of less than 5 hours of sleep per night, or several days in a row of less than 6 hours of sleep per night are associated with intermittent involuntary lapses in attention and reduced affect regulation. Functional magnetic resonance imaging comparison indicated that, compared to a well-rested state, amygdala response to images of trauma is 60% greater after sleep deprivation. Physicians who defer normal sleep—a regular mandate of many postgraduate training programs—suffer greater emotional distress from trauma they face in the course of their duty and greater risk of harming a patient due to decreased cognitive performance. The case below illustrates several cultural factors that contribute to physicians' de-prioritization of self-care and sleep deprivation specifically.

Case Illustration 1.1

Dr. Stephens, a third-year surgery resident, graduated from an Ivy League undergraduate school, finished at the top of his medical school class, and trained at one of the most competitive surgical residency programs in North America. His patients loved him, and he had a reputation for a tireless work ethic and an upbeat, constantly cheerful personality. He would often say to medical students and interns "Do you know what the worst thing about every other night call is? You miss half of the good cases."·

One morning, he was not his usual self. The previous evening, he had worked particularly late for a post-call day, finally leaving the hospital at 4:00 PM. He stayed because a patient he had been caring for went into surgery at 10:00 AM, and he wanted the additional operating room experience. He also felt personally responsible for the patient's care. The chief resident initially said Dr. Stephens should not assist with the surgery because he was post-call, but he smiled and looked the other way when Dr. Stephens continued to scrub in. The difficult surgery went well, and Dr. Stephens felt particularly good about the opportunity to play an important part in the life-saving care of his patient. Dr. Stephens knew he would not be in trouble for going over maximum allowed work hours because he regularly underreported hours to ensure his report was consistent with mandated limits. When he was an intern, his senior resident taught him that this was common practice and a necessary compromise in order to get through residency *without any problems*. He was exhausted as he drove home. He fell asleep at a traffic light and woke up when someone honked after the light turned green. When he got home, he slept for 90 minutes but got up in order to get ready to go to a Broadway play with his wife. He had canceled similar plans with his wife twice in the past 3 months due to work demands. After driving home from the play, getting something to eat as quickly as he could, and getting ready for bed, he had 4 hours to sleep before getting up to make it back to the hospital in time to scrub in for an early morning surgery case his attending had suggested he help with.

Following surgery, he stopped to check on a patient, a high-ranking politician, who would soon be going home. As he walked down the hall to the patient's room, a nurse handed him a file with the patient's name on it containing printed material on postoperative care and specific discharge instructions, including follow-up care appointments for diagnosed problems. The nurse explained that she was shorthanded and asked Dr. Stephens if he could please deliver these materials to the patient.

Before he got to the patient's room, Dr. Stephens got a page from a colleague. His colleague had some extra pizza in the cafeteria and would share with Dr. Stevens if he hurried. Dr. Stephens was hungry and hurried to the cafeteria. He put the file down on the seat beside him as he ate. When he finished, he went to see his patient, but he forgot about the file and left it behind. A few minutes later, he noticed that he had forgotten the file and ran back to the cafeteria. The file was gone. A worker in the cafeteria had noticed a teenage boy laughing and taking a photo of the contents of the folder with his phone. The worker turned the file in but was unable to catch the teenage boy who took the photograph. A notified privacy officer called the nursing unit caring for the high-ranking politician and quickly learned that Dr. Stephens was the last health-care professional to have the file before leaving it in a public space. The privacy officer informed Dr. Stephens that he would soon face significant discipline, including possible termination at work as well as possible heavy civil court penalties. He could even face criminal penalties for his negligence in violation of Federal HIPAA legislation. Dr. Stephens usually exhibited immaculate organization skills and was very aware of the harsh HIPAA-related penalties that health-care organizations and health-care workers may face to if they fail to protect personal health information. He was stunned that he had forgotten the file. He did not feel like himself.

As part of a public response to the incident, hospital administration later orchestrated Dr. Stephens' dismissal. Dr. Stephens left his residency program with $300,000 in debt from medical school loans and uncertainty regarding federal court penalties he may soon face. A prominent provider of the online annual HIPAA education required of all physicians subsequently added details of Dr. Stephens' error and punishment as an example of what can happen to health-care professionals who violate HIPAA policy.

Even if not sleep-deprived, physicians who subvert their own needs in the service of others to the point of burnout are likely to deliver worse care to the patients they serve. One report indicates that each standard deviation increase in physicians' scores on the Maslach Burnout Inventory depersonalization subscale is associated with a 0.5 standard deviation longer posthospital discharge recovery time for the patients they cared for during hospitalization (Halbesleben and Rathert 2008). The study reports a standard deviation in posthospital discharge recovery time of 25 days. This means that each standard deviation increase in physicians' depersonalization is associated with an increase of more than 12 days in patients' post-discharge recovery time. Several other reports demonstrate medical errors and other indicators of lower quality of care delivered by physicians experiencing work exhaustion and depersonalization or interpersonal disengagement (Wallace et al. 2009).

Shaming Intolerance of Error

When physicians do make a mistake, they are at risk of shaming litigation and devastating personal and professional consequences. Independent of litigation risk, physicians suffer when they make a mistake that could or does hurt a patient (Schwappach and Boluarte 2009). Professional mistakes are never pleasant. In the culture of medicine, physicians often react to their own mistakes with intolerant shame and self-disparagement. As with deferment of self-care in the service of others, physicians' harsh response to their own errors is associated with increased risk of burnout and other indicators of worsening clinical performance.

Compassion in Addressing Personal Well-Being and Health-Care Quality Improvement

The cultural influences driving deferment of self-care and shaming response to errors create mental health risks affecting physicians in particular. Both of these culturally normative

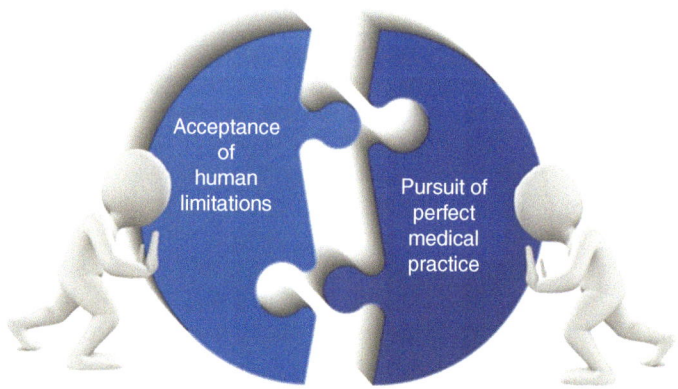

FIGURE 1.1 Acceptance of human limitations and pursuit of perfect medical practice are two sides of the same high clinical performance coin. (Source: Patty Purpur deVries. © Board of Trustees of the Leland Stanford University. All Rights Reserved)

failures of self-compassion—deferment of self-care and self-deprecating or shame-and-blame response to errors—are addressable at individual and institutional levels. Individual physicians can learn that acceptance of human limitations and pursuit of perfect medical practice are two sides of the same high clinical performance coin (Fig. 1.1). Physicians can engage in the practice of medicine accordingly—with balanced attention to self-care and a hopeful, intent-to-improve growth mind-set in response to mistakes.

Compassion in Addressing Personal Wellbeing

Personal and professional growth overlap with the concept of self-care and include the attitudes and skills Stephen Covey refers to in the concept of "sharpening the saw" (Covey 2013). Essentially, taking time to care for self and sharpen tools of personal efficacy contributes to greater professional efficiency, in a way that is analogous to taking time to sharpen a saw before cutting through a thick log. Physicians who may otherwise not prioritize self-care in the context of persistent patient care demands may engage in self-care more consistently through discovery of objective data or through their own subjective experience as they learn of the positive effects that self-care renders to clinical performance. Doctors who are aware that healthy sleep affects clinical performance may be more likely to prioritize sleep. Similarly, surgeons may be more likely to prioritize adequate nutrition during busing surgery days if they believe that healthy food choices and fluid intake will improve their performance in the operating room. Messages about the value of good self-care may be more salient and persuasive to medical students, residents, and attending physicians when framed in the context of benefits to clinical performance. Physicians who are engaged in health behaviors consistent with good self-care will be more likely to counsel their patients to do the same (Frank et al. 2013; Lobelo et al. 2009). Physicians have a high capacity for behavioral change when motivated by evidence that healthy behaviors improve clinical performance. Physicians also have above-average capacity to benefit from cognitive reframing methods to mitigate self-castigating reactions to mistakes.

Cognitive reframing methods that draw from physicians' well-cultivated capacity for compassion toward others may be particularly helpful. One method asks participants to engage in the following ten steps:

1. At the top of a piece of paper, write a one-line description of a moment when you felt badly about a mistake you made at work.
2. In the left margin, write the emotions you experienced during that moment. Examples of emotions people may experience during these moments include worry or fear, sadness or despair, hopelessness or frustration, isolation or loneliness, rejection or scorn, and guilt or shame.
3. In the right margin, write the negative thoughts that may have been going through your mind in that moment—the specific thoughts related to the specific emotions you identified earlier. As you write, leave two or three lines between each thought (for later use at step 7).

4. Rate the intensity of each emotion you identified on a scale of 1–10.

5. Imagine a physician exactly like you sitting next to you, a physician who has gone through the exact same experience and is reflecting on the exact same moment. Would you say the same thoughts you had about yourself to this physician? If so, you may have a balanced capacity to be as kind in your self-talk as you are toward others. Most physicians are more compassionate toward others' mistakes than they are toward their own. If you find yourself in this majority, you may be able to draw on the more compassionate standard you have for others in order to create a more healing growth mind-set response to your own mistakes—and benefit from improved mood and clinical performance in the process. If this seems reasonable to you, continue with this exercise.

6. Return to the list of thoughts that were running through your mind when affected by the mistake you made. If another physician's thoughts after making the same mistake were exactly like yours, what might you offer as more compassionate replacement thoughts for him/her?

7. Write these more compassionate replacement thoughts for that physician in the space you left between thoughts recorded during step 3. Try to write these more compassionate thoughts in response to your initial thoughts even if they are difficult for you to accept for yourself at this point.

8. Consider the advantages and disadvantages of accepting these more compassionate thoughts to replace some or all of the negative thoughts you identified in your own self-talk.

9. Do you see more advantages than disadvantages in accepting the more compassionate thoughts for yourself?

10. To finish this exercise, look at the emotion intensity ratings you indicated earlier for each emotion you identified. Re-rate the intensity of each emotion now. If you noticed a helpful shift in the intensity of difficult emotions, you have benefited from this brief cognitive reframing exercise.

In our experience, most physicians benefit to some degree from practicing this kind of cognitive reframing exercise (see Case Illustration 1.2). For many, it may be easier to create a healthy perspective than to maintain it. Regular practice can help, with the support of a coach or therapist if needed. A more complex and equally compelling opportunity is systematic, collaborative efforts to replace fear-based reactions to mistakes with more helpful perspectives and practice at collective organizational, local, and national policy levels.

Case Illustration 1.2

Dr. George was a productive trauma surgeon. She was highly esteemed by her colleagues and care teams for her capacity to care compassionately for patients and her highly developed surgical skills. After a particularly long day in the OR, she accidentally omitted the typical insulin protocol orders for her diabetic patient when writing the admission orders for a patient she had just treated for multiple stab wounds to the abdomen. The patient was 8 months pregnant and had been brutally attacked by her husband. Dr. George and her colleagues were not able to save the baby. Six hours after admission, a nurse called Dr. George concerned by the diabetic patient's glucose level, which was now in the 400 s. Dr. George quickly ordered the usual insulin protocol and asked for an endocrinology consultation to help manage the recovering patient's blood sugar levels. The patient subsequently developed a methicillin-resistant staph infection at her surgical site. Dr. George worried that her temporary spike in blood sugar level may have contributed to the infection. The infection protracted her recovery and hospitalization.

Dr. George's thoughts about this incident included "I'm not emotionally strong enough to be a trauma surgeon," "I deserve to be sued," and "I'm an unsafe doctor." She developed insomnia and extreme symptoms of burnout. She eventually called her employee assistance program, which referred her to a local therapist. The therapist had experience working with surgeons, and Dr. George found her to be helpful. In time, Dr. George realized that while she would never feel good about making a significant mistake in the course of her medical care, some rate of error may be unavoidable. She was also able to recognize that, by focusing on what she could learn, a growth mind-set allowed her to recover from mistakes, which are excruciatingly hard to face. She accepted the reality that a growth mind-set perspective is qualitatively different from the self-disparaging conclusions that prohibit personal growth and learning. Dr. George still felt badly whenever she remembered her patient and the added financial difficulties she faced due to her medical complications. She partly wished that her patient would sue her so that her patient's financial suffering might be remedied. She eventually came to terms with the fact that there were few options for her to provide redress for this patient directly. Instead, she used her experience and dedication to her patients to join a local state effort to create a medical no-fault malpractice system so that patients who are in need of financial help due to medical injuries would be more likely to receive such help.

Compassion in Health-Care Quality Improvement

Responding to physicians' mistakes with public shaming via civil litigation and draconian penalties for the mishandling of health information is consistent with the assumption that health providers' fidelity in performance must be motivated by fear of harsh retribution for errors. Evidence does not support this assumption (Frakes and Jena 2016). US physicians face greater risk of malpractice litigation than most of their international colleagues. Yet instead of achieving a reduction in errors, the US health-care system often tallies the highest number of medical errors in cross-national comparisons (Schoen et al. 2009). Available evidence suggests that HIPAA legislation creates a culture of privacy paranoia that erects unintended barriers to the sharing of health information pertinent to patient care and correlates with an increased number of patient complaints about privacy breaches, even as intuitions have instituted comprehensive and expensive efforts to become HIPAA compliant (Wilkes 2014). It seems unlikely that the threat of punishment improves the quality of care that physicians deliver to their patients and unlikely that organizations built on a culture of paranoia provide a safer and more healing health-care environment. A more plausible hypothesis is that threat of punishment contributes to defensive medicine, a culture of fear, health-care worker burnout, and degradation in quality of patient care.

At an organizational level, transparent quality improvement processes based on collectively shared values and intent on delivering skilled, high-quality care are far more effective in preventing errors than blaming and embarrassing or punishing individuals for their mistakes (Leape et al. 2009). One barrier in shifting to and maintaining a culture where quality improvement is driven by compassion for patients, colleagues, and self is obvious: Health-care teams often face traumatic patient experiences in their work to prevent and alleviate suffering. This exposure to trauma, if left unchecked, leads to fear that increases likelihood of blame and aggressive behavior when things go badly. The antidotes to this constant cultural pathology threat are mindful systematic support of colleagues in medicine who have been involved in an adverse clinical event, community building, and cultivation of a culture of mutual respect and appreciation. These group efforts and characteristics comprise what we refer to as a "culture of wellness" (see Chap. 2) and are robust determinants of professional fulfillment (Trockel et al. 2017b).

Cultivating compassion at work strengthens the heart of a culture of wellness where optimal team performance depends on strong bonds between team members, particularly during times of stress. Skills that promote compassion at work are those that allow individuals and groups to (1) notice others' distress and (2) act to alleviate their distress (Kanov et al. 2004). Personal and group normative values, attitudes, experiences, habits, and skills affect the probability of noticing others' distress and affect the likelihood and efficacy of responses to alleviate distress. Individuals and organizations engaged in the cultivation of compassion and the concomitant integration of the pursuit of perfect performance with an acceptance of human limitations are likely to achieve their personal and organizational best.

References

Brazeau CM, Shanafelt T, Durning SJ, Massie FS, Eacker A, Moutier C, et al. (2014) Distress among matriculating medical students relative to the general population. Acad Med 89: 1520–1525.

Covey SR (2013) The 7 habits of highly effective people: Powerful lessons in personal change, Simon and Schuster, New York

Davis M, Detre T, Ford DE, Hansbrough W, Hendin H, Laszlo J, et al. (2003) Confronting depression and suicide in physicians: a consensus statement. JAMA 289: 3161–3166.

Dyrbye LN, West CP, Satele D, Boone S, Tan L, Sloan J, et al. (2014) Burnout among US medical students, residents, and early career physicians relative to the general US population. Acad Med 89: 443–451.

Frakes M, Jena AB (2016) Does medical malpractice law improve health care quality? J Public Econ 143: 142–158.

Frank E, Dresner Y, Shani M, Vinker S (2013) The association between physicians' and patients' preventive health practices. CMAJ 185: cmaj.121028.

Halbesleben JR, Rathert C (2008) Linking physician burnout and patient outcomes: exploring the dyadic relationship between physicians and patients. Health Care Manage Rev 33: 29–39.

Kanov JM, Maitlis S, Worline MC, Dutton JE, Frost PJ, Lilius JM (2004) Compassion in organizational life. Am Behav Sci 47: 808–827.

Krause AJ, Simon EB, Mander BA, Greer SM, Saletin JM, Goldstein-Piekarski AN, et al. (2017) The sleep-deprived human brain. Nat Rev Neurosci 18: 404.

Leape L, Berwick D, Clancy C, Conway J, Gluck P, Guest J, et al. (2009) Transforming healthcare: a safety imperative. BMJ Quality Safety 18: 424–428.

Lobelo F, Duperly J, Frank E (2009) Physical activity habits of doctors and medical students influence their counselling practices. Br J Sports Med 43: 89–92.

Murthy V (2017) One Nation Under Stress: Improving Emotional Well-being in America. American Conference on Physician Health. San Francisco, CA.

Schoen C, Osborn R, How SK, Doty MM, Peugh J (2009) In chronic condition: experiences of patients with complex health care needs, in eight countries, 2008. Health Affairs 28: w1–w16.

Schwappach DL, Boluarte TA (2009) The emotional impact of medical error involvement on physicians: a call for leadership and organisational accountability. Swiss Med Weekly 139: 9.

Shanafelt TD, Hasan O, Dyrbye LN, Sinsky C, Satele D, Sloan J, et al. (2015) Changes in burnout and satisfaction with work-life balance in physicians and the general US working population between 2011 and 2014. Mayo Clinic Proceedings, Elsevier, Philadelphia, pp 1600–1613.

Trockel M, Bohman B, Lesure E, Hamidi MS, Welle D, Roberts L, et al. (2017a) A brief instrument to assess both burnout and professional fulfillment in physicians: reliability and validity, including correlation with self-reported medical errors, in a sample of resident and practicing physicians. Acad Psychiatry. 2018;42(1):11–24.

Trockel M, Hamidi M, Murphy ML, De Vries PP, Bohman B (2017b) 2016 Physician Wellness Survey Full Report [Online]. Available: https://pdfs.semanticscholar.org/4223/cd552b5c3c15f9f91d2c-8982dad8779724e4.pdf [Accessed July 11 2018].

Wallace JE, Lemaire JB, Ghali WA (2009) Physician wellness: a missing quality indicator. Lancet 374: 1714–1721.

Weinstein MS (2018) Out of the Straitjacket. N Engl J Med 378: 793–795.

Wilkes J (2014) The creation of HIPAA culture: Prioritizing privacy paranoia over patient care. BYU Rev: 2014(5), 1213–1250.

Chapter 2
Creating a Culture of Wellness

Nikitha Krishna Menon and Mickey Trockel

I've learned that people will forget what you said, people will forget what you did, but people will never forget how you made them feel.
– Dr. Maya Angelou

Physician wellbeing can be most effectively promoted through comprehensive, systematic organizational strategies that address all three reciprocal domains outlined by the Stanford model of wellbeing and professional fulfilment: personal resilience, culture of wellness, and efficiency of practice (Fig. 2.1). Chapter 1 introduced cultural norms that affect physician wellness. This chapter continues where the previous chapter left off and addresses strategies to improve the organizational culture of wellness, which we define as "a set of normative values, attitudes, and behaviors that promote self-care, personal and pro-

N. K. Menon
Stanford University School of Medicine, Department of Psychiatry and Behavioral Sciences, Palo Alto, CA, USA

M. Trockel (✉)
Stanford Hospital and Clinics, Department of Psychiatry and Behavior Science, Palo Alto, CA, USA

School of Medicine, Stanford University, Palo Alto, CA, USA
e-mail: trockel@stanford.edu

© Springer Nature Switzerland AG 2019   19
L. Weiss Roberts, M. Trockel (eds.),
The Art and Science of Physician Wellbeing,
https://doi.org/10.1007/978-3-319-42135-3_2

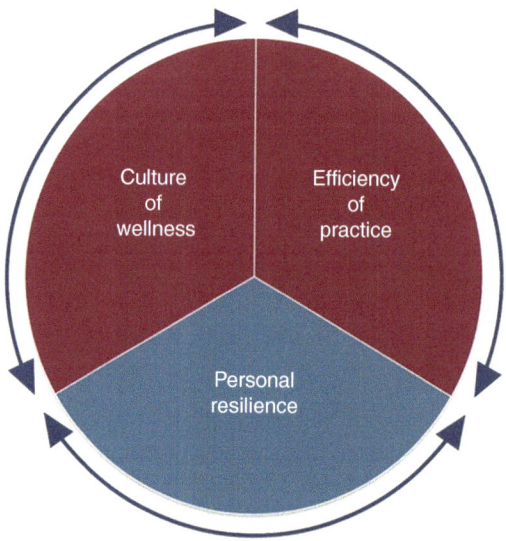

FIGURE 2.1 The reciprocal domains of physician wellbeing. (Source: Patty Purpur deVries. © Board of Trustees of the Leland Stanford University. All Rights Reserved)

fessional growth, and compassion for colleagues, patients, and self" (Bohman et al. 2017).

Intervention at the cultural level is more likely to be aimed at everyone who is a member of the group and more likely to focus on group-level norms, interpersonal communication, and the way members of the group feel about and treat one another. In the process, group norms that support wellbeing are likely to increase individual adoption of attitudes and behaviors that promote personal wellness and resilience. In addition, physicians who are immersed in and contribute to a culture of wellness at work are more likely to engage in opportunities to improve workflow and team-based care initiatives that increase efficiency of their medical practice. There are compelling reasons to establish a culture of wellness at organizations where physicians hope to provide a healing environment for patients. There are also compelling reasons not to do so. Were this not so, medical training and practice settings would already be consistent models of all aspects of a culture of wellness. We therefore begin this chapter by reviewing three barriers to a culture of wellness and discussing possible solutions for each.

Barriers to a Culture of Wellness Common in Medical Training and Practice

Belief that Deferring Self-Care Equals Dedication to Patients

Medical training and practice culture often perpetuates the view that self-sacrifice equals dedication to patients and self-care equals weakness. The primary strategy to overcome this barrier is consistent review of the evidence linking self-care and wellbeing to clinical performance parameters in order to establish self-care as a cultural norm. Social marketing efforts that disseminate education on the effects of self-care on performance may be helpful. Medical school and postgraduate training leaders and health-care organization leaders have immense influence to establish self-care as a social norm when they model good self-care habits themselves.

Belief that Shaming and Punishment in Response to Errors Promote Safety in Health Care

Long-standing US legal policy and recent privacy policies based on federal HIPAA legislation have normalized fear-based strategies to ensure safety in health care (see Chap. 1). Physician wellbeing will benefit from increased reliance on compassion-grounded motivators in the practice of medicine in lieu of strategies that rely on fear to motivate compliance and quality. Collective efforts can achieve concomitant reduction in organizational, local, and national policy reliance on reactive and unnecessary fear-based strategies to motivate quality of patient care.

Replacing fear-based motivators for quality improvement with compassion may require the collective perception that caring for people at work increases their propensity to give

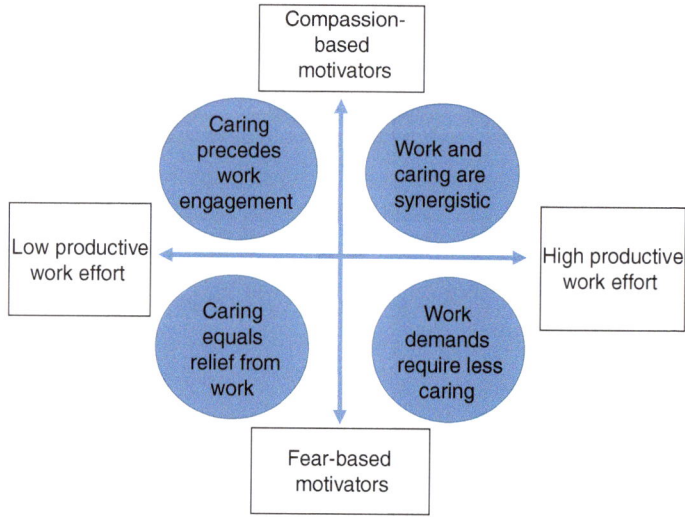

FIGURE 2.2 Compassion motivators integrate caring and performance

their best efforts. A recent *Harvard Business Review* article positioned "Caring" and "Results" on opposite ends of a cultural analysis graph, suggesting these two cultural commodities are difficult to achieve in the same workplace environment (Groysberg et al. 2018). The validity of this perception depends on the balance between compassion-based versus fear-based motivation at the heart of organizational culture. In a system that relies on fear to motivate, caring for people and garnering results may be competing aims. In a health-care system that cultivates motivation by compassion, caring for team members and garnering optimal results are synergistic aims (Fig. 2.2).

Stigma Suggesting that Physicians Who Seek Mental Health Help Are Less Fit for Duty

Another obvious barrier to physician health is the cultural stigma of seeking help for mental health. In many states, the physician licensure process requires disclosure of prior mental health history that leads many physicians to avoid seeking help (Gold et al. 2016). We know less about the degree to which state medical boards actually deny medical licensure to physicians based on their self-reported mental health history. Nevertheless, eliminating this real or perceived barrier is essential in order for physicians to access mental health care when needed. In most states, first steps may include public service campaigns and political advocacy to support medical board policy change. Leaders in medicine may also influence change by sharing their own positive experiences receiving mental health support.

In addition, leadership modeling vulnerability, self-disclosure, and self-care is an important step toward a culture of wellness where exposing vulnerability to seek help is normative rather than systematically discouraged. Professional athletes often have sports psychologists capable of helping them cultivate high-level mental health for optimal performance and overcoming significant stressors when needed. Messages from leaders normalizing the use of mental health support may lessen the current stigma that keeps some physicians from seeking help.

Overcoming the barriers that slow progress toward a culture of wellness will facilitate cultivation of the cultural factors that drive professional fulfilment and prevent burnout. Several of these factors warrant specific attention.

Promoting Specific Culture of Wellness Factors for Physician WellBeing

Psychological Safety

Unfortunately, the current climate of medical culture often reacts to human error with shame and blame (see Chap. 1). This creates a toxic environment in which physicians do not feel comfortable being human or making mistakes. This also fosters maladaptive perfectionism, which is associated with burnout in health care (Chang 2012). Psychological safety, a collective trust within a group that there is safety in taking interpersonal risks (Edmondson 1999), contributes to a culture of wellness in medicine. Institutions can facilitate psychological safety at many levels. At a departmental level, physician leaders can be transparent about their own human limitations and strategies to improve. For example, a department leader can share stories of her personal errors and associated improvement and/or coping strategies with colleagues. This sets the precedent that successful physicians are human and that humanity is not a negative trait. Similarly, a department leader can honestly inform his colleagues when he is taking a day off to look after his mental health. At the state or national level, psychological safety may be markedly improved for physicians by development and implementation of a no-fault malpractice system (Kessler 2011). This would allow compassionate, capable physicians to heal their patients without fear of reactive punishment for unavoidable human errors.

Inclusive Leadership Style

When physicians lead with an inclusive style, collaborating with their staff to provide the best care possible, everyone wins. Perception of collaborative relationships predicts physician job satisfaction (Chang et al. 2009). Promoting an inclusive leadership style in physicians as they guide their teams can improve team behaviors and reduce medical error (Morey et al. 2002). Efforts to cultivate inclusive leadership style and other supportive leadership skills are likely to render important dividends for health-care provider wellness and for quality of patients' care.

Leadership Support

Cultivating leadership support for physicians is conducive to a culture of wellness and is associated with increased satisfaction and lower burnout (Shanafelt et al. 2015). Effective support includes efforts from immediate supervisors to inform, engage, inspire, develop, and recognize physicians (Shanafelt et al. 2015). When physicians feel connected with and heard by their leaders, they are better able to cope with the stress inherent in medical practice.

Regularly scheduled and thoughtfully conducted annual reviews offer one mechanism for physician leaders to demonstrate effective support for those they lead. Effectiveness of an annual review may be optimized by attention to four components: (1) recognition of the individual's specific professional contributions and successes, (2) transparent communication to inform, (3) career development coaching, and (4) humble inquiry to seek suggestions for leadership and organizational improvement (Shanafelt and Swensen 2017).

A "Listen, Act, Develop" approach to organizational improvement offers a framework to engage front-line physician in collaboration with leadership to improve organizational practices and mitigate burnout (Swensen et al. 2016). As the name implies, this approach systematically uses basic effective leadership strategies to train and empower division or small department-level physician leaders. First, physician leaders "Listen" in order to learn about the malleable factors that contribute to professional burnout and to ascertain front-line physicians' ideas for practical solutions to mitigate these factors. Designated physician leaders then "Act" to mobilize group resources for development and implementation of strategies that can be accomplished locally and to collaborate with the larger organization leadership to develop and implement promising strategies that require larger organization collaboration. This process is an ideal opportunity to "Develop" new physician leaders. Repeated cycles of the "Listen, Act, Develop" process, concurrent with effective transparent communication, will lead to successful organizational improvement efforts in many instances and indicate to all physicians that the organization cares about reducing unnecessary work-stress—even when rapid improvement is not realized.

Case Illustration 2.1

As newly appointed Division Chief of Hospital Medicine at Avery-Grey Healthcare, Dr. Aguilar wanted to provide her faculty with areas to voice constructive workplace suggestions. She did so by issuing, collecting, and carefully reviewing feedback cards. These cards questioned what was going right, what was going wrong, and what could be done better in the department. She encouraged inpatient hospitalists in her division to honestly, anonymously complete these cards at monthly meetings. As she reviewed the responses, she discovered that a great number of comments shared a common recommendation. The comments described hospitalists using a large amount of time for non-clinical functions that other members of the patient care team could spearhead, given the opportunity. In particular, many hospitalists indicated they were spending much of their time making follow-up care arrangements for patients. They suggested offloading this to another trained employee, such as a social worker.

Dr. Aguilar promptly responded to these concerns by working with the administration to hire a social worker, Mr. Altman, for her division. Mr. Altman eagerly collaborated with the hospitalists and quickly became adept at arranging follow-up care for hospitalized patients. This facilitated larger caseloads for the physicians and increased productivity to meet the needs of a growing number of patients. The increased billing revenue of the division eventually exceeded Mr. Altman's salary. Furthermore, inpatient hospitalists went home half an hour earlier on average per day, and many of them felt supported by Dr. Aguilar. One such physician, Dr. Lee, pulled Dr. Aguilar aside at a meeting a number of months after Mr. Altman began working in the division.

Dr. Lee privately informed Dr. Aguilar that he had considered leaving the institution during the past year as a result of burnout. He had felt that his work was losing meaning and that he did not have time for his family.

However, he stated that this changed when Dr. Aguilar hired Mr. Altman in response to the feedback he had provided. Hiring Mr. Altman had given Dr. Lee an increased sense of having a supportive work environment and allowed him more time with his loved ones. Dr. Lee thanked Dr. Aguilar for making him feel heard and respected. Dr. Aguilar was grateful that he felt comfortable sharing his experience with her. A number of physicians shared similar stories—in person, and anonymously through the cards—following this change. At the end of the fiscal year, her department chair praised her for the marked increase in team morale and increase in revenue within her department.

Values Alignment

A medical culture of wellness requires values alignment. Individuals engaged in the mission, vision, and values of an institution are more motivated to make changes that further align themselves with these components. Aligning individual values to those of their leaders and institutions is integral to producing lasting organizational change (Branson 2008). Support from leadership is associated with values alignment and perceived appreciation. Both values alignment and perceived appreciation may mediate the relationship between support from leadership and professional fulfillment (Trockel et al. 2017).

Appreciation and Gratitude

A sense of appreciation stands out as perhaps the strongest driver of professional fulfillment (Trockel et al. 2017) that facilitates kindness and collaboration in medicine. Health-care providers who implement personal gratitude practices are likely to experience lower levels of stress and improved mood (Cheng et al. 2015). Gratitude at work can also reduce burnout (Chan 2011) and is associated with increased resilience (Dwiwardani et al. 2014) and achievement (Froh et al. 2007) (see Chap. 3).

Case Illustration 2.2

To optimize communication in their clinic, Drs. Brown, Williams, and Lin held a daily huddle with their team members. Typically, they covered agenda items such as clinic-related changes and particular cases during this time. They also frequently engaged in group social activities. Thanking one another for contributions became a social norm in their group.

On a rare day when Dr. Lin was homesick with a high fever, she contacted her patients for the day and attempted to reschedule them. Most of her patients sympathized and were able to see her another day, but one could not reschedule because he would be traveling for work. Dr. Lin emailed Dr. Williams and asked if he would be able to see her patient that day. He immediately called Dr. Lin and agreed to see her patient.

All members of the expanded work team experienced high professional fulfillment and felt connected to—and grateful for—their colleagues every day.

Fairness/Equity

Unfairness and lack of equity in the workplace contributes to burnout by creating cynicism (Maslach et al. 2001). A culture of wellness can thrive in a fair and equitable work environment, and a myriad of policies and expectations can facilitate this. For example, an organization can implement blind hiring and promotion processes in order to prevent unconscious biases from deterring worthy candidates. This would involve using software systems to blind the hiring team from the ethnicity, race, gender, and other discriminatory factors of candidates. This would improve the diversity of the organization and set an expectation of merit-based rewards and fairness in promotion. Furthermore, a department could implement salary transparency among its employees. This would promote the reduction of the gender gap by arming female physicians with the information necessary to receive fair pay. Attention to fairness may help reduce the current gender gap in physician wellness in the United States, where female physicians experience greater burnout than their male counterparts (Linzer et al. 2002).

Flexibility and Work-Life Integration

Work-home interference directly increases burnout in physicians (Linzer et al. 2001). A medical culture of wellness requires acknowledging that physicians are human beings with obligations outside of their clinical duties. Physicians are less susceptible to burnout when given the opportunity to fulfill their obligations and maintain relationships outside of work without being penalized for it. Team-based care strategies that increase efficiency of physicians' medical practice may improve work-life integration for some physicians (Sinsky et al. 2013). Institutions can also improve work-home integration by providing adequate maternity and paternity leaves and encouraging the use of vacation time.

Peer Support

Effective peer support can reduce burnout and encourage a culture of wellness. Increased emotional exhaustion in physicians is associated with increased need for support, and physicians often prefer one-on-one support from a colleague (Bruce et al. 2005). Effective peer support programs offer confidential conversations with a physician colleague matched by specialty. Minimal training—added to already extant interpersonal competency most physicians have developed—is typically sufficient to empower physicians to serve in a peer support role for colleagues who have experienced an adverse patient care event or other situational stress. When peer support programs are commissioned and overseen by medical staff leaders as part of ongoing quality improvement efforts, the confidential conversations that peer supporters offer physicians dealing with patient care-related distress are protected from legal discovery in many states. If properly marketed, encouraged, and sustained, peer support programs may mitigate distress during times when physicians are at critically increased risk for burnout.

Community/Collegiality

Approximately 60% of resident physicians cite relationships with their colleagues as the most rewarding aspect of their work (Levy 2018). A strong sense of collegiality in medicine can engage physicians and strengthen their bonds with one another. As burnout is often characterized by interpersonal disengagement (Trockel et al. 2018), cultivating a supportive community in medical culture may assist in mitigating burnout. Social support also moderates the impact of stress on burnout (Etzion 1984).

Conclusion

A Culture of Wellness Is Achievable

Creating a culture of wellness begins with understanding the current climate of a medical culture and the barriers to change. It is imperative that this understanding of a medical culture comes from the views of the physicians within it; the culture is created, owned, and modified by physicians within it. Systematic approaches to improve the culture of wellness and evaluation research to assess efficacy of promising approaches are needed. Intervention at the cultural level is different from health promotion at the individual level even when similar intervention mechanisms are employed. For example, a positive psychology-based program directed at individual physician wellbeing may invite physicians to keep a gratitude journal where they keep a daily record of things that they are grateful for. A positive psychology-based program directed at work-group culture change may invite an entire team to keep a gratitude journal where they record daily thoughts about specific things that they are grateful someone did, contributed, or achieved at work.

References

Bohman B, Dyrbye L, Sinsky CA, Linzer M, Olson K, Babbott S, et al. (2017) Physician Well-Being: The Reciprocity of Practice Efficiency, Culture of Wellness, and Personal Resilience. NEJM Catalyst [Online]. Available from: catalyst.nejm.org/physician-well-being-efficiency-wellness-resilience/ [Accessed June 2017].

Branson CM (2008) Achieving organisational change through values alignment. Journal of Educational Administration 46: 376–395.

Bruce S, Conaglen H, Conaglen J (2005) Burnout in physicians: a case for peer-support. Intern Med J 35: 272–278.

Chan DW (2011) Burnout and life satisfaction: Does gratitude intervention make a difference among Chinese school teachers in Hong Kong? Educational Psychology 31: 809–823.

Chang WY, Ma JC, Chiu HT, Lin KC, Lee PH (2009) Job satisfaction and perceptions of quality of patient care, collaboration and teamwork in acute care hospitals. J Adv Nurs 65: 1946–1955.

Chang Y (2012) The relationship between maladaptive perfectionism with burnout: Testing mediating effect of emotion-focused coping. Personality and Individual Differences 53: 635–639.

Cheng S-T, Tsui PK, Lam JH (2015) Improving mental health in health care practitioners: Randomized controlled trial of a gratitude intervention. Journal of Consulting and Clinical Psychology 83: 177.

Dwiwardani C, Hill PC, Bollinger RA, Marks LE, Steele JA, Doolin HN, et al. (2014) Virtues Develop From a Secure Base: Attachment and Resilience as Predictors of Humility, Gratitude, and Forgiveness. J Psychol Theol 42.

Edmondson A (1999) Psychological safety and learning behavior in work teams. Administrative Science Quarterly 44: 350–383.

Etzion D (1984) Moderating effect of social support on the stress–burnout relationship. J Appl Psychol 69: 615–622.

Froh JJ, Miller DN, Snyder SF (2007) Gratitude in children and adolescents: Development, assessment, and school-based intervention. School Psychology Forum, Citeseer.

Gold KJ, Andrew LB, Goldman EB, Schwenk TL (2016) "I would never want to have a mental health diagnosis on my record": A survey of female physicians on mental health diagnosis, treatment, and reporting. General Hospital Psychiatry 43: 51–57.

Groysberg B, Lee J, Price J, Cheng J (2018) The Leader's Guide to Corporate Culture How to Manage the Eight Critical Elements of Organizational Life. Harvard Business Review 96: 44–52.

Kessler DP (2011) Evaluating the medical malpractice system and options for reform. Journal of Economic Perspectives 25: 93–110.

Levy S (2018). Residents Lifestyle and Happiness Report 2017. Available: https://www.medscape.com/slideshow/residents-lifestyle-report-2017-6008988 [Accessed July 14, 2018].

Linzer M, McMurray JE, Visser M, Oort FJ, Smets E (2002) Sex differences in physician burnout in the United States and the Netherlands. J Am Med Women Assoc (1972) 57: 191–193.

Linzer M, Visser MRM, Oort FJ, Smets EMA, McMurray JE, De Haes HCJM (2001) Predicting and preventing physician burnout: results from the United States and the Netherlands. Am J Med 111: 170–175.

Maslach C, Schaufeli WB, Leiter MP (2001) Job burnout. Ann Rev Psychol 52: 397–422.

Morey JC, Simon R, Jay GD, Wears RL, Salisbury M, Dukes KA, Berns SD (2002) Error Reduction and Performance Improvement in the Emergency Department through Formal Teamwork Training: Evaluation Results of the MedTeams Project. Health Services Res, 37: 1553–1581.

Shanafelt T, Swensen S (2017) Leadership and Physician Burnout: Using the Annual Review to Reduce Burnout and Promote Engagement. Am J Med Qual 32: 563–565.

Shanafelt TD, Gorringe G, Menaker R, Storz KA, Reeves D, Buskirk SJ, et al. (2015) Impact of organizational leadership on physician burnout and satisfaction. Mayo Clin Proc 90(4):432–40.

Sinsky CA, Willard-Grace R, Schutzbank AM, Sinsky TA, Margolius D, Bodenheimer T (2013) In search of joy in practice: a report of 23 high-functioning primary care practices. Ann Fam Med 11: 272–8.

Swensen S, Kabcenell A, Shanafelt T (2016) Physician-Organization Collaboration Reduces Physician Burnout and Promotes Engagement: The Mayo Clinic Experience. J Healthc Manag 61: 105–27.

Trockel M, Bohman B, Lesure E, Hamidi MS, Welle D, Roberts L, et al. (2018) A brief instrument to assess both burnout and professional fulfillment in physicians: reliability and validity, including correlation with self-reported medical errors, in a sample of resident and practicing physicians. Acad Psychiatry 42: 11–24.

Trockel M, Hamidi M, Murphy ML, De Vries PP, Bohman B (2017) 2016 Physician Wellness Survey Full Report [Online]. Available: https://pdfs.semanticscholar.org/4223/cd552b5c3c15f9f91d2e-8982dad8779724e4.pdf [Accessed July 11 2018].

Chapter 3
Compassion Cultivation

Robert Horowitz

If you want others to be happy, practice compassion.
If you want to be happy, practice compassion.

– The Dalai Lama

Introduction

There is a quiet crisis in modern health care: studies suggest that over half of physicians are affected by burnout (Shanafelt et al. 2015). The core symptoms are exhaustion and disengagement from work – "an erosion of the human soul" – that manifest as cynicism, loss of meaning, and depersonalization of coworkers and patients (Maslach and Leiter 2008; Demerouti and Bakker 2008). For many physicians, the susceptibility to burnout is compounded by lack of training in emotion regulation and by the influences of a professional culture that encourages emotional distancing, prioritizes clinical responsibilities over self-care, and tacitly endorses cynical attitudes toward patients (Shapiro 2013; Montgomery 2014). Studies indicate that physicians who have trouble recognizing and managing their emotional distress and have difficulty empathizing with others are more prone to burnout; in contrast, doctors who are aware of their feelings, consider

R. Horowitz (✉)
Stanford University School of Medicine, Stanford Prevention Research Center, Palo Alto, CA, USA

© Springer Nature Switzerland AG 2019
L. Weiss Roberts, M. Trockel (eds.),
The Art and Science of Physician Wellbeing,
https://doi.org/10.1007/978-3-319-42135-3_3

33

the perspectives of other people, and express more empathic concern and altruism toward others have been shown to enjoy greater satisfaction and less burnout from their work (Gleichgerrcht and Decety 2013; Lamothe et al. 2014). Findings such as these are shedding a new light on the value of compassion: when we bring warmth and kindness to the stressful feelings of ourselves and others, we heal too, making us more resilient and fulfilled.

Compassion has been formally defined as "being moved by another's suffering and wanting to help" (Lazarus 1991). The experience of compassion is complex and involves multiple components: the awareness of another's plight; assessments of the other person and their predicament; appraisals of our own perspectives, capabilities, and resources; and the psychophysical correlates of concern, caring, and motivation to help (Goetz and Simon-Thomas 2017). We can also direct compassion inwardly – self-compassion – by offering the same kindness to ourselves that we would show to a dear friend in our situation (Germer and Neff 2013b). Compassion has been practiced in Buddhist traditions for 2500 years and is regarded as an important foundation for emotional healing (Makransky 2012). Emerging evidence suggests that a compassionate orientation toward others benefits our own psychological, social, and physical wellness (Millar et al. 1988; Krause et al. 1992; Schwartz et al. 2003; Post 2005; Sprecher and Fehr 2006). For example, people who spent money on others appeared to experience greater happiness than those who spent it on themselves (Dunn et al. 2008), and volunteering for altruistic reasons was linked to longer life expectancy than volunteering for self-oriented motives (Konrath et al. 2012).

Self-compassion is gaining recognition as a healthy way to relate to ourselves. Psychologist Kristin Neff conceptualizes self-compassion as the interplay of mindfulness, common humanity, and self-kindness (Neff 2003). In a stressful situation, mindfulness allows us to attend to our unpleasant feelings instead of avoiding them or taking them too personally. Common humanity recognizes that we're not alone: everyone experiences challenges and has limitations. Self-kindness comforts us with an inner friendliness rather than berating us with harsh self-criticism or unrealistic demands.

Self-compassion has been linked to higher levels of happiness, optimism, and life satisfaction (Allen et al. 2012; Hall et al. 2013; Homan 2016; Neff et al. 2007; Neff 2011; Neff 2012) and less anxiety, depression, and shame (Barnard and Curry 2011; MacBeth and Gumley 2012; Johnson and O'Brien 2013). In medical trainees and physicians, self-compassion correlates positively with wellbeing and resilience and inversely with burnout and disturbed sleep (Kemper et al. 2015; Olson et al. 2015). The 2016 Stanford Physician Wellness Survey reported that lack of self-compassion was the strongest predictor of burnout of all variables assessed (Trockel et al. 2016).

Compassion is often regarded as a relatively fixed endowment, but millenia-old contemplative traditions and recent scientific research indicate that it is malleable and amenable to training. A time-honored method is loving-kindness meditation, in which friendly warmth and affection are engendered for others while repeating phrases such as "May you be safe" and "May you be happy" (Kornfield 2008). Substantial evidence suggests that loving-kindness and compassion meditations increase wellbeing, positive emotions, self-compassion, and social connectedness, while reducing negative affect such as depression (Fredrickson et al. 2008; Hofmann et al. 2011; Galante et al. 2014; Seppälä et al. 2014; Shonin et al. 2015; Weng et al. 2013; Zeng et al. 2015). Similarly, inducing self-compassion experimentally appears to enhance happiness, promote positive behavior changes, and diminish depression (Kelly 2010; Shapira and Mongrain 2010).

Several compassion training programs have been developed to teach perspectives and skills that support a compassionate lifestyle using psychoeducational and meditative approaches. While most courses are intended for general audiences and do not include content specific to health-care providers, some physicians find them attractive and participate in public and organizational settings. This article reviews representative programs to illustrate themes and variations in methods of cultivating compassion with relevant research findings. Readers seeking general reviews of compassion training are referred to several recent publications (Brito 2014; Kirby 2016; Skwara et al. 2017).

How Is Compassion Cultivated

The remarkably prosocial nature of human beings (Simpson and Beckes 2010; Marsh 2016) is thought to be an evolutionary legacy that favored parental caregiving and societal collaboration (Goetz et al. 2010; Decety and Svetlova 2011). On a personal and practical level, compassion can feel challenging and unreliable, however, due to its emotional and cognitive costs (Condon and Feldman Barrett 2013; Hodges and Klein 2001) and variability in different contexts (Stellar and Keltner 2014). A primary goal of compassion training is to transform kindhearted tendencies into a more robust, dependable, and expansive compassion that inspires and guides daily life (Jinpa 2015).

Training programs foster compassion through mutually reinforcing strategies: (1) focusing and stabilizing attention in the midst of emotional distress; (2) fortifying affective ("felt") compassion; (3) developing facilitative cognitive perspectives; (4) building preconditions for compassion, such as a sense of common humanity; (5) reducing barriers to compassion (e.g., biases and misconceptions); and (6) expanding compassion to a wider range of individuals, groups, and situations. As an example, compassion is generally easiest for us to feel toward those closest and most similar to us and less available for strangers and members of outgroups (Stellar and Keltner 2014). Sensing commonality with others, even by tapping in time to music together (Valdesolo and Desteno 2011), can stimulate feelings of connectedness and efforts to assist one another. Compassion training leverages this principle by identifying values and experiences shared with others – our common humanity – to promote appreciation and kindness.

Current compassion training programs are usually conducted as weekly group meetings over 8–10 weeks or as brief intensive courses. Curricula offer a combination of psychoeducation – which clarifies the relationship between thoughts, emotions, and habitual patterns – and meditative practices. A variety of meditation techniques are taught to nurture the affective and cognitive aspects of compassion. Practicing mindfulness is central to all programs. Mindfulness is described as the awareness that arises when we pay attention to the experience of the present moment without judging or conceptualizing it (Kabat-Zinn 2003); mindfulness enables us to face stressful feelings with less reactivity and more equanimity and can be fortified through meditation. Mindfulness meditation has been linked to reductions in physician burnout, stress, anxiety, and depression and improvements in mood and emotional stability (Krasner et al. 2009; Fortney et al. 2013; West et al. 2016). Mindfulness is discussed in more depth in Chap. 12.

Compassion meditations rely on attention, imagination, perspective-taking, language, and somatosensory experience to evoke compassion and its antecedents. One common technique directs the words and goodwill of compassionate phrases (e.g., "May you be free from suffering") to a progression of increasingly challenging targets: yourself, a loved one, a neutral person, a difficult person, and, ultimately, all beings. Another method is the Tibetan Buddhist practice of *tonglen,* in which we imagine taking away the suffering of another person and sending them our own happiness and wellbeing (Jinpa 2015). Program participants are encouraged to practice daily formal meditations (often available as audio recordings) and informal "on-the-spot" techniques to enhance their abilities.

Social neuroscience is providing insights into emotion regulatory effects of compassion training that are relevant to clinicians. A central concept is empathy, which may be described as a constellation of social capabilities that enable us to share and understand another person's emotional or physical state (Goetz and Simon-Thomas 2017). Neuroimaging studies consistently demonstrate that when we witness someone's pain, our brain emulates their brain's pain-related activation patterns, effectively simulating their experience in our own neural systems (Singer and Lamm 2009). Empathizing with someone's predicament may therefore be distressing, particularly if we imagine ourselves to be in their shoes (Decety and Lamm 2011). Compassion training shows promise in protecting against this effect. In one study, subjects practiced empathically identifying with the suffering of others in a 1-day session, followed 1 week later by a day of compassion training (Klimecki et al. 2014). After building empathy, participants responded to video clips of human suffering with increased negative affect and brain imaging patterns characteristic of empathic pain. In comparison, compassion training was associated with increased positive affect, even while viewing upsetting material, and activation of brain regions linked to love, positive affect, and reward. Other recent findings suggest that compassion training may also contribute to emotion regulation by promoting acceptance rather than reduction of negative affect (Engen and Singer 2015; Goldin and Jazaieri 2017).

Compassion Training Programs

This section describes several popular compassion training programs that attract physicians interested in self-development. With the exception of Being With Dying, a course for healthcare professionals engaged in end-of-life care described later, the curricula are general and do not specifically address issues encountered in clinical practice. An experimental training program configured to encourage physician participation is also presented as a case study in program design. Each program synopsis includes related research findings.

Cognitively-Based Compassion Training

Cognitively-Based Compassion Training (CBCT) was developed at Emory University in response to growing depression in undergraduates; it was later adapted for the general public and special populations, such as foster children and breast cancer survivors, to promote compassion, resilience, and well-being (Ozawa-de Silva et al. 2012; Dodds et al. 2015). Emory School of Medicine offers dedicated CBCT classes to faculty, staff, and medical students.

CBCT is a modern secular program heavily influenced by Tibetan Buddhist traditions of mind training and spiritual development but avoids explicit references to Buddhist concepts such as karma and reincarnation (Ozawa-de Silva and Negi 2013; Mascaro et al. 2016; Lavelle 2016). Analytic inquiry is used as a primary tool to deconstruct biases that undermine our sense of similarity and connectedness to other people (Lavelle 2017).

CBCT is generally delivered in 8–10 weekly sessions. Participants begin by learning to stabilize their attention and gain insight into their thoughts, feelings, and emotions (Lavelle 2017; Mascaro et al. 2017). Self-compassion is nurtured by differentiating helpful from harmful mental states and habits. The curriculum then develops compassion for others systematically. By examining our interdependence with countless other people, we are inclined to feel gratitude and appreciation for them; reflecting on the shared human desire to be well and avoid distress reveals our common humanity. This leads to greater affection and empathic concern for others, which naturally engenders the compassionate wish that they be free from distress. Finally, this wish is transformed into an active commitment to relieve others of suffering.

Several studies have investigated the physiological and psychological effects of CBCT. A randomized controlled trial of 6 weeks of CBCT reported significant reductions in the immune/inflammatory marker interleukin [IL]-6 and behavioral distress responses to a psychosocial stressor in CBCT participants who had accrued greater than the median meditation practice time (Pace et al. 2009). In another study, CBCT participants viewed negative images and showed an upward trend in activation of the right amygdala (a brain region related to emotion regulation) that correlated significantly with reduced depression scores (Desbordes et al. 2012). Mascaro et al. found that CBCT was linked to improvements in empathic accuracy (the ability to correctly infer others' thoughts and emotions) (Mascaro et al. 2012).

One of the few studies of compassion training in a healthcare setting tested the feasibility and psychological benefits of CBCT in preclinical medical students at Emory School of Medicine (Mascaro et al. 2016). Almost 45% of second-year students chose to enroll and were randomized to CBCT (10 weekly 1.5-hour classes) or a wait-list control; 70% of the CBCT participants completed the study. The CBCT arm showed decreases in depression and loneliness and increases in compassion that were most marked in students with high initial depression scores; in contrast, controls with high depression scores showed reductions in compassion.

Compassion Cultivation Training

Compassion Cultivation Training (CCT) is an 8-week program that teaches general audiences methods to enhance wellbeing and promote compassion for themselves and others (Goldin and Jazaieri 2017). The curriculum was developed at Stanford University by a team of neuroscientists, psychologists, and contemplative scholars (Jinpa and Weiss 2013). Stanford Healthcare and Sharp Healthcare systems are among the health-care systems that offer CCT to their providers.

To nurture compassion, CCT combines psychoeducation, secular meditation practices, and interactive exercises; these are supported by inspirational stories and poetry and home practice (Jinpa and Weiss 2013). Like CBCT, the curriculum is strongly influenced by Tibetan Buddhist traditions but places greater emphasis on direct compassion training practices such as loving-kindness meditation and less on analytic inquiry. The frameworks share similarities in their progression through mindfulness, self-compassion, and compassion for others. CCT establishes the foundational perspectives of common humanity and interconnectedness to engender compassion, which is gradually expanded to include all humanity (Goldin and Jazaieri 2017). Participants practice *tonglen* to move their compassion to action by envisioning themselves taking away the suffering of others and sending them wellbeing. The last session presents a comprehensive meditation that integrates the core techniques of the course, constituting a regular practice after the program ends (Goldin and Jazaieri 2017).

Stanford researchers investigated the psychological effects of CCT in a single cohort of community-dwelling adults randomized to CCT or a waitlist control group. The results were reported in several publications. CCT was associated with greater self-compassion and reductions in fears of compassion for others, from others, and for oneself compared to controls (Jazaieri et al. 2013); other researchers have linked fears of compassion to self-criticism, depression, and lack of self-compassion (Gilbert et al. 2011). The effects of CCT on emotion regulation have also been explored. In one analysis, CCT participants showed improvements in mindfulness and happiness and decreases in worry and emotional suppression compared to controls (Jazaieri et al. 2014). In another article, CCT participants showed increased calmness and diminished anxiety over the course of the program (Jazaieri et al. 2017). An intriguing finding was that despite feeling more able to regulate their negative affect, participants were less inclined to do so. They increasingly accepted stress and anxiety rather than suppressing it. Finally, CCT was associated with increased self-caring behaviors (Jazaieri et al. 2015). Specifically, practicing compassion meditation correlated with less mind-wandering to unpleasant topics and more mind-wandering to pleasant topics; these, in turn, predicted more caring behaviors for oneself and others.

Mindful Self-Compassion (MSC)

Mindful Self-Compassion (MSC) is a program devoted to teaching attitudes and skills of self-compassion that enable us to meet life experiences, particularly difficult ones, with an inner kindness, comfort, and support (Germer and Neff 2013a). MSC is often taught as an 8-week program or a 5-day intensive course; newer options include online and 2-day core skills training.

The curriculum engages the class in a journey of self-discovery through didactic presentations, meditative and informal practices, and reflective and interactive exercises (Germer and Neff 2013a). After laying the conceptual foundations for self-compassion, participants are taught core mindfulness and loving-kindness meditations adapted to nurture self-compassion. They learn to motivate themselves with kindness rather than self-criticism and to use self-compassion to live in accord with their core values. A half-day retreat in the latter half of the program consolidates and deepens skills. Participants then learn to approach difficult emotions and challenging relationships – including compassion fatigue in caregivers – with mindfulness and self-compassion. The program finishes with an exploration of the supportive positive practices of savoring, gratitude, and self-appreciation and offers suggestions for maintaining the practice of self-compassion going forward.

MSC was evaluated in a study of community-based adults randomized to MSC or a waitlist control (Neff and Germer 2012). Compared to controls, MSC participants showed greater improvements in self-compassion, compassion for others, mindfulness, and life satisfaction and larger reductions in depression, anxiety, stress, and avoidance of difficult thoughts and feelings. All gains from the 8-week program were maintained at 1-year follow-up.

Being with Dying (BWD)

Being With Dying (BWD) is a training program in compassionate end-of-life care and provider self-care intended for health-care professionals (Halifax 2013; Rushton et al. 2009). The course is taught as an 8-day residential intensive course hosted by the Upaya Zen Center in Santa Fe.

BWD differs from the previously discussed programs in commingling compassion training with clinically relevant material (from the area of palliative care). Compassion is conceptualized as a process that emerges from complex interactions of attention and affect, intention and insight, and embodiment and engagement, which represent targets for training (Halifax 2012). Woven through the curriculum are a rich set of contemplative and reflective approaches that include: (1) practicing focused attention and open awareness; (2) developing insight into values and priorities, ethics, and attitudes toward altruism, pain, suffering, and death; (3) practicing deep listening and staying present with pain and suffering; (4) cultivating prosocial qualities, such as empathy, compassion, and sympathetic joy; and (5) gaining familiarity with subjective psychophysical aspects of sickness, dying, and death (Halifax 2013). These are elaborated through didactic expositions, group explorations, and other interactive exercises.

In a study of the impact of BWD on past participants (Rushton et al. 2009), four major themes emerged from confidential telephone interviews supported by an anonymous online survey: (1) the power of being present to the suffering of patients and families; (2) cultivation of a more stable, balanced compassion for others and oneself; (3) recognition and management of one's own grief; and (4) the importance of self-care. All themes had at least some physician endorsement, although physicians comprised only 25% of the interviewees (the remainder were primarily nurses, social workers, and chaplains). Many participants reported improved resilience and less burnout.

Brief Compassion Training for Physician Well-Being: A Case Study in Program Design

Despite positive reports from compassion training programs, the requisite time commitments (Shapiro et al. 2005) and formal meditation practices may deter participation by many physicians. Recently, abbreviated meditation curricula have been created that appear to be beneficial to health-care providers (Gilmartin et al. 2017). In 2015, I developed a physician wellness program with colleagues at the Stanford Prevention Research Center that promotes participation by prioritizing convenience and emphasizes self-compassion to enhance resilience and self-care. This project is presented as a case study in configuring compassion training around specific characteristics such as type, length, and accessibility of training.

The program is designed around several guiding principles. First, barriers to participation are reduced by delivering training in clinical work settings and minimizing class and practice time. Second, the primary goal is to instill a mind-set of self-compassion supported by just-in-time tools that mediate self-kindness and self-care in stressful situations. Mind-sets shape behavior (Crum and Zuckerman 2017) and can empower significant, persistent motivational change from relatively small interventions (Yeager and Walton 2011). Third, physicians are recruited as established clinical teams rather than as individuals to improve participation and legitimize self-compassion.

The program begins with a 45-min orientation followed by 8 weekly, 30-min sessions. After a brief check-in, each session presents a topic and an exercise intended to evoke self-compassion at stressful times during the day. Participants are initially guided through a 7- to 10-min version of the exercise followed by a 3-min version to demonstrate how the process can be expedited. The core practices include (1) Settling Down (mindful breathing); (2) Compassionate Person (visualizing and receiving compassion from a kindhearted person); (3) Basic Compassion (loving-kindness); (4) Self-Compassion Break[1] (self-compassion during an upsetting situation); (5) Common Humanity (sharing human limitations with others); and (6) One for Me, One for You[1] (breathing compassion in for yourself and out for another person). Participants receive laminated cards as visual reminders of the exercises and have access to online recordings of the material.

A pilot study to test the feasibility of the program enrolled five primary care practices (26 physicians, 81% women) in Santa Clara County, CA. Overall attendance was 75%. As a primary care physician, longtime meditator, and Trained Teacher of Mindful Self-Compassion, I was the sole trainer for the program. Participants completed pre- and post-intervention surveys of empathy, compassion, and self-compassion based on items from validated instruments and of self-efficacy for skills taught in the program. All items used 5-point Likert scales (1 = strongly disagree, 5 = strongly agree). Statistically significant increases were observed in median differences (MD) before and after training for self-compassion (self-kindness) (MD = 1, p = 0.002); 61% of responses to "I'm kind to myself when I'm experiencing suffering" were negative before training, while 70% of responses were positive after training. Significant changes were also observed in self-efficacies for mindful breathing (MD = 1,

1 Adapted from Mindful Self-Compassion by K. Neff and C. Germer.

$p = 0.005$); recognizing common humanity (MD = 1, $p = 0.008$); and evoking self-compassion (MD = 1, $p = 0.002$).

Participants reported that that the program was appealing and convenient, and that self-compassion was valuable for their self-care. The brevity of the exercises and convenience of training in the workplace was key to engaging many of the providers. Those with little or no meditation experience were challenged initially but were typically able to apply the training by the completion of the program.

The following narrative illustrates one physician's experience during the program.

Case Illustration 3.1

A female physician participated in the Brief Compassion Training for Physician Well-Being program with practice partners at her primary care clinic. Managing the demands of career and family, her stresses were primarily at home. After learning a simple mindful breathing exercise ("Settling Down") in the first session, she began taking a breath before entering her house after work. In the fourth week of the program, she reported an epiphany: "the world is not going to stop turning if I slow down. I sat on the floor playing blocks with my son and my taxes were in view. And I thought, 'The taxes are not going anywhere.' And that was really nice." In the next session, she described the class as "a time to take a breath and to rethink the frenetic pace that we live in. The world doesn't stop if I take a break for 30 minutes to slow down and breathe and I actually feel re-energized." Near the end of the program, she summarized: "My usual MO is to say I should probably check my emails and get on the EMR. And now what happens is the 'I should do that' goes 'Well, should I do that?' Maybe it would be better for me to read People Magazine. And shockingly, you wake up feeling better the next day and can do your emails and EMR." Several weeks after completing the training, she taught a patient about self-compassion.

The limitations of this pilot study include lack of a control group and follow-up, small sample size, a single trainer, and modifications to the program during the pilot. Future studies with measures of wellbeing and burnout, larger cohorts, and multiple trainers in randomized controlled trials are recommended to more adequately assess the effectiveness of the intervention.

The Brief Compassion Training for Physician Well-Being shows promise in lowering barriers to physician participation in a self-compassion program. Next steps will focus on teacher training and maintenance of perspectives and skills acquired during the program.

Conclusion

A growing body of research suggests that a compassionate lifestyle is good for our psychological, social, and physical wellbeing. Self-compassion is a healthy way to relate to ourselves and has been linked to resilience and reduced burnout in health-care providers. Several compassion training programs are available to cultivate compassion and self-compassion by combining meditative and psychological methods. Although most curricula were not explicitly designed for physicians, reported gains in positive mood, life satisfaction, and self-compassion and reductions in anxiety and depression could be beneficial to health-care practitioners. Of special relevance to doctors is emerging evidence that compassion training may enhance emotion regulation and buffer against empathic distress, a contributor to physician burnout. More research is needed to delineate the effectiveness and limitations of compassion training in physician cohorts. Tailoring curricula to the challenges faced by providers in clinical settings, as in the Being With Dying program, may improve applicability in medical practice. Preliminary research suggests that designing for the convenience of health-care practitioners may broaden the appeal of compassion training and extend its benefits to a wider audience. In an era of epidemic physician burnout, compassion training is a promising approach to fostering resilience and wellbeing by helping physicians to take better care of themselves.

References

Allen AB, Goldwasser ER, Leary MR (2012) Self-Compassion and Well-being among Older Adults. Self Identity 11:428–453.

Barnard LK, Curry JF (2011) Self-compassion: Conceptualizations, Correlates, & Interventions. Review of General Psychology 15:289–303.

Brito G (2014) Secular Compassion Training: An Empirical Review. Journal of Transpersonal Research 6:61–71.

Condon P, Feldman Barrett L (2013) Conceptualizing and experiencing compassion. Emotion 13:817–821.

Crum A, Zuckerman B (2017) Changing Mindsets to Enhance Treatment Effectiveness. JAMA 317:2063–2064.

Decety J, Lamm C (2011) Empathy versus Personal Distress: Recent Evidence from Social Neuroscience. In: Decety J, Ickes W (eds) The Social Neuroscience of Empathy. MIT Press.

Decety J, Svetlova M (2011) Putting together phylogenetic and ontogenetic perspectives on empathy. Developmental Cognitive Neuroscience 2:1–24.

Demerouti E, Bakker AB (2008) The Oldenburg Burnout Inventory: A good alternative to measure burnout and engagement. In: Halbesleben JRB (ed) Handbook of Stress and Burnout in Health Care. Nova Science, Hauppauge, NY.

Desbordes G, Negi LT, Pace TWW, Wallace BA, Raison CL, Schwartz EL (2012) Effects of mindful-attention and compassion meditation training on amygdala response to emotional stimuli in an ordinary, non-meditative state. Front Hum Neurosci 6:292.

Dodds SE, Pace TWW, Bell ML, Fiero M, Negi LT, Raison CL, Weihs KL (2015) Feasibility of cognitively-based compassion training (CBCT) for breast cancer survivors: a randomized, wait list controlled pilot study. Supportive Care in Cancer 23:3599–3608.

Dunn EW, Aknin LB, Norton MI (2008) Spending money on others promotes happiness. Science 319:1687–1688.

Engen HG, Singer T (2015) Compassion-based emotion regulation up-regulates experienced positive affect and associated neural networks. Soc Cogn Affect Neurosci 10:1291–1301.

Fortney L, Luchterhand C, Zakletskaia L, Zgierska A, Rakel D (2013) Abbreviated mindfulness intervention for job satisfaction, quality of life, and compassion in primary care clinicians: a pilot study. Ann Fam Med 11:412–420.

Fredrickson BL, Cohn MA, Coffey KA, Pek J, Finkel SM (2008) Open hearts build lives: positive emotions, induced through loving-kindness meditation, build consequential personal resources. J Pers Soc Psychol 95:1045–1062.

Galante J, Galante I, Bekkers MJ, Gallacher J (2014) Effect of kindness-based meditation on health and well-being: a systematic review and meta-analysis. J Consult Clin Psychol 82:1101–1114.

Germer CK, Neff KD (2013a) The mindful self-compassion training program. In: Singer T, Bolz M (eds) Compassion: Bridging practice and science: A multimedia book. Max Planck Institute for Human Cognitive and Brain Sciences, Leipzig.

Germer CK, Neff KD (2013b) Self-compassion in clinical practice. J Clin Psychol 69:856–867.

Gilbert P, McEwan K, Matos M, Rivis A (2011) Fears of compassion: Development of three self-report measures. Psychology and Psychotherapy: Theory, Research and Practice 84:239–255.

Gilmartin H, Goyal A, Hamati MC, Mann J, Saint S, Chopra V (2017) Brief Mindfulness Practices for Healthcare Providers - A Systematic Literature Review. Am J Med 130:1219.e1–1219.e17.

Gleichgerrcht E, Decety J (2013) Empathy in clinical practice: how individual dispositions, gender, and experience moderate empathic concern, burnout, and emotional distress in physicians. PLoS One 8:e61526.

Goetz JL, Keltner D, Simon-Thomas E (2010) Compassion: an evolutionary analysis and empirical review. Psychol Bull 136:351–374.

Goetz JL, Simon-Thomas E (2017) The Landscape of Compassion: Definitions and Scientific Approaches. In: Seppälä EM, Simon-Thomas E, Brown SL, Worline MC, Cameron CD, Doty JR (eds) Oxford Handbook of Compassion Science. Oxford University Press, New York.

Goldin PR, Jazaieri H (2017) The Compassion Cultivation Training (CCT) Program. In: Seppälä EM, Simon-Thomas E, Brown SL, Worline MC, Cameron CD, Doty JR (eds) Oxford Handbook of Compassion Science. Oxford University Press, New York.

Halifax J (2012) A heuristic model of enactive compassion. Curr Opin Support Palliat Care 6:228–235.

Halifax J (2013) Being with dying: Curriculum for the professional training programme in compassionate end-of-life-care. In: Singer T, Bolz M (eds) Compassion: Bridging practice and science: A multimedia book. Max Planck Institute for Human Cognitive and Brain Sciences, Leipzig.

Hall CW, Row KA, Wuensh KL, Godley KR (2013) The role of self-compassion in physical and psychological well-being. The Journal of Psychology 147:311–323.

Hodges SD, Klein KJK (2001) Regulating the costs of empathy: the price of being human. The Journal of Socio-economics 30:437–452.

Hofmann SG, Grossman P, Hinton DE (2011) Loving-kindness and compassion meditation: Potential for psychological interventions. Clinical Psychology Review 31:1126–1132.

Homan KJ (2016) Self-Compassion and Psychological Well-Being in Older Adults. J Adult Dev 23:111–119.

Jazaieri H, Jinpa GT, McGonigal K, Rosenberg EL, Finkelstein J, Simon-Thomas E, Cullen M, Doty JR, Gross JJ, Goldin PR (2013) Enhancing Compassion: A Randomized Controlled Trial of a Compassion Cultivation Training Program. J Happiness Stud 14:1113–1126.

Jazaieri H, Lee IA, McGonigal K, Jinpa T, Doty JR, Gross JJ, Goldin PR (2015) A wandering mind is a less caring mind: Daily experience sampling during compassion meditation training. The Journal of Positive Psychology 11:37–50.

Jazaieri H, McGonigal K, Jinpa T, Doty JR, Gross JJ, Goldin PR (2014) A randomized controlled trial of compassion cultivation training: Effects on mindfulness, affect, and emotion regulation. Motivation and Emotion 38:23–35.

Jazaieri H, McGonigal K, Lee IA, Jinpa T, Doty JR, Gross JJ, Goldin PR (2017) Altering the Trajectory of Affect and Affect Regulation: the Impact of Compassion Training. Mindfulness 9:283–293.

Jinpa T (2015) A Fearless Heart: How the Courage to Be Compassionate Can Transform Our Lives. Hudson Street Press, New York.

Jinpa T, Weiss L (2013) Compassion Cultivation Training (CCT). In: Singer T, Bolz M (eds) Compassion: Bridging practice and science: A multimedia book. Max Planck Institute for Human Cognitive and Brain Sciences, Leipzig.

Johnson EA, O'Brien KA (2013) Self-compassion soothes the savage ego-threat system: Effects on negative affect, shame, rumination, and depressive symptoms. Journal of Social and Clinical Psychology 32:939–963.

Kabat-Zinn J (2003) Mindfulness-based interventions in context: past, present, and future. Clinical Psychology: Science and Practice 10:144–156.

Kelly AC (2010) Training in self-compassion: Reducing distress and facilitating behaviour change. Dissertation, McGill University.

Kemper KJ, Mo X, Khayat R (2015) Are Mindfulness and Self-Compassion Associated with Sleep and Resilience in Health Professionals. J Altern Complement Med 21:496–503.

Kirby JN (2016) Compassion interventions: The programmes, the evidence, and implications for research and practice. Psychol Psychother 90:432–455.

Klimecki OM, Leiberg S, Ricard M, Singer T (2014) Differential pattern of functional brain plasticity after compassion and empathy training. Soc Cogn Affect Neurosci 9:873–879.

Konrath S, Fuhrel-Forbis A, Lou A, Brown S (2012) Motives for volunteering are associated with mortality risk in older adults. Health Psychol 31:87–96.

Kornfield J (2008) The Art of Forgiveness, Lovingkindness, and Peace. Bantam Books, New York.

Krasner MS, Epstein RM, Beckman H, Suchman AL (2009) Association of an educational program in mindful communication with burnout, empathy, and attitudes among primary care physicians. JAMA 302:1284–1293.

Krause N, Herzog A, Baker E (1992) Providing support to others and well-being in later life. Journal of Gerontology 47:P300–P311.

Lamothe M, Boujut E, Zenasni F, Sultan S (2014) To be or not to be empathic: the combined role of empathic concern and perspective taking in understanding burnout in general practice. BMC Family Practice 15:15.

Lavelle BD (2016) Against One Method: Contemplation in Context. In: Purser R, Forbes D, Burke A (eds) Handbook of Mindfulness: Culture, Context, and Social Engagement. Springer International Publishing.

Lavelle BD (2017) Compassion in Context: Tracing the Buddhist Roots of Secular, Compassion-Based Contemplative Programs. In: Seppälä EM, Simon-Thomas E, Brown SL, Worline MC, Cameron CD, Doty JR (eds) Oxford Handbook of Compassion Science. Oxford University Press, New York.

Lazarus RS (1991) Emotion and Adaptation. Oxford University Press, New York.

MacBeth A, Gumley A (2012) Exploring compassion: A meta-analysis of the association between self-compassion and psychopathology. Clinical Psychology Review 32:545–552.

Makransky J (2012) Compassion in Buddhist psychology. In: Germer CK, Siegel RD (eds) Compassion and Wisdom in Psychotherapy. Guilford Press, New York.

Marsh AA (2016) Neural, cognitive, and evolutionary foundations of human altruism. Wiley Interdisciplinary Reviews: Cognitive Science 7:59–71.

Mascaro JS, Kelley S, Darcher A, Negi LT, Worthman C, Miller A, Raison C (2016) Meditation buffers medical student compassion from the deleterious effects of depression. The Journal of Positive Psychology 13:133–142.

Mascaro JS, Negi LT, Raison CL (2017) Cognitively Based Compassion Training: Gleaning Generalities from Specific Biological Effects. In: Seppälä EM, Simon-Thomas E, Brown SL, Worline MC, Cameron CD, Doty JR (eds) Oxford Handbook of Compassion Science. Oxford University Press, New York.

Mascaro JS, Rilling JK, Negi LT, Raison CL (2012) Compassion meditation enhances empathic accuracy and related neural activity. Soc Cogn Affect Neurosci 8:48–55.

Maslach C, Leiter MP (2008) The Truth About Burnout: How Organizations Cause Personal Stress and What to Do About It. Jossey-Bass, San Francisco.

Millar MG, Millar KU, Tesser A (1988) The effects of helping and focus of attention on mood states. Personality and Social Psychology Bulletin 14:536–543.

Montgomery A (2014) The inevitability of physician burnout: Implications for interventions. Burnout Research 1:50–56.

Neff KD (2003) Self-compassion: An alternative conceptualization of a healthy attitude toward oneself. Self and Identity 2:85–101.

Neff KD (2011) Self-Compassion, Self-Esteem, and Well-Being. Social and Personality Psychology Compass 5:1–12.

Neff KD (2012) The science of self-compassion. In: Germer CK, Siegel RD (eds) Compassion and Wisdom in Psychotherapy. Guilford Press, New York.

Neff KD, Germer CK (2012) A pilot study and randomized controlled trial of the mindful self-compassion program. Journal of Clinical Psychology 69:28–44.

Neff KD, Rude SS, Kirkpatrick KL (2007) An examination of self-compassion in relation to positive psychological functioning and personality traits. Journal of Research in Personality 41: 908–916.

Olson K, Kemper KJ, Mahan JD (2015) What factors promote resilience and protect against burnout in first-year pediatric and medicine-pediatric residents. J Evid Based Complementary Altern Med 20:192–198.

Ozawa-de Silva B, Negi LT (2013) Cognitively-based compassion training (CBCT)–Protocol and key concepts. In: Singer T, Bolz M (eds) Compassion: Bridging practice and science: A multimedia book. Max Planck Institute for Human Cognitive and Brain Sciences, Leipzig.

Ozawa-de Silva BR, Dodson-Lavelle B, Raison CL, Negi LT, Silva BRO, Phil D (2012) Compassion and ethics: scientific and practical approaches to the cultivation of compassion as a foundation for ethical subjectivity and well-being. Journal of Healthcare, Science and the Humanities 2:145–161.

Pace TW, Negi LT, Adame DD, Cole SP, Sivilli TI, Brown TD, Issa MJ, Raison CL (2009) Effect of compassion meditation on neuroendocrine, innate immune and behavioral responses to psychosocial stress. Psychoneuroendocrinology 34:87–98.

Post SG (2005) Altruism, happiness, and health: It's good to be good. International Journal of Behavioral Medicine 12:66–77.

Rushton CH, Sellers DE, Heller KS, Spring B, Dossey BM, Halifax J (2009) Impact of a contemplative end-of-life training program: Being with dying. Palliative and Supportive Care 7:405–414.

Schwartz C, Meisenhelder JB, Ma Y, Reed G (2003) Altruistic Social Interest Behaviors Are Associated With Better Mental Health. Psychosomatic Medicine 65:778–785.

Seppälä EM, Hutcherson CA, Nguyen DTH, Doty JR, Gross JJ (2014) Loving-kindness meditation: a tool to improve healthcare provider compassion, resilience, and patient care. J of Compassionate Health Care 1:5.

Shanafelt TD, Hasan O, Dyrbye LN, Sinsky C, Satele D, Sloan J, West CP (2015) Changes in Burnout and Satisfaction With Work-Life Balance in Physicians and the General US Working Population Between 2011 and 2014. Mayo Clin Proc 90:1600–1613.

Shapira LB, Mongrain M (2010) The benefits of self-compassion and optimism exercises for individuals vulnerable to depression. The Journal of Positive Psychology 5:377–389.

Shapiro J (2013) The feeling physician: educating the emotions in medical training. European Journal for Person Centered Healthcare 1:310–316.

Shapiro SL, Astin JA, Bishop SR, Cordova M (2005) Mindfulness-based stress reduction for health care professionals: results from a randomized trial. International Journal of Stress Management 12:164–176.

Shonin E, Gordon WV, Compare A, Zangeneh M (2015) Buddhist-derived loving-kindness and compassion meditation for the treatment of psychopathology: a systematic review. Mindfulness 6:1161–1180.

Simpson JA, Beckes L (2010) Evolutionary perspectives on prosocial behavior. In: Mikulincer M, Shaver PR (eds) Prosocial Motives, Emotions, and Behavior: The Better Angels of Our Nature. American Psychological Association, Washington.

Singer T, Lamm C (2009) The social neuroscience of empathy. Ann N Y Acad Sci 1156:81–96.

Skwara AC, Brandon GK, Saron CD (2017) Studies of Training Compassion: What Have We Learned; What Remains Unknown? In: Seppälä EM, Simon-Thomas E, Brown SL, Worline MC, Cameron CD, Doty JR (eds) Oxford Handbook of Compassion Science. Oxford University Press, New York.

Sprecher S, Fehr B (2006) Enhancement of mood and self-esteem as a result of giving and receiving compassionate love. Current Research in Social Psychology 11:227–242.

Stellar JE, Keltner D (2014) Compassion. In: Tugade M, Shiota L, Kirby L (eds) Handbook of Positive Emotion. Guilford Press, New York.

Trockel M, Hamidi M, Murphy M, Purpur de Vries P, Bohman B (2016) Stanford 2016 Physician Wellness Survey. https://wellmd.stanford.edu/content/dam/sm/wellmd/documents/Full-2016-Physician-Wellness-Survey-Report-16-Aug-2017-Final-rd.pdf. Accessed 24 Mar 2018.

Valdesolo P, Desteno D (2011) Synchrony and the social tuning of compassion. Emotion 11:262–266.

Weng HY, Fox AS, Shackman AJ, Stodola DE, Caldwell JZ, Olson MC, Rogers GM, Davidson RJ (2013) Compassion training alters altruism and neural responses to suffering. Psychol Sci 24:1171–1180.

West CP, Dyrbye LN, Erwin PJ, Shanafelt TD (2016) Interventions to prevent and reduce physician burnout: a systematic review and meta-analysis. Lancet 388:2272–2281.

Yeager DS, Walton GM (2011) Social-Psychological Interventions in Education: They're Not Magic. Review of Educational Research 81:267–301.

Zeng X, Chiu CP, Wang R, Oei TP, Leung FY (2015) The effect of loving-kindness meditation on positive emotions: a meta-analytic review. Front Psychol 6:1693.

Part II
Recognizing Threats to Physician Wellbeing

Chapter 4
Mistreatment

Jessica Rainey-Clay and Rebecca Smith-Coggins

Case Illustration
I would like to put on the record that Dr. X was the physician whom I saw verbally abuse and humiliate a medical student. This medical student came into the OR, stood at the foot of the bed, and was completely ignored for about 15 minutes. He finally spoke up and said 'So, Dr. X, you're doing a procedure today?' Dr. X started mocking and verbally ridiculing him. The student stood at the foot of the bed for the remainder of the surgery and continued to be unacknowledged after this episode. – Anonymous medical student

Introduction

Given the many demands in the medical arena, it is not surprising that there is, at times, a suboptimal learning environment. Patient care needs take priority over education.

J. Rainey-Clay · R. Smith-Coggins (✉)
Stanford University, Department of Emergency Medicine,
Stanford, CA, USA
e-mail: smithcog@stanford.edu

© Springer Nature Switzerland AG 2019   57
L. Weiss Roberts, M. Trockel (eds.),
The Art and Science of Physician Wellbeing,
https://doi.org/10.1007/978-3-319-42135-3_4

What may be striking is that, according to national reports, there is an abusive culture that exists within medical education. Abusive behavior in the medical domain has become known as "mistreatment," and it tends to follow hierarchical lines of responsibility. Learners on the lower end of the power differential report feeling publicly humiliated and experience being the subjects of degrading comments. This behavior directly impacts the learner's sense of wellbeing. Mistreatment most likely arises from a lack of wellness on the educator's part. It may play a role in the quality of care that a patient receives as well.

History and Prevalence

The phenomenon of medical student abuse was first described by Silver et al. in 1982 (Silver 1982). As a pediatrician, Dr. Silver's research focused on child abuse. He noticed that medical students at the University of Colorado exhibited some of the same behaviors as children from abusive homes. He asked medical students at the University of Colorado about their experience with abuse in a questionnaire. A total of 46% of all students and 80.6% of seniors who responded reported feeling abused at some point during their medical education. Of those students who reported abuse, 69% reported at least one incident that they considered of "major importance and very upsetting."

At that time, Silver defined learner abuse as unnecessary or avoidable acts or words of a negative nature inflicted on another person or persons. Additionally, he compared medical students to abused children in a rather disconcerting way. He noted that medical students are in vulnerable positions, emotionally and hierarchically. Often the "abusers," medical educators, like abusive parents, do not recognize or appreciate their behaviors or their effects on the learners. The mistreating educator is unwittingly perpetuating a culture of mistreatment and an unhealthy power dynamic that often reflects his or her prior educational experience on the lower end of the hierarchy. This seems to parallel how abused, victimized children can develop abusive behaviors (Rosenberg and Silver 1984).

Anyone who has completed medical school and residency has most likely experienced or witnessed mistreatment. Data from the Accreditation Council for Graduate Medical Education (ACGME) surveys from nearly 20 years ago estimate that up to 80% of medical school graduates report abuse during training (Silver and Glicken 1990). More recent literature and survey analysis estimate that 59–76% of medical students and residents report mistreatment (Fnais et al. 2014; Cook et al. 2014). Today, similar surveys find that the prevalence of reported mistreatment is persistently high despite an increased awareness of mistreatment within medical education (Fried et al. 2012). In fact, the ACGME and the Association of American Medical Colleges (AAMC) have adopted mistreatment questions in their annual surveys of residents and medical students, respectively.

Types of Mistreatment

According to the AAMC:

> ...it must be acknowledged that the social and behavioral diversity of students, faculty, residents, and staff, combined with the intensity of the interactions between them, will, from time to time, lead to alleged, perceived or real incidents of inappropriate behavior or mistreatment of individuals. Examples of mistreatment include sexual harassment; discrimination or harassment based on race, religion, ethnicity, gender, sexual orientation, physical handicap or age; humiliation, psychological or physical punishment and the use of grading and other forms of assessment in a punitive manner. (Petersdorf 1992)

These behaviors are considered by the AAMC to be indicative of student mistreatment:

- Public humiliation
- Requiring a student to perform personal services
- Physical harm or threatening with physical harm
- Denial of opportunities for training or rewards based solely on gender, race, ethnicity, or sexual orientation

- Giving lower evaluations or grades solely because of gender, race, ethnicity, or sexual orientation
- Use of racially or ethnically offensive remarks
- Use of offensive remarks/names related to sexual orientation
- Use of offensive sexist remarks
- Unwanted sexual advances
- Asking to exchange sexual favors for grades or other rewards

Sources of Mistreatment

The individuals who resort to disrespectful behavior in the medical arena are from all disciplines. According to the most recent AAMC graduation questionnaire, medical students reported that interns and residents (14.4%) are almost as likely to be the sources of mistreatment as the faculty (17.7%) (Association of American Medical Colleges 2016). However, nurses and fellow medical students have been reported as well. Mullan et al. note that interns reported nurses as the most frequent source of disruptive behavior while attending physicians primarily reported other physicians (Mullan et al. 2013).

In addition to medical personnel, patients and families have been reported to be sources of mistreatment (Crutcher et al. 2011; Whitgob et al. 2016). These studies note that 40–67% of reported incidents of mistreatment were due to patients and families.

The Interplay of Wellness and Mistreatment

Certain influences on individuals may create a climate conducive to disrespectful behavior. A physician's sense of wellbeing is most likely one such influence. As an educator becomes hungry, fatigued, or burned out, his/her patience diminishes. At that point, he or she may lash out at another individual, who is likely to be lower in the medical hierarchy. This disrespectful behavior will almost certainly decrease the abused person's sense of wellbeing. The educating physician may end up feeling worse too.

Impact on Learners

The current medical culture seems to perpetuate mistreatment and learner abuse as the accepted socialization process. Patient care team structure may be a significant part of the problem. The patient care team structure has evolved over time to provide continuity of care, maximize exposure of cases for resident education, facilitate workload delegation, and enhance connections among consistent team members. By switching rotations regularly, learners have increased educational opportunities; however, the constantly changing environment can be stressful. Additionally, the continual influx of new, inexperienced medical students on the team forces medical students to function inefficiently from the periphery (Bynum and Lindeman 2016). Medical students are forced into a passive role, and their learning is often through observation. In reality, the medical student, by virtue of inexperience and frequent rotational changes, may make more work for the typically already overworked and stressed resident team members. Medical students are outside of the group, not fully incorporated into the team dynamics, and often are perceived as being minimally contributory to the team. Thus, medical students find themselves ignored and disrespected. They are negatively impacted by the unprofessional behavior of their superiors.

When medical students are disrespected, medical student wellbeing suffers. The suboptimal learning environment can lead to increased feelings of stress, depersonalization, objectification, and self-doubt (Richman et al. 1992). Studies show that students who have been exposed to mistreatment and poor professionalism during their education have higher rates of depression and stress (Haglund et al. 2009). Individuals in this cascade of burnout often progress to unhealthy and self-destructive behavior, as many medical learners do not have the ability to recognize burnout or to implement mechanisms for recovery or prevention.

From this suboptimal learning environment, students may also learn that unprofessional behavior is acceptable. Some may perceive disrespect as the norm. The mistreated learner may unknowingly adopt similar patterns, ultimately perpetuating an abusive culture within medicine. By developing unprofessional tendencies, students may find that their personal and professional relationships are compromised, which in turn may impact their wellbeing and further interfere with their educational opportunities. The cycle of disrespect, unprofessionalism, and loss of wellbeing supports the prevalence and persistence of learner mistreatment in the culture of medicine.

Impact on Mistreater

Another important consideration is the effect on the person who is the source of the mistreatment. Anecdotal evidence reveals that many residents and faculty are remorseful and surprised at the perception of their actions when they are informed that they have mistreated students. Some become defensive or blame modern medical culture for coddling students too much. Mistreatment behaviors are often out of character. These educators often care deeply about their students' education and put concerted effort into their educational endeavors. A combination of educator fatigue, a stressful work environment, concern for unstable patients, and a lack of formal education in teaching may lead to disrespectful behaviors. Hence, mistreatment may be born from diminished educator wellbeing and may in turn cause worsening educator morale. When learners give anonymous feedback about incidents of perceived mistreatment, educators may become demoralized and decide to pull away from teaching and interacting with learners. What once brought educators a sense of purpose and reward can result in feelings of resentment or feelings of being unappreciated and misunderstood. Physician compensation is generally lower in the academic setting than in private practice, and negative feedback can have a detrimental impact on educators' appointments, promotions, bonuses, and opportunities. Although compensation varies widely by specialty, estimates suggest an average of a 13%

lower compensation for academic compared to nonacademic providers (Davis 2016).

Solutions

To help enact change, below is a set of recommendations compiled from both the literature and ongoing educational programs. First and foremost, education is critical for both learners and educators in order to increase awareness of mistreatment and how to report it. Institution-wide transparency about the effects of reporting mistreatment is important. One of the reasons listed in institutional, AAMC, and ACGME surveys for not reporting mistreatment is that learners feel that no significant action would be taken. As modeled by the Stanford medical student mistreatment program, a detailed and transparent system can encourage learners to report mistreatment. The Stanford program ensures that the mistreating educator is coached with constructive feedback initially, with mandated education if a second incident occurs, and with a more aggressive rehabilitative intervention if recurrent mistreatment incidents occur (Smith-Coggins et al. 2017).

With disrespectful behavior playing a significant role in our medical education, it is important to approach this issue from multiple angles to find solutions that will decrease the severity and prevalence of mistreatment. Learners can be given the skills to interact in a professionally constructive manner at the time of disrespectful behavior so that it can be acknowledged and resolved contemporaneously. Mistreatment recognition, management, and prevention should be incorporated in the didactic curricula of both students and residents. Both learners and educators who experience or witness mistreatment should be empowered to speak up without fear of retaliation and with the assurance that their concerns will be heard and acted upon.

Programs have been developed to attempt to lessen mistreatment within the institutional framework (Smith-Coggins et al. 2017; Lau et al. 2017). Any evidence of retribution by an educator must be handled swiftly and decidedly in order to show that the medical culture does not allow for mistreatment. Students need to be able to report mistreatment anonymously without fear of reprisal. A two-tiered feedback mechanism would be useful so that learners could give constructive feedback to educators, formative feedback could go to the educator, and summative feedback could be kept in the educator's file.

Educators need to be coached in methods of avoiding disrespectful behavior. Residents, while still very much in the learner role, are often faced with the sudden expectation of teaching students, without recognition of this dichotomy by the system or education on how to balance these new roles. A clear and thorough description of learner roles and responsibilities at the outset of a rotation can avoid many misunderstandings that are perceived as mistreatment. An understanding of the importance of patient care as a priority, especially when a patient is unstable, can avoid resentments.

A focus on educator well-being will be immensely beneficial. In addition, organizations must be able to recognize when negative faculty behavior is not driven by fatigue or burnout but rather relates to character pathology in which the faculty member exploits a position of power to abuse others. This said, organizations must recognize system problems that contribute to a stressful work environment and proactively take measures to protect the wellbeing of educators. Specific mandatory rehabilitative interventions need to be established and enforced at the departmental and institutional level for repetitive mistreatment behavior by individuals. Each institution should work to establish a program for safe confidential reporting that is linked to resources for reporter support and debriefing. A secure system needs to be established to keep track of mistreatment incidents. Individuals should be assisted with feedback to increase awareness of their behavior and its effect on learners. They should also be provided with resources for professional development through coaching by trained senior faculty. All educators benefit from an educational approach where they are informed of mistreatment behaviors, the reporting process, and educational interventions for recurrent incidences. This quality improvement model can provide hope for the healing of our medical culture. In this hopeful paradigm, dynamics driven by stress, trauma, and fear perpetuating mistreatment can be replaced with a supportive training culture defined by compassion and respect for educators and students that includes high expectations for competent, professional, and compassionate behavior from both, even in the face of stress.

To lessen the prevalence and subsequent effects of mistreatment of health-care professionals by patients and families, physicians and trainees need to learn to address these situations in a professional manner. One study describes team debriefing and critical reflection as strategies to better understand and respond to these denigrating experiences (Whitgob et al. 2016).

Conclusion

Mistreatment is so prevalent in medical education that it is often assumed, by both trainees and educators alike, to be socially and professionally acceptable. Mistreatment of learners is never appropriate and is counterproductive to the goal of training successful, effective, and healthy medical professionals. The field of medicine needs a sweeping cultural revision at all levels, including learners, educators, and institutions, in order to have a meaningful and lasting impact on the system. Learners need to be taught how to manage and respond to mistreatment, as well as how to provide constructive feedback to their educators. Educators and the institutions that employ them need to take the initiative to recognize signs of burnout and find ways to help manage stress so that educators can provide constructive, meaningful education to their learners. In a health-care system in which abuse is pervasive, team structure and teaching methods need to be examined thoroughly, and the numerous factors leading to mistreatment need to be addressed. Ultimately, learner mistreatment negatively affects clinical wellness, which negatively affects patient care. In addition, the distress that mistreatment causes renders mistreated clinicians at higher risk of mistreating future learners, and a vicious cycle is perpetuated.

In summary, medical learner mistreatment occurs at all levels of education, from medical students and interns through more senior house staff, fellows, and attending physicians. Mistreatment can cause detrimental effects on the health and wellbeing of health-care professionals and can lead to adverse consequences for hospital efficiency and patient care.

References

Association of American Medical Colleges. (2016, July). Medical school graduation questionnaire: 2016 all schools summary report. Retrieved June 2017, from AAMC: https://www.aamc.org/download/464412/data/2016gqallschoolssummaryreport.pdf

Bynum WE, Lindeman B (2016). Caught in the middle: a resident perspective on influences from the learning environment that perpetuate mistreatment. Acad Med 91: 301–304.

Cook AF, Arora VM, Rasinski KA, Curlin FA, Yoon JD (2014). The prevalence of medical student mistreatment and its associating with burnout. Acad Med 89: 749–754.

Crutcher RA, Szafran O, Woloschuk W, Chatur F, Hansen C (2011). Family medicine graduates' perceptions of intimidation, harassment, and discrimination during residency training. BMC Med Educ 11: 88.

Davis J. (2016, July). We analyzed 35,000 physician salaries. Doximity (blog). https://blog.doximity.com/articles/we-analyzed-35-000-physician-salaries-here-s-what-we-found.

Fnais N, Soobiah C, Chen MH, Lillie E, Perrier L, Tashkhandi M, Straus SE, et al. (2014). Harassment and discrimination in medical training: A systematic review and meta-analysis. Acad Med 89: 817–827.

Fried JM, Vermillion M, Parker NH, Uijtdehaage S (2012). Eradicating medical student mistreatment: A longitudinal study of one institution's efforts. Acad Med 87: 1191–1198.

Haglund ME, aan het Rot M, Cooper NS, Nestadt PS, Muller D, Southwick SM, et al. (2009). Resilience in the third year of medical school: A prospective study of the associations between stressful events occurring during clinical rotations and student well-being. Acad Med(84: 258–268.

Lau JN, Mazer LM, Leibert CA, Merrell SB, Lin DT, Harris I. (2017, July) A Mixed-Methods Analysis of a Novel Mistreatment Program for the Surgery Core Clerkship. Acad Med 92(7) : 1028–1034.

Mullan CP, Shapiro J, McMahon GT (2013, March). Interns' experiences of disruptive behavior in an academic medical center. Journal of Graduate Medical Education: 25–30.

Petersdorf RG. Student Mistreatment. Association of American Medical Colleges. Washington DC. 28 July 1992. Memo. https://www.aamc.org/members/gsa/54690/gsa_mistreatment.html

Richman JA, Flaherty JA, Rospenda KM, Christensen ML (1992). Mental health consequences and correlates of reported medical student abuse. JAMA 267(5): 692–694.

Rosenberg DA, Silver HK (1984, Feb). Medical Student Abuse: An Unnecessary and Preventable Cause of Stress. JAMA 251(6): 739–742.

Smith-Coggins R, Prober CG, Wakefield K, Farias R. (2017, April). Zero Tolerance: Implementation and Evaluation of the Stanford Medical Student Mistreatment Prevention Program. Acad Psychiatry 41(2): 195–199.

Silver HK. (1982). Medical students and medical schools. JAMA 247: 309–310.

Silver HK, Glicken AD (1990). Medical Student Abuse. Incidence, Severity, and Significance. JAMA 263: 527–532.

Whitgob EE, Blankenburg RL, Bogetz AL (2016). The discriminatory patient and family: strategies to address discrimination towards trainees. Acad Med 91: s64–s69.

Chapter 5
Burnout

Jessica A. Gold

Case Illustration

Jane, a 28-year-old second-year internal medicine resident, hits her alarm clock at 5 AM to go to the hospital. When it goes off, she lets out a sigh and feels very little motivation to get out of bed. Yet, like she has done for almost 2 years, she gets out of bed and drives to work. While at work, she rounds on her patients, snapping at one who asks her for a glass of water, and dismissing a family member who tries to ask her a question. A peer who has noticed that Jane has been a lot more negative lately and has not been acting like herself asks Jane what is wrong. Jane replies, "I just hate everything about being here and I have another full year to go."

J. A. Gold (✉)
Washington University in St. Louis, Department of Psychiatry,
St. Louis, MO, USA
e-mail: jgold@wustl.edu

© Springer Nature Switzerland AG 2019
L. Weiss Roberts, M. Trockel (eds.),
The Art and Science of Physician Wellbeing,
https://doi.org/10.1007/978-3-319-42135-3_5

Part I: What Is Burnout?

In 1974, a psychologist named Herbert Freudenberger coined a term to describe job dissatisfaction related to work stress. He named it "burnout" (Freudenberger 1974). Since that time, our understanding of burnout as a syndrome has evolved. Broadly speaking, the World Health Organization defines it as a "state of vital exhaustion" (Fralick and Flegel 2014), and it is commonly understood to be a state of mental and physical exhaustion related to work (Ishak et al. 2009). More specifically, burnout is often broken down into three domains as described by Maslach and Jackson (1981): emotional exhaustion, depersonalization, and reduced personal accomplishment (Maslach and Jackson 1981).

To better understand the meaning of the domains of burnout, Jane's case will serve as an example. Jane has very little enthusiasm to get out of bed and go to work and describes "hating" her job and feeling trapped ("I have another full year to go"). These are symptoms of emotional exhaustion, often caused by prolonged stress, which can lead to feelings of helplessness, defeat, and loss of enthusiasm at work. Jane is also indifferent toward her patients and negative toward her colleagues and her profession. She is therefore also exhibiting signs of depersonalization. The final domain, reduced personal accomplishment, is represented by detachment from one's job and withdrawal from responsibilities. In Jane's case, this happens when she does not want to get out of bed. It also shows itself more subtly in her interactions and enjoyment with day-to-day work (Maslach and Jackson 1981; Schaufeli et al. 1996). Therefore, by definition, Jane is burned out, a constellation of symptoms that could be quantified further using the scale developed by Maslach and Jackson (1981). While burnout or burnout syndrome gives a name to what Jane is suffering from, burnout is not yet a diagnosis and is not included in diagnostic classification systems like the International Statistical Classification of Diseases and Related Health Problems (ICD)-10 or the Diagnostic and Statistical Manual of Mental Disorders (DSM)-5.

Part II: Epidemiology of Burnout

Like Jane, approximately one-half of US physicians will experience burnout throughout their careers, a number that has been increasing from 2011 to 2014 (Shanafelt et al. 2015b). It is present in all stages of training, affecting 28–45% of medical students and 27–75% of residents (Ishak et al. 2009), and varies across specialties. In fact, the highest rates are seen in physicians that are considered to be on the "front lines" of care, or those who practice family medicine, internal medicine, and emergency medicine (Shanafelt et al. 2012). It is clear that burnout is a significant issue in physicians and physicians-in-training.

To better understand the uniqueness of burnout to physician-hood, studies have compared physician populations with matched population controls. The data suggest that medical students, residents and fellows, and early-career physicians are all statistically more likely to be burned out than their matched samples (Dyrbye et al. 2014). Physicians were also more likely than working adults in the US to be dissatisfied with their work-life balance (Shanafelt et al. 2012). In fact, being a physician or physician-in-training is a risk factor for burnout. While those with higher levels of education and professional degrees were found to have lower rates of burnout compared to high school graduates, this was not the case for MD or DO degrees. Instead, simply having a degree in medicine increases burnout (Shanafelt et al. 2012) suggesting that an MD or DO degree is not protective like other professional degrees but instead is a risk.

Burnout also varies across physicians' careers, starting even before medical school. One study noted higher rates of burnout in premedical students than in other college students (Fang et al. 2012), yet in a different study, matriculating medical students had lower burnout rates than age-similar college graduates (Brazeau et al. 2014). It is uncertain from this data whether higher risk students choose to enter medical school in the first place or if medical school training itself leads to burnout. What is certain, however, is the high frequency of burnout in this group; in one study of 4287 medical students, 49.6% reported burnout (Dyrbye et al. 2008). Rates of burnout seem to peak after medical school and in residency. The data suggest that overall burnout and higher feelings of depersonalization and fatigue were the most prevalent in residents and fellows, as compared to early-career (EC) physicians and medical students (Dyrbye et al. 2014). Rates also vary largely by specialty and year of training, with highest rates in OB-GYN residents and in first-year residents in one study (Martini et al. 2004). When controlling for age, sex, relationship status, and career stage, being a resident or fellow was associated with increased odds of burnout (Dyrbye et al. 2014).

Looking beyond training and into physician-hood, burnout continues to vary over the course of one's career, peaking in the middle. Studies have also shown a variation by gender, with one study noting higher rates of burnout in women (38.5% vs. 28%) (Trockel et al. 2016). While early-career physicians had the highest rates of depersonalization, physicians had the most emotional exhaustion and the most burnout in the middle of their careers. This was seen across genders, specialties, and practice types (Dyrbye et al. 2013). In fact, physicians in the middle of their careers were most likely to consider leaving medicine in the next 24 months for reasons other than retirement (12.5%), when compared to early- (4.8%) and late- (5.2%) career physicians, respectively (Dyrbye et al. 2013). Ultimately, burnout is a significant factor in all stages of a physician's career and is becoming a much more prevalent and significant problem over time.

Part III: Causes of Burnout

With a clear understanding of the breadth of the problem, it is important to consider the causes or drivers of burnout in physicians. Some typical causes include high workload, lack of efficiency, lack of autonomy, challenges with work-life integration, and lack of meaning in work (Shanafelt et al. 2016c). These drivers can then be influenced by the individual physician, the team at work, the organization (the hospital, the university), and national factors (like insurance or reimbursement) (Shanafelt et al. 2016c). Given the high rates (over 50% of physicians), burnout is much more likely to be rooted in global causes like the work environment and the care delivery system, rather than personal factors or personal characteristics (Shanafelt et al. 2012), though both can contribute.

Analyzing the physician's day-to-day environment, one can identify many causes for increased stress. Studies have found that long hours (Martin 2002), job demands (Alarcon 2011), heavy work load (Shanafelt et al. 2003), sleep impairment (Trockel et al. 2016), and inefficiency due to excessive administrative work (Shanafelt et al. 2003) increase rates of burnout. In fact, physicians who used the electronic health record (EHR) were often less satisfied with the amount of time they spent on administrative work and were subsequently more likely to be burned out (Shanafelt et al. 2016a). Significant workload, with long hours and frequent clerical work, can also contribute to a loss of a sense of meaning from work, which has also been associated with higher rates of burnout (Shanafelt et al. 2003). In one study, the time a physician spent on their "most meaningful activity" was the largest predictor of burnout, or, more specifically, those who spent less than 20% of their time working on the activity they found the most meaningful had significantly higher rates of burnout (Shanafelt et al. 2009b). As most physicians reported that they derived the most meaning from patient care (68%) (Shanafelt et al. 2009b) and EHRs can often distract from clinical tasks (33% of work clinical and 49% clerical) (Sinsky et al. 2016), it is perhaps not surprising that EHRs may themselves be contributing to the rise in physician burnout (see Chap. 6).

Loss of autonomy often created by the constraints of the team and institution is also associated with high rates of burnout (Shanafelt et al. 2003). Studies have shown that constraining organizational structure, low quality and safety standards (Lee et al. 2013) and low organizational commitment (Alarcon 2011) lead to higher emotional exhaustion.

For example, rules around the scheduling of vacation, sick leave, call, and clinic start and end times can limit flexibility, and the rigid application of practice guidelines can limit clinical decision-making (Shanafelt et al. 2016c). Additionally, compensation determined entirely on billing (i.e., number of direct clinical hours) (Shanafelt et al. 2009a) and insurance regulations around note writing, prescriptions, and referrals all contribute to loss of autonomy by physicians (Shanafelt et al. 2016c). Given the effect of the organization on one's autonomy, it is perhaps not surprising that the reverse would also be true; a culture of wellness— which included things like perceived appreciation, personal alignment with the organization, and peer supportiveness—could increase professional fulfillment and thus help prevent burnout (Trockel et al. 2016) (see Chap. 2).

An additional cause of burnout is difficulty integrating one's personal and professional lives (Shanafelt et al. 2003), or work-life balance. This was found to be a much more significant contributor to burnout in the US than in Europe (Lee et al. 2013). Work-life balance can be affected on the individual level by one's spouse or children, at the level of the team due to coverage and leave, and at the level of the organization-given rules around part-time work and licensing requirements (Shanafelt et al. 2016c). In a population of surgeons, having children and working more than 60 hours a week was associated with higher levels of burnout (Shanafelt et al. 2009a). Additionally, family stress and being unmarried were associated with higher burnout in residents (Martini et al. 2004), and a positive life event, like a marriage, was associated with lower burnout in medical students (Dyrbye et al. 2009). It is important to note that causes of burnout may differ in different stages of training and career. Medical students might have fewer opportunities for meaning in their roles and thus might have a low sense of personal efficacy that will lead to burnout. Their learning climate, including being on the wards or a rotation with call, can also contribute to burnout (Dyrbye et al. 2009). Residents, however, may be burdened by new work responsibilities and the new day-to-day stress of life as a physician (Dyrbye et al. 2014). All years are affected by burnout; no stage of training or career is immune.

Part IV: Outcomes of Burnout

Why do we even care about burnout?

High rates of burnout can lead to significant consequences for physicians both personally and professionally. This, in turn, can lead to poor health outcomes for patients and systemic problems for a hospital system.

First, let's examine how burnout affects the individual physician. Studies have shown that burnout is associated with worsened mental health (Asai et al. 2007), problematic alcohol use (Shanafelt et al. 2003; Oreskovich et al. 2012), tobacco use (Soler et al. 2008), psychotropic medication use (Soler et al. 2008), and stress-related health problems (Martini et al. 2004). Burnout is also associated with suicidal ideation (Shanafelt et al. 2011). In fact, in medical school, burnout has a dose-response relationship with suicidal ideation, i.e., the higher the burnout, the more likely one is to be suicidal (Dyrbye et al. 2008). Yet, as burnout has also been associated with higher stigma and lower likelihood of seeking mental health care (Dyrbye et al. 2015), burnout becomes a serious threat to physicians' livelihood, mental health, and life.

Burnout can lead to low job satisfaction, which can have significant effects on the medical workforce. Studies have shown that higher stress can increase physician's intention to withdraw from practice (Williams et al. 2010), and increased burnout is related to early retirement (Leenders and Henkens 2010). Higher burnout is also associated with intention to leave a current position (Dewa et al. 2014b), intention to quit a specialty (Dewa et al. 2014b), and intention to leave academic medicine (Shanafelt et al. 2009b). One study showed that physicians with lower job satisfaction and higher levels of emotional exhaustion were more likely to reduce their full-time equivalent (FTE) over the following 24 months in a dose-response relationship (Shanafelt et al. 2016c). More specifically, when controlling for age, sex, and specialty, for every 1-point increase in emotional exhaustion and 1-point decrease in satisfaction, there was a 43% and 34% higher likelihood of reducing FTE, respectively (Shanafelt et al.

2016c). In another hospital, 21% of physicians who reported burnout in 2013 no longer worked at that hospital by 2015. The number of physicians with burnout who had left the hospital was more than two times the number of those without burnout who had left the hospital (Trockel et al. 2016). In medical students, one study showed that those with burnout were three times more likely to have serious thoughts of dropping out of medical school (Dyrbye et al. 2010c), with burnout always preceding thoughts of dropping out (Dyrbye et al. 2010c). Interestingly, when students "recovered" from burnout, their thoughts of wanting to drop out returned to baseline frequency (Dyrbye et al. 2010c).

As all domains of burnout have also been associated with more use of sick leave (Soler et al. 2008), it is clear burnout is a significant cost to productivity (Dewa et al. 2014b). Decrease in staff and productivity also carries a high price tag. One study found the cost of burnout-related departure of staff alone to be between US $22 and US $88 million (Trockel et al. 2016). Another study estimated the cost of burnout for the Canadian health-care system by surveying all physicians in Canada (more than 60,000 participated) and assessing the net difference between retirement and cutbacks in services between those physicians who were very dissatisfied and those who were not. Their results, which they emphasized were likely a conservative measurement, found the cost to be about 213 million Canadian dollars ($185.2 million due to early retirement and $27.9 million due to reduced clinical hours) or approximately US $159 million (Dewa et al. 2014a). Ultimately, burnout significantly affects a hospital system.

Besides decreasing the workforce, burnout can also affect patient care. Studies have shown that increased burnout is associated with decreased quality of care (Klein et al. 2010), decreased amount of time devoted to patient care (Shanafelt et al. 2016c), and self-reported suboptimal patient care in residents (Shanafelt et al. 2002). Burnout is also associated with more medical errors, with higher self-report of errors in residents who are burned out (West et al. 2006). In medical students, burnout was associated with self-reported unprofessional conduct and less altruistic professional goals and values

(Dyrbye et al. 2010a). Perhaps because of the difference in care provided or difference in empathy from the provider, job satisfaction and burnout can also affect patient adherence to recommended therapy (Dimatteo et al. 1993) and the degree of trust and confidence that patients have in their physician (Haas et al. 2000). Having higher satisfaction with one's own job can lead to higher satisfaction ratings by patients (Haas et al. 2000). Those who are burned out are not at all satisfied.

Part V: Prevention/Intervention Strategies

As burnout can be caused by the individual, the team, the organization, or the system, it is perhaps not surprising that strategies at both individual and structural or organizational levels are warranted to reduce burnout (West et al. 2016). A systematic review indicated that both individual- and organizational-level strategies produced meaningful reductions in burnout (West et al. 2016). We will briefly examine different interventions to both prevent and decrease burnout in physicians (Shanafelt et al. 2017).

Individual-Level Interventions

Several interventions at the individual level have been published in the literature. One such group of interventions focuses on enabling physicians to recognize their own needs and ask for help. Evidence suggests that providers who seek help or use coping strategies have lower emotional exhaustion (Ito and Brotheridge 2003). This might be easier said than done, however, given high levels of stigma in burned-out physicians. Only one-third of burned-out medical students seek help (Dyrbye et al. 2015). As motivation to get help is limited, it might be necessary instead to provide physicians with the knowledge and skills to better help themselves. One might hypothesize that simply educating medical students on self-care and burnout would be an effective intervention to change health habits; however, one such intervention study yielded no effects on depression, alcohol use, or stress (Ball and Bax 2002). Instead, it seems most effective to teach skills to physicians.

There are many different types of skills that have helped decrease burnout in physicians. Teaching mindfulness and enhancing self-awareness are the most studied. For medical students, a ten-session mindfulness meditation course improved mood as compared to controls (Rosenzweig et al. 2003). Another study found that an all-day stress management workshop for residents decreased emotional exhaustion, with effects still present 6 weeks after the intervention (McCue and Sachs 1991). For physicians at other levels of training or practice, mindfulness has also been proven effective. In one study, physicians were trained in four key mindfulness practices and were subsequently found to have significantly decreased burnout and enhanced mental well-being (Goodman and Schorline 2012). Another study included a 19-session, biweekly discussion group consisting of mindfulness and self-reflection for physicians. Following these sessions, physicians found work more meaningful and experienced reduced depersonalization; effects were sustained 12 months later (West et al. 2014). An additional program involved an intensive, yearlong (52-hour) curriculum on narrative medicine and mindfulness meditation. Participating physicians had large and sustained improvements in burnout, mood, and empathy (Krasner et al. 2009). Exercise was also trialed as an intervention. Twelve physicians were found to have reduced emotional exhaustion after completing 12 one-hour aerobic sessions (Gerber et al. 2013). With minimal time investment in learning new skills, individual physicians experienced significant gain and improvement in burnout. For more information on mindfulness training, see Chap. 3.

In addition to skills building, reflection groups also seem to be effective interventions for physicians. In one study, Balint sessions were found to be preventative against stress and burnout (Benson and Magraith 2005). At the Mayo Clinic, providing physicians with 1 hour of protected time to meet over food and discuss physician-hood improved meaning and reduced burnout (West et al. 2015). At Stanford, the

Balance in Life Program allows surgical residents to practice team dynamics and receive leadership training with a process group led by a clinical psychologist (Joseph 2017). Self-development groups have been effective at reducing burnout (Williams et al. 2015). Though more outcome measurements are needed to determine the best type of group to address burnout, groups are a promising intervention.

There are several other avenues at the individual level that might be effective in burnout reduction but have not yet been studied. Brief web-based cognitive behavioral interventions were found to be effective in reducing suicidal ideation (Guille et al. 2015); however, no such brief intervention has looked at the effect of skills learning on burnout. It is possible that in-person courses on mindfulness might be translated into online modules for clinicians with less time to participate (see Chap. 3). It is also possible that knowledge-based interventions that were ineffective previously might be more effective as online resources. In-person groups might translate to confidential online forums or virtual support groups where many rely on the support of others virtually. Facebook groups like the Physician Moms Group, for example, could perhaps function to reduce burnout through validation or a decrease in social isolation. Though unstudied, peer advocates (Robledo-Gil et al. 2018), who are most often sought out for mental health and relationship issues, might also help decrease burnout for trainees. Ultimately, however, at the individual level, promoting personal resilience is often preferred. While skills teaching and in-person groups have been proven effective at reducing burnout, there are many more avenues of promising interventions that warrant further investigation and interest.

Organizational-Level Interventions

While individual interventions are important, organizational interventions are key to burnout reduction. In one hospital, over 60% of physicians rated potential organizational strategies, including leadership development and collaborative practice improvement, as helpful or extremely helpful (Trockel et al. 2016). In fact, a combination of both personal and organizational interventions was found to have much longer-lasting effects (12 months or more) (Awa et al. 2010) than either alone.

Simply acknowledging that burnout is a problem, measuring burnout as a performance measure, and coming up with ways to intervene are key to overall reduction in burnout in physicians (Shanafelt and Noseworthy 2017). One primary care clinic prioritized wellbeing to the same extent as quality of care. They analyzed the factors affecting wellbeing and implemented plans for improvement. Following the implementation, physicians were found to have less emotional exhaustion (Dunn et al. 2007). At Mayo Clinic, different work units focused on specific issues that were leading to burnout and developed interventions to improve them. Each unit, no matter what the specific intervention, had a significant reduction in burnout (Swensen et al. 2016). Even at the level of the American Medical Association, the STEPS Forward Program has online modules aimed to educate physicians on how to streamline workflow, boost efficiency, and reduce administrative burden (Joseph 2017) with hopes of lowering burnout. The governing bodies of graduate medical education have also called attention to burnout by holding symposia on wellbeing and collecting educational resources for training programs to use to respond to resident suicide and encourage wellness (Joseph 2017).

The organization is also responsible for creating the learning and working environment. Studies have shown a strong dose-response relationship between the level of support (from family, friends, peers, and the medical school) and satisfaction with the environment. Higher satisfaction, in turn, was found to be protective against burnout (Dyrbye et al. 2010b). One factor that contributes to a supportive environment for trainees is the leadership and role modeling of faculty. An environment where student education was perceived as a priority for faculty was associated with recovery from burnout (Dyrbye et al. 2010b). Additionally, a focus on leadership development can lower burnout, as an increased score in leadership is related to decreased burnout (Shanafelt and Noseworthy 2017; Shanafelt et al. 2015a).

The working environment may also be improved upon by other organizational interventions. Duty hour restrictions created by the Accreditation Council for Graduate Medical Education (ACGME) have been effective in reducing burnout (Williams et al. 2015; Shanafelt et al. 2016b; Shanafelt et al. 2017). Residents benefit from access to a refrigerator full of energizing food options (see Chap. 14) and a home base area where they can relax and build a sense of community and belonging (Joseph 2017). Regulatory reform can help decrease clerical burden (Shanafelt et al. 2016a). Changing incentive and reward structure (i.e., not having salary simply based on patients and face-to-face time) has also been shown to reduce burnout (Shanafelt and Noseworthy 2017). Strategies like aligning values with culture and pass/fail grading (Shanafelt and Noseworthy 2017) have also been effective.

Hypothesized organizational-level solutions to improve burnout are wide reaching. Workspaces and offices should be optimized to see whether there is a design that may ease burnout (e.g., printers in rooms, e-card readers, windows). Organizations often provide vouchers for free rides home if residents feel unsafe to drive, and this, along with call room design, meal vouchers, and availability and utility of nap pods, should be studied. Additionally, though the electronic medical record contributes to physician burnout (Shanafelt et al. 2016a), more information is needed to formulate targeted potential interventions to ease physician workflow. Solutions like hiring scribes and administrative assistants for clerical work, such as prescriptions, should be further studied, particularly their cost-effectiveness considering burnout cost reduction. Given the importance of leadership and role modeling, it is important to look at the workplace culture as an avenue for intervention (see Chap. 2). Physicians should be encouraged to admit their own limitations, and adjustments should be made to value balance over hours worked.

Implementation of culture change is perhaps one of the hardest interventions, but promoting faculty who prioritize prevention and mitigation of burnout in medical trainees might be a start (Dyrbye et al. 2010b).

The evidence suggests that burnout is a significant problem in physicians, increasing in frequency, and prevalent at all stages of training. It is associated with negative personal and professional outcomes (to the hospital and to the patient) and needs to be sufficiently and urgently addressed. The American Medical Association now has a fourth aim, in addition to lower cost, enhanced quality, and increased access: professional satisfaction (Joseph 2017). Prioritizing physician wellness and job satisfaction at the organizational level is a key first step to improving burnout. However, other interventions are needed at the individual, team, and organizational levels to effectively address, prevent, and decrease the burnout epidemic in our physicians.

References

Alarcon GM (2011) A meta-analysis of burnout with job demands, resources, and attitudes. J Voca Behav 79:549–62.

Asai M, Morita T, Akechi T et al (2007) Burnout and psychiatric morbidity among physicians engaged in end-of-life care for cancer patients: a cross-sectional nationwide survey in Japan. Psychooncology 16:421–28.

Awa WL, Plaumann M, Walter U (2010) Burnout prevention: a review of intervention programs. Patient Educ Couns 78: 184–90.

Ball S, Bax A (2002) Self-care in medical education: effectiveness of health-habits interventions for first-year medical students. Acad Med 77: 911–7.

Benson J, Magraith K (2005) Compassion fatigue and burnout: the role of Balint groups. Aust Fam Physician 34:497–8.

Brazeau CM, Shanafelt T, Durning S, et al (2014) Distress among matriculating medical students relative to the general population. Acad Med 89:1520–5.

Dewa CS, Jacobs P, Thanh NX, et al (2014a) An estimate of the cost of burnout on early retirement and reduction in clinical hours of practicing physicians in Canada. BMC Health Serv Res 14: 254.

Dewa CS, Loong D, Bonato S, et al (2014b) How does burnout affect physician productivity? A systematic literature review. BMC Health Serv Res 14: 325.

Dimatteo MR, Sherbourne CD, Hays RD, et al (1993) Physicians' characteristics influence patients' adherence to medical treatment: results from the Medical Outcomes Study. Health Psychol 12:93–102.

Dunn PM, Arnetz BB, Christensen JF, et al (2007) Meeting the imperative to improve physician well-being: assessment of an innovative program. J Gen Intern Med 22:1544–52.

Dyrbye LN, Thomas MR, Massie FS Jr, et al (2008) Burnout and suicidal ideation among U.S. medical students. Ann Intern Med 149:334–41.

Dyrbye LN, Thomas MR, Harper W, et al (2009) The learning environment and medical student burnout: a multicentre study. Med Educ 43:274–82.

Dyrbye LN, Massie FS Jr, Eacker A, et al (2010a) Relationship between burnout and professional conduct and attitudes among US medical students. JAMA 304:1173–80.

Dyrbye LN, Power DV, Massie FS Jr, et al (2010b) Factors associated with resilience to and recovery from burnout: a prospective, multi-institutional study of US medical students. Med Educ 44: 1016–26.

Dyrbye LN, Thomas MR, Power DV, et al (2010c) Burnout and serious thoughts of dropping out of medical school: a multi-institutional study. Acad Med 85: 94–102.

Dyrbye LN, Varkey P, Boone SL, et al (2013) Physician satisfaction and burnout at different career stages. Mayo Clin Proc 88:1358–67.

Dyrbye LN, West CP, Satele D, et al (2014) Burnout among U.S. medical students, residents, and early career physicians relative to the general U.S. population. Acad Med 89: 443–51.

Dyrbye LN, Eacker A, Durning SJ, et al (2015) The impact of stigma and personal experiences on the help-seeking behaviors of medical students with burnout. Acad Med 90: 961–9.

Fang DZ, Young CB, Golshan S, et al (2012) Burnout in premedical undergraduate students. Acad Psychiatry 36: 11–6.

Fralick M & Flegel K (2014) Physician burnout: Who will protect us from ourselves? CMAJ 186:731.

Freudenberger HJ (1974) Staff burnout. J Soc Issues 30:159–65.

Gerber M, Brand S, Elliot C, et al (2013) Aerobic exercise training and burnout: a pilot study with male participants suffering from burnout. BMC Res Notes 6:78.

Goodman MJ & Schorline JB (2012) A mindfulness course decreases burnout and improves well-being among healthcare providers. Int J Psychiatry Med 43:119–28.

Guille C, Zhao Z, Krystal J et al (2015) Web-based cognitive behavioral therapy intervention for the prevention of suicidal ideation in medical interns: a randomized clinical trial. JAMA Psychiatry, 72(12): 1192–1198.

Haas JS, Cook EF, Puopolo AL, et al (2000) Is the professional satisfaction of general internists associated with patient satisfaction? J Gen Intern Med 15:122–8.

Ishak WW, Lederer S, Mandili C, et al (2009) Burnout during residency training: a literature review. J Grad Med Educ 1: 236–42.

Ito JK, Brotheridge CM (2003) Resources, coping strategies, and emotional exhaustion: A conservation of resources perspective. J Vocat Behav 63: 490–509.

Joseph R (2017, March 15) Performance Training and Public Health for Physician Burnout. In:NEJM Access. Available via http://catalyst.nejm.org/performance-training-public-health-burnout/. Accessed 11 April 2017.

Klein J, Grosse Frie K, Blum K, et al (2010) Burnout and perceived quality of care among German clinicians in surgery. Int J Qual Health Care 22:525–30.

Krasner MS, Epstein RM, Beckman H, et al (2009) Association of an educational program in mindful communication with burnout, empathy, and attitudes among primary care physicians. JAMA 302: 1284–93.

Lee RT, SEo B, Hladkyj S, et al (2013) Correlates of physician burnout across regions and specialties: a meta-analysis. Hum Resour Health 11:48.

Leenders MV, Henkens K (2010). Burnout, work characteristics and retirement intentions. Tijdschr Gerontol Geriatr 41:136–45.

Martin S (2002) More hours, more tired, more to do: results from the CMA's 2002 Physician Resource Questionnaire. Cmaj 167: 521–2.

Martini S, Arfken CL, Churchill A, et al (2004) Burnout comparison among residents in different medical specialties. Acad Psychiatry 28:240–2.

Maslach C, Jackson SE (1981) The measurement of experienced burnout. J Organ Behav 2: 99–113.

Mccue JD, Sachs CL (1991) A stress management workshop improves residents' coping skills. Arch Intern Med 151: 2273–7.

Oreskovich MR, Kaups KL, Balch CM, et al (2012) Prevalence of alcohol use disorders among American surgeons. Arch Surg 147:168–74.

Robledo-Gil T, Guo XM., Horien C, et al (2018) Utilization and effectiveness of a peer advocate program for medical students. Acad Psych 42(1): 168–170.

Rosenzweig S, Reibel DK, Greeson JM, et al (2003) Mindfulness-based stress reduction lowers psychological distress in medical students. Teach Learn Med 15: 88–92.

Schaufeli WB, Maslach C, Jackson SE (1996) Maslach Burnout Inventory-General Survey. In: The Maslach burnout inventory-test manual, Consulting Psychologists Press, Palo Alto, CA.

Shanafelt TD, Noseworthy JH (2017) Executive leadership and physician well-being: nine organizational strategies to promote engagement and reduce burnout. Mayo Clin Proc 92:129–46.

Shanafelt TD, Bradley KA, Wipf JE, et al (2002) Burnout and self-reported patient care in an internal medicine residency program. Ann Intern Med 136:358–67.

Shanafelt TD, Sloan JA, Habermann TM (2003) The well-being of physicians. Am J Med 114:513–9.

Shanafelt TD, Balch CM, Bechamps GJ, et al (2009a) Burnout and career satisfaction among American surgeons. Ann Surg 250: 463–71.

Shanafelt TD, West CP, Sloan JA, et al (2009b) Career fit and burnout among academic faculty. Arch Intern Med 169:990–5.

Shanafelt TD, Balch CM, Dyrbye L, et al (2011) Special report: suicidal ideation among American surgeons. Arch Surg 146:54–62.

Shanafelt TD, Boone S, Tan L, et al (2012) Burnout and satisfaction with work-life balance among US physicians relative to the general US population. Arch Intern Med 172:1377–85.

Shanafelt TD, Gorringe G, Mcnakcr R, ct al (2015a) Impact of organizational leadership on physician burnout and satisfaction. Mayo Clin Proc 90:432–40.

Shanafelt TD, Hasan O, Dyrbye LN, et al (2015b) Changes in burnout and satisfaction with work-life balance in physicians and the general US working population between 2011 and 2014. Mayo Clin Proc 90: 1600–13.

Shanafelt TD, Dyrbye LN, Sinsky C, et al (2016a) Relationship between clerical burden and characteristics of the electronic environment with physician burnout and professional satisfaction. Mayo Clin Proced 91:836–48.

Shanafelt TD, Dyrbye LN, West CP, et al (2016b) potential impact of burnout on the US physician workforce. Mayo Clin Proc 91:1667–8.

Shanafelt TD, Mungo M, Schmitgen J, et al (2016c)Longitudinal study evaluating the association between physician burnout and changes in professional work effort. Mayo Clin Proc 91:422–31.

Shanafelt TD, Dyrbye LN, West CP (2017) Addressing physician burnout: the way forward. JAMA 317:901–2.

Sinsky C, Colligan L, Li L, et al (2016)Allocation of physician time in ambulatory practice: a time and motion study in 4 specialties. Ann Intern Med 165:753–60.

Soler JK, Yaman H, Esteva M, et al (2008) Burnout in European family doctors: the EGPRN study. Fam Pract 25: 245–65.

Swensen S, Kabcenell A, Shanafelt TD (2016) Physician organization collaboration reduces physician burnout and promotes engagement:the Mayo Clinic experience. J Healthc Manag 61: 105–27.

Trockel M, Hamidi M, Murphy M, et al. (2016) Physician wellness survey full report. Stanford Medicine: Well MD Center.

West CP, Huschka MM, Novotny PJ, et al (2006) Association of perceived medical errors with resident distress and empathy: a prospective longitudinal study. JAMA 296: 1071–8.

West CP, Dyrbye LN, Rabatin JT, et al (2014) Intervention to promote physician well-being, job satisfaction, and professionalism: a randomized clinical trial. JAMA Intern Med 174: 527–33.

West C, Dyrbye L, Satele D, et al (2015) A randomized controlled trial evaluating the effect of COMPASS (Colleagues Meeting to Promote And Sustain Satisfaction) small group sessions on physician well-being, meaning, and job satisfaction. J Gen Intern Med, 30.

West CP, Dyrbye LN, Erwin PK, et al (2016) Interventions to prevent and reduce physician burnout: a systematic review and meta-analysis. Lancet 388: 2272–2281.

Williams D, Tricomi G, Gupta J, et al (2015) Efficacy of burnout interventions in the medical education pipeline. Acad Psychiatry 39:47–54.

Williams ES, Konrad TR, Scheckler WE, et al (2010) Understanding physicians' intentions to withdraw from practice: the role of job satisfaction, job stress, mental and physical health 2001. Health Care Manage Rev 35: 105–15.

Chapter 6
The Electronic Health Record

Christopher Sharp and Lindsay Stevens

The Promise of the Electronic Health Record

The promise of electronic health records (EHRs) was great. Other industries had used information technology (IT) to enable "mass customization" with the efficient and reliable production of goods and services according to the highly personalized needs of individual customers, but healthcare was lagging in uptake. Safety concerns were forefront, and the risk of harm caused by medical care was receiving increased scrutiny (Kohn et al. 2000). The EHR and related information technology created an opportunity for physicians to prevent errors and adverse events, facilitate more rapid responses, and provide feedback aligned with the tenets of the profession. IT capabilities could improve communication, create ubiquitous access to information and calculations, assist with decision support, and improve medication safety (Bates and Gawande 2003). Further, the EHR offered a vehicle to optimize reimbursements through improved

C. Sharp (✉)
Stanford Health Care, Stanford University School of Medicine
Department of Medicine, Stanford, CA, USA
e-mail: csharp@stanfordhealthcare.org

L. Stevens
Lucile Packard Children's Hospital and Stanford University School of Medicine Department of Pediatrics, Stanford, CA, USA

© Springer Nature Switzerland AG 2019   87
L. Weiss Roberts, M. Trockel (eds.),
The Art and Science of Physician Wellbeing,
https://doi.org/10.1007/978-3-319-42135-3_6

documentation, increase productivity, automate routine manual tasks, and meet regulatory requirements (Edwardson et al. 2017). Additionally, population health management across health systems requires working with large data sets, which is only possible with digitization. With these opportunities, it was hypothesized that healthcare would improve for patients, and thus adoption was encouraged through market forces and the incentives of the Health Information Technology for Economic and Clinical Health Act (HITECH) of 2009 (Mennemeyer et al. 2015). The physician experience when delivering care in such a complex environment was not a widespread consideration; at the time, the stakes to improve care through the digital transformation of the practice of medicine were high.

The proliferation of EHRs has been dramatic. In 2008, less than 16% of medical practices used basic EHRs. Today, this number approaches 90% — with EHRs that are certified to have a comprehensive set of capabilities (The Office of the National Coordinator for Health Information Technology 2017). In the hospital and the outpatient setting, physicians have experienced a myriad of changes beyond the use of the technology itself. These include changes in social relationships and communication patterns when face-to-face interactions were replaced by electronic ones and transformational changes in work relationships, such as when more senior physicians found themselves less adept than those more junior, received scrutiny from administrators due to new visibility into clinical actions, and experienced new expectations from patients for immediacy and transparency (Wachter 2015). Today, headlines that tie the impact of the EHR directly to physician dissatisfaction, frustration, and burnout are abundant. Headlines such as "Doctors are burning out because electronic medical records are broken" come from the Dean of a major academic institution (Minor 2017). Perspectives emerge in the published medical literature describing the "building resentment against the shackles of the present EHR" (Zulman et al. 2016). Popular videos that illustrate the sense of frustration gain internet viewership (ZDoggMD 2015). What is behind this remarkable response?

The Experience of the EHR

Unfortunately, there is good evidence that the experience of the EHR is associated with a rising level of burnout in physicians in the United States (Shanafelt et al. 2016). There are many contributors to this relationship: EHRs have contributed to an undue clerical burden in the delivery of care. Regulatory requirements and external oversight which contribute to loss in a provider's sense of autonomy can be driven through EHR interactions, such as the requirement to use specific diagnosis terminology or structure computer order entry (Ommaya et al. 2018). Changes in work allocation require more time spent with computer interactions and less time spent directly with patients. Increased interaction with the computer may decrease meaningful interactions with colleagues, patients, and staff, as an email cannot replace the value of a direct discussion. Providers may be inadequately trained to use these systems and lack sufficient proficiency and self-confidence. Lastly, patients expect more access to their personal health data and expect electronic communication with their care team, adding new interaction points for providers to manage.

Imagine the experiences of two physicians in the following cases.

Case Illustration 6.1

A 65-year-old pediatric nephrologist at an academic medical center has spent the last 30 years of his career documenting his visits on paper and/or dictating his notes through a phone transcription system. His nurse handled calling in prescriptions and billing only required a check mark or two on a slip of paper. He could order labs by ticking off a few boxes on a standardized paper form. It was difficult to get records from other institutions or to know exactly what may have been done by another physician, but his records at this institution were in his paper file. For the last 10–15 years, he has been able to search for lab results in an online portal, but that has been the extent of his computer interaction.

He isn't a very fast typist. This year, his clinic is going live with a fully integrated EHR. He will now have to document his entire visit electronically: (1) he will have to review all of the patient medications in the EHR system and click all of the requisite boxes; (2) he will have to manually enter all of the patient's family and social history in the designated fields; (3) he will have to type up his note or use a complicated template; (4) he will have to order all labs and medications electronically, and he will have to manually search for each thing and fill out a bunch of fields before he can move on; (5) he will have to fill out his billing and send the documentation to the referring provider by clicking through several additional fields; and (6) everything will have to be done completely before he will be able to "close" the visit; if he doesn't close the visit in a reasonable amount of time, he will be notified by hospital leadership. All of this means he will be spending an extra 2 hours at work each day and finishing up charting on his weekends. He still enjoys his patients, but he thinks he might retire early because the extra effort isn't worth it.

Case Illustration 6.2

A 30-year-old new attending physician is joining an existing internal medicine practice. She grew up using computers, the hospital that she worked at in residency had an EHR, and she knows how to navigate the system quickly. She created a bunch of quick links and dot phrases in the EHR to make documenting faster. She can type even when not looking at the computer. She does have to make sure she checks several boxes for the compliance department, but she's gotten used to it, and it doesn't slow her down that much. She likes that she can see what her colleagues have done, and she uses decision-support tools to help her make better decisions. She would like it if she didn't have to write such long notes, but overall, she views the EHR as part of her job.

One could imagine how these different experiences with the EHR contribute to the physicians' overall sense of wellbeing and satisfaction with their jobs. We will discuss the aforementioned negative impacts of the EHR in further detail.

Clerical Burden

Clerical tasks are a reality of modern medical practice in the United States. Interactions with payers, regulatory bodies, legal oversight, and government entities require descriptive and supporting documentation. The EHR has reinforced many of these requirements as part of the physician's daily work. Physicians who use EHRs and Computerized Provider Order Entry (CPOE) have lower satisfaction with the amount of time spent on clerical tasks and higher rates of burnout in primary care and across specialties (Shanafelt et al. 2016; Babbott et al. 2014). While physicians believe that EHRs can improve access to patient information and lead to improvements in quality of care conceptually, the EHR has been identified as significantly worsening professional satisfaction due to poor usability, increased time required for data entry, and inefficient and less fulfilling work (Friedberg et al. 2014).

Clerical burden may be defined as "administrative tasks" — the processes, procedures, and requirements with which physicians are required to comply that affect, directly or indirectly, the provision of medical care services. While physicians appreciate the necessity of some level of clerical burden, clerical burden is commonly seen as peripheral to core professional values and the direct care for the patient. Clerical burden is manifested through EHR interactions such as medication reconciliation, e-prescribing of medications, complex billing requirements, and highly specific data selection. This specificity and burden have become required of physicians over time due to the influence of various stakeholders on the development of the EHR (Table 6.1). With an aim to reduce clerical burden, a major physician professional society has proposed a framework to analyze administrative tasks through a review of their source, intent, effects, and solutions. This provides a method to evaluate new and existing administrative requirements, regulations, or programs to deter-

TABLE 6.1 The EHR from the perspective of various stakeholders (Erickson et al. 2017)

Perspective	Example
Payers…the source of billing documentation	Specific, legible documentation permanently available for scrutiny and review
Healthcare enterprises…a way to ensure compliance with organizational directives	Concurrent review by coding and quality personnel with requests for clarification
Legal system…a statement of legal facts	Specific, legible documentation permanently available for scrutiny and review
Public health…a method to collect their data at drastically reduced costs	Mandatory reporting of specific diagnoses, results, or immunizations
Measurement entities…a tool to automate the collection of measurement data	Quality measurement derived directly from EHR documentation and actions
Government entities…a way to observe and enforce compliance regulations	EHR design to assure federal and state laws are followed such as privacy considerations

mine whether they should be challenged, undergo revision, or be eliminated entirely. However, this framework and its application is far more recent than the proliferation of EHRs (Erickson et al. 2017).

Clerical work may be quantified using the data generated through the EHR itself. Much clerical work occurs outside of the time the provider is with the patient. In a study that evaluated the activity records in the EHR at a large ambulatory multispecialty practice, time allocated in face-to-face visits was found to be equal to time spent in "desktop medicine" (patient messages, refills, ordering tests, reviewing results) (Tai-Seale et al. 2017). This is not surprising considering studies show that primary care physicians may receive inbox notifications up to 75 times per day (Murphy et al. 2016). Importantly, staffing and scheduling models, as well as provider payment models for primary care practice, may not support or reward this "desktop" activity adequately despite its growth—leading to further clerical burden and associated profession dissatisfaction caused by a change in the content of professional work.

Autonomy and Work Control

Greater physician autonomy and greater control over the pace and content of clinical work are associated with better professional satisfaction (Friedberg et al. 2014). The use of the EHR brings about greater regulation and monitoring of practice, which erodes control and autonomy. For example, the Medicare Access and CHIP (Children's Health Insurance Program) Reauthorization Act (MACRA) served to merge multiple programs by the Center for Medicare and Medicaid Services (CMS) into an even larger and more complex program called the Merit-Based Incentive Payment System and Alternative Payment Models (Merit-based Incentive Payment System 2018). Regulations require physicians to document specific items in order to prove quality care has been delivered. In response to the complexity of these programs, the American Medical Association and many other medical societies have raised warning over the regulatory burden on physicians (American Medical Association 2016).

Importantly, adverse effects on work-life integration can result in decreased professional satisfaction. When surveyed for recertification, family medicine physicians identified personal and practice characteristics that most strongly associate with burnout, including less control over workload, lack of sufficient time for documentation, and more time spent on EHR at home (Rassolian et al. 2017).

Time Spent with the Computer

The time spent with a computer during the delivery of care is only partially valuable for clinicians. While actions such as review of pertinent data and careful documentation of clinical attributes are beneficial, issues of data overload, usability, and excessive documentation burden contribute to a significant time spent with the computer. Current observations show that for every hour physicians provide direct clinical face time in ambulatory practices, they spend 1–2 additional hours on EHR and desk work (Tai-Seale et al. 2017; Sinsky et al. 2016). Through the evaluation of EHR log data, primary care physicians were found to spend more than one-half of their workday, nearly 6 hours, interacting with the EHR during and after clinic hours (Arndt et al. 2017). In the hospital, residents spend 36% of working time per day using the EHR (Ouyang et al. 2016). Emergency medicine physicians spent a majority of time on the computer performing data entry, with computer use at nearly 4000 mouse-clicks per shift (Hill et al. 2013). In the eyes of physicians, this amount of computer time is excessive for the practice of medicine.

In addition to significant use of the computer during the clinical day, an erosion of work-life balance is noted. More after-hours time spent on the EHR is associated with burnout and less work-life satisfaction in primary care residents and faculty (Robertson et al. 2017). Physicians report 1–2 hours of after-hours work each night, devoted mostly to EHR tasks (Sinsky et al. 2016; Arndt et al. 2017).

Meaningful Interactions

Increased interaction with the computer affects the meaningful interactions that providers have with their patients, colleagues, and staff. The introduction of computers into the examination room changes the physicians' focus and interaction with the patient. This ritual of attention or "presence" is a long-described source of meaning for both physicians and patients (Verghese 2016). It appears that the computer may have either a positive or negative effect depending on how the computer is integrated into the encounter (Silverman et al. 2014). As observed in the room with patients, however, physicians spent ~50% on direct clinical face time and ~40% on EHR and desk work (Sinsky et al. 2016). The time spent looking at the patient ("gaze time") by a provider becomes split between the patient and the EHR. Higher "gaze time" is associated with greater patient satisfaction (Farber et al. 2015). "Gaze time" has the potential to be improved by the placement of the computer in the room and specific training to address the skills needed to multitask while continuing to engage the patient, but it is not clear that training is widely available (Duke et al. 2013). Further, physicians may spend more time reviewing case data and less time interviewing patients and listening to their stories. Interactions with colleagues and staff have been described to change with the introduction of the EHR (Payne 2014). The need to congregate at the nursing unit or engage in "radiology rounds" is no longer required to access critical patient information now that it is documented in the EHR. Resident physicians are more likely found huddling with their computers in a "bunker" where they focus on the virtual chart instead of direct interactions with the patient and other caregivers (Verghese 2008).

Proficiency in EHR Use

EHRs are notoriously complex to use. Unlike other consumer electronics which typically do not include training or even a user manual, EHRs commonly require multiple hours of classes, both for initial training and for ongoing educational updates. Some physicians attain more proficiency than others, although it is not clear that this is due to experience alone (Clarke et al. 2014). Recall the differing experiences of Physician 1 and Physician 2; younger physicians are generally more satisfied with their electronic environment and CPOE. Older physicians have had to adjust to a new system, whereas the EHR may be all that younger physicians have ever experienced (Taft et al. 2015). Proficiency may be an important modifiable factor as related to efficiency and burnout.

Democratization Through Digitization

Access to health information has been significantly changed. Patients have increasingly facile mechanisms to access general health information that is specific to their needs. Further, patients have more access to their own health data through direct-to-consumer technologies and their own health records, which have been made readily accessible through EHR technology due to regulatory and consumer trends—including the physician's note (Topol 2015; Walker et al. 2014). This creates new challenges for physicians, who now have to address more informed patients. Online direct scheduling by patients and open ability for patients to send electronic messages to their physicians are aligned with patient demand as consumers, but it may contribute to increased burden and a lack of control in the work environment if inadequately supported.

Moving Ahead with the EHR

Given these issues, how can interactions with the EHR be improved in order to enhance physician wellbeing?

Institutions have started tackling the issue by testing possible interventions. At Stanford University and its affiliated hospitals and clinics, leaders have attempted to address inadequate proficiency and decreased efficiency problems by creating a training program tailored to the individual provider (Stevens et al. 2017). In this program, dedicated trainers address the areas of specific concern for each physician in a systemized way, helping to familiarize them with system functionality and more efficient ways of accomplishing their routine tasks (DiAngi et al. 2019).

Other institutions have invested in supports to decrease the documentation burden on the physician. One such support is the use of scribes who observe the visit and document as the physician interacts with the patient. Scribes can be present in person (Guo et al. 2017) or can observe the visit virtually through wearable face-mounted video computing technology such as Google Glass (Verger 2017). Scribes have been shown to improve physician interactions with patients and overall physician satisfaction (Bank et al. 2013; Gellert et al. 2015; Gidwani et al. 2017), but it is important to address the interpersonal relationship between the physician and the scribe as well as other administrative requirements before implementing such an intervention (Yan et al. 2016).

Voice-to-text services, augmenting dictation services, or speech recognition software can be effective for physicians who are inefficient typists, but proven evidence supporting their use remains weak (Hodgson and Coiera 2016). Team-based care models can distribute some of the physician's workload to nurses and other support staff where possible (Contratto et al. 2017). This requires attention to the scope of practice so that all members of the team can appropriately work to the best of their abilities. In the ambulatory setting, advanced care team models may be a powerful strategy. Clinically trained individuals (nurses, medical assistants, or specialty technicians) may assist with visit documentation, non-physician order entry, inbox management, health coaching, and care coordination. Nursing support can triage and respond to electronic communications from patients. This has been described in high-functioning primary care practices (Shipman and Sinsky 2013). More research is needed to describe how the EHR relates to physician wellness—and to better describe and quantify all issues of physician wellness (Ommaya et al. 2018; Brigham et al. 2018; Dyrbye et al. 2017).

While these solutions address some of the burden on the physician, the core issue of a large documentation requirement remain. Further, EHR systems are complex and often require numerous steps to document the required information. The Center for Medicare and Medicaid Services (CMS) has reassessed the evaluation and management (E/M) documentation guidelines and has acknowledged that the regulatory burden for providers may be excessive and may not be contributing to improved documentation (Centers for Medicare & Medicaid Services 2018). In the future, perhaps physicians may create shorter, more meaningful notes.

Future solutions should focus on improved EHR usability and design and more innovative interactions and functions. Novel usability improvements, natural language processing, artificial intelligence, and machine learning may contribute to a new and improved EHR experience for clinicians. Revisions of age-old workflows and improved patient interactions will surely be necessary for physicians and patients to reap the opportunities brought forward by EHRs and the digitization of care (Jones et al. 2012). Monitoring and adjusting for professional well-being is paramount to bring forward a best working and caring environment for physicians and the patients they serve.

References

American Medical Association. Merit-Based Incentive Payment System (MIPS) and Alternative Payment Model (APM) Incentive Under the Physician Fee Schedule, and Criteria for Physician-Focused Payment Models; Proposed Rule (CMS-5517-P). Letter to Andrew Slavitt, June 24, 2016. [Internet]. 2016 [cited 2017 Oct 16]. Available from: https://download.ama-assn.org/resources/doc/washington/macra-state-speciality-sign-on-letter.pdf

Arndt BG, Beasley JW, Watkinson MD, Temte JL, Tuan W-J, Sinsky CA, et al. (2017) Tethered to the EHR: Primary Care Physician Workload Assessment Using EHR Event Log Data and Time-Motion Observations. Ann Fam Med. Sep 15(5):419–26.

Babbott S, Manwell LB, Brown R, Montague E, Williams E, Schwartz M, et al. (2014) Electronic medical records and physician stress in primary care: results from the MEMO Study. J Am Med Inform Assoc JAMIA. Feb;21(e1):e100–106.

Bank A, Obetz C, Konrardy A, Khan A, Pillai K, McKinley B, et al. (2013) Impact of scribes on patient interaction, productivity, and revenue in a cardiology clinic: a prospective study. Clin Outcomes Res. Aug;399.

Bates DW, Gawande AA. (2003) Improving safety with information technology. N Engl J Med. Jun 19;348(25):2526–34.

Brigham T, Barden C, Legreid Dopp, Anna, Kaplan, Jay, Malone, Beverly, Martin, Christina, et al. (2018) A Journey to Construct an All-Encompassing Conceptual Model of Factors Affecting Clinician Well-Being and Resilience. Natl Acad Med [Internet]. 2018 Jan 29 [cited 2018 Jan 31]; Available from: https://nam.edu/journey-construct-encompassing-conceptual-model-factors-affecting-clinician-well-resilience/

Centers for Medicare & Medicaid Services. (2018) Proposed Policy, Payment, and Quality Provisions Changes to the Medicare Physician Fee Schedule for Calendar Year 2018 [Internet]. 2017 [cited 2017 Sep 5]. Available from: https://www.cms.gov/Newsroom/MediaReleaseDatabase/Fact-sheets/2017-Fact-Sheet-items/2017-07-13-2.html

Clarke MA, Belden JL, Kim MS. (2014) Determining differences in user performance between expert and novice primary care doctors when using an electronic health record (EHR): EHR usability gaps between doctors. J Eval Clin Pract. Dec 20(6):1153–61.

Contratto E, Romp K, Estrada CA, Agne A, Willett LL. (2017) Physician Order Entry Clerical Support Improves Physician Satisfaction and Productivity. South Med J. May 110(5):363–8.

DiAngi YT, Stevens LA, Pageler NM, Halpern-Felsher B, Lee TC. (2019) Electronic Health Record (EHR) Training Program Identifies a New Tool to Quantify the EHR time Burden and Improves Providers' Perceived Control over their workload in the EHR. JAMIO. (In Press)

Dyrbye LN, Trockel M, Frank E, Olson K, Linzer M, Lemaire J, et al. (2017) Development of a Research Agenda to Identify Evidence-Based Strategies to Improve Physician Wellness and Reduce Burnout. Ann Intern Med. May 16;166(10):743–4.

Duke P, Frankel RM, Reis S. (2013) How to integrate the electronic health record and patient-centered communication into the medical visit: a skills-based approach. Teach Learn Med. 25(4):358–65.

Edwardson N, Kash BA, Janakiraman R. (2017) Measuring the Impact of Electronic Health Record Adoption on Charge Capture. Med Care Res Rev. 2017 Oct 1;74(5):582–94.

Erickson SM, Rockwern B, Koltov M, McLean RM, Medical Practice and Quality Committee of the American College of Physicians. (2017) Putting Patients First by Reducing Administrative Tasks in Health Care: A Position Paper of the American College of Physicians. Ann Intern Med. May 2;166(9):659–61.

Farber NJ, Liu L, Chen Y, Calvitti A, Street RL, Zuest D, et al. (2015) EHR use and patient satisfaction: What we learned. J Fam Pract. Nov 64(11):687–96.

Friedberg MW, Chen PG, Van Busum KR, Aunon F, Pham C, Caloyeras J, et al. (2014) Factors Affecting Physician Professional Satisfaction and Their Implications for Patient Care, Health Systems, and Health Policy. Rand Health Q;3(4):1.

Gellert GA, Ramirez R, Webster SL. (2015) The Rise of the Medical Scribe Industry: Implications for the Advancement of Electronic Health Records. JAMA. Apr 7;313(13):1315.

Gidwani R, Nguyen C, Kofoed A, Carragee C, Rydel T, Nelligan I, et al.(2017) Impact of Scribes on Physician Satisfaction, Patient Satisfaction, and Charting Efficiency: A Randomized Controlled Trial. Ann Fam Med. Sep;15(5):427–33.

Guo U, Chen L, Mehta PH. (2017) Electronic health record innovations: Helping physicians - One less click at a time. HIM J. Jan 1;1833358316689481.

Hill RG, Sears LM, Melanson SW. (2013) 4000 Clicks: a productivity analysis of electronic medical records in a community hospital ED. Am J Emerg Med. Nov;31(11):1591–4.

Hodgson T, Coiera E. (2016) Risks and benefits of speech recognition for clinical documentation: a systematic review. J Am Med Inform Assoc. Apr;23(e1):e169–79.

Jones SS, Heaton PS, Rudin RS, Schneider EC. (2012) Unraveling the IT Productivity Paradox — Lessons for Health Care. N Engl J Med. Jun 14;366(24):2243–5.

Kohn LT, Corrigan J, Donaldson MS, editors. (2000) To err is human: building a safer health system. Washington, D.C: National Academy Press; 287 p.

Mennemeyer ST, Menachemi N, Rahurkar S, Ford EW.(2015) Impact of the HITECH act on physicians' adoption of electronic health records. J Am Med Inform Assoc. Jul 30;0:1–6.

Merit-based Incentive Payment System (MIPS) Overview - QPP [Internet]. [cited 2018 Apr 2]. Available from: https://qpp.cms.gov/mips/overview

Minor L, Medicine SUS of. (2017) Doctors are burning out because electronic medical records are broken [Internet]. Quartz. [cited 2017 Oct 15]. Available from: https://qz.com/1061322/doctors-are-burning-out-because-electronic-medical-records-are-broken/

Murphy DR, Meyer AN, Russo E, Sittig DF, Wei L, Singh H. (2016) The Burden of Inbox Notifications in Commercial Electronic Health Records. JAMA Intern Med. Apr 1;176(4):559–60.

The Office of the National Coordinator for Health Information Technology. (2017) Office-based Physician Electronic Health Record Adoption [Internet]. [cited 2017 Oct 15]. Available from: https://dashboard.healthit.gov/quickstats/pages/physician-ehr-adoption-trends.php

Ommaya AK, Cipriano PF, Horvath KA, Paz HL, DeFrancesco MS, Hingle ST, Butler S, Sinsky CA. (2018) Care-Centered Clinical Documentation in the Digital Environment: Solutions to Alleviate Burnout. Natl Acad Med [Internet]. 2018 Jan 29 [cited 2018 Jan 30]; Available from: https://nam.edu/care-centered-clinical-documentation-digital-environment-solutions-alleviate-burnout/

Ouyang D, Chen JH, Hom J, Chi J. (2016) Internal Medicine Resident Computer Usage: An Electronic Audit of an Inpatient Service. JAMA Intern Med. Feb;176(2):252–4.

Payne T. (2014) Practical guide to clinical computing systems. Boston, MA: Elsevier, New York.

Rassolian M, Peterson LE, Fang B, Knight HC, Peabody MR, Baxley EG, et al. (2017) Workplace Factors Associated With Burnout of Family Physicians. JAMA Intern Med. Jul 1;177(7):1036–8.

Robertson SL, Robinson MD, Reid A. (2017) Electronic Health Record Effects on Work-Life Balance and Burnout Within the I(3) Population Collaborative. J Grad Med Educ. Aug;9(4):479–84.

Shanafelt TD, Dyrbye LN, Sinsky C, Hasan O, Satele D, Sloan J, et al. (2016) Relationship Between Clerical Burden and Characteristics of the Electronic Environment With Physician Burnout and Professional Satisfaction. Mayo Clin Proc. Jul;91(7):836–48.

Shipman SA, Sinsky CA. (2013) Expanding primary care capacity by reducing waste and improving the efficiency of care. Health Aff Proj Hope. Nov;32(11):1990–7.

Silverman H, Ho Y-X, Kaib S, Ellis WD, Moffitt MP, Chen Q, et al. (2014) A novel approach to supporting relationship-centered care through electronic health record ergonomic training in pre-clerkship medical education. Acad Med J Assoc Am Med Coll. Sep;89(9):1230–4.

Sinsky C, Colligan L, Li L, Prgomet M, Reynolds S, Goeders L, et al. (2016) Allocation of Physician Time in Ambulatory Practice: A Time and Motion Study in 4 Specialties. Ann Intern Med. Dec 6;165(11):753.

Stevens LA, DiAngi YT, Schremp JD, Martorana MJ, Miller RE, Lee TC, et al. (2017) Designing An Individualized EHR Learning Plan for Providers. Appl Clin Inform. Sep 6;8.

Taft T, Lenert L, Sakaguchi F, Stoddard G, Milne C. (2015) Effects of electronic health record use on the exam room communication skills of resident physicians: a randomized within-subjects study. J Am Med Inform Assoc Jan;22(1):192–8.

Tai-Seale M, Olson CW, Li J, Chan AS, Morikawa C, Durbin M, et al. (2017) Electronic Health Record Logs Indicate that Physicians Split Time Evenly Between Seeing Patients and Desktop Medicine. Health Aff (Millwood). Apr 1;36(4):655–62.

Topol EJ. (2015) The patient will see you now: the future of medicine is in your hands. New York: Basic Books; 350 p.

Verger R. (2017) Doctors are wearing the new Google Glass while seeing patients | Popular Science [Internet]. 2017 [cited 2017 Sep 5]. Available from: http://www.popsci.com/google-glass-doctors-office

Verghese A. (2016) The Importance of Being. Health Aff (Millwood). Oct 1;35(10):1924–7.

Verghese A. Culture Shock — Patient as Icon, Icon as Patient. N Engl J Med. 2008 Dec 25;359(26):2748–51.

Wachter RM. (2015) The digital doctor: hope, hype, and harm at the dawn of medicine's computer age. New York: McGraw-Hill Education; 330 p.

Walker J, Darer JD, Elmore JG, Delbanco T. (2014) The road toward fully transparent medical records. N Engl J Med. Jan 2;370(1):6–8.

Yan C, Rose S, Rothberg MB, Mercer MB, Goodman K, Misra-Hebert AD. (2016) Physician, Scribe, and Patient Perspectives on Clinical Scribes in Primary Care. J Gen Intern Med. Sep;31(9):990–5.

ZDoggMD. (2015) EHR state of mind [Internet]. 2015 [cited 2017 Oct 2]. Available from: http://zdoggmd.com/ehr-state-of-mind/

Zulman DM, Shah NH, Verghese A. (2016) Evolutionary Pressures on the Electronic Health Record: Caring for Complexity. JAMA. Sep 6;316(9):923–4.

Chapter 7
Financial Anxiety

David J. Peterson and Jeffrey G. Miller

Financial distress (or anxiety) has been described as an individual's reaction to the condition of their personal financial situation (Prawitz et al. 2006). Although there can be many causes for anxiety, according to a CNBC survey (Brown 2016), financial anxiety is a leading cause of stress in relationships, and according to a survey by the American Psychological Association, financial worry is the "number one cause of stress in America today" (American Psychological Association 2015). One factor contributing to financial anxiety today are memories of the Great Recession, the worst global financial crisis since the Great Depression (Wikipedia 2017). Occurring between December 2007 and June 2009, the Great Recession resulted in the "collapse of the financial sector," with some of this collapse evidenced by an average 30% decline in housing prices, rising unemployment, and over a 50% drop in the S&P 500 Index (Wikipedia 2017). More fallout from the Great Recession such as declines in personal income, cascading bank failures, and a general economic malaise certainly contributed to a financial anxiety that lingers to this day, despite robust rebounds since 2009.

D. J. Peterson (✉) · J. G. Miller
Medical College of Wisconsin, Department of Psychiatry
and Behavioral Medicine, Milwaukee, WI, USA
e-mail: peterson@mcw.edu

© Springer Nature Switzerland AG 2019   103
L. Weiss Roberts, M. Trockel (eds.),
The Art and Science of Physician Wellbeing,
https://doi.org/10.1007/978-3-319-42135-3_7

Some physicians might think that they are immune from financial anxiety because of the high salaries they will earn resulting from the demand for their unique training coupled with the simple fact that everyone needs health care. But according to the APA survey, "money is a somewhat or very significant amount of stress for the majority of Americans" (American Psychological Association 2015). In fact, some physicians might find themselves more susceptible to financial anxiety due to the significant student debt that they carry because of their unique and long training. Becker's Healthcare reports that the median medical student debt in 2014 was $180,000 and 43% of medical student graduates surveyed had debt totaling "$200,000 or more" (Wood 2015). This level of educational debt only contributes to the usual anxiety-provoking financial pressures of managing the debt attached to home ownership, raising a family, building a financial future, and planning for retirement.

Contributors to financial anxiety change with age (Wells 2016). What was important in one's 20s and 30s fades as new priorities emerge as one enters one's 40s, 50s, and beyond. Careful understanding, foresight, and planning can help mitigate the money worries that contribute to financial anxiety. To help with this understanding and planning, "personal income management, personal investment management and personal risk management" tools exist to address the risks that can threaten a physician's economic and emotional well-being (Peterson and Strode 2013). These "tools" include compensation and benefits, investments and savings, insurances, wills, and powers of attorney, to name a few.

Financial issues and pressures result in increased worry and even anxiety. In 2005, O'Neill, et al. (2005) reported that the effects of financial distress have been found to include anxiety, insomnia, headaches, and depression. Anxiety is a normal part of everyday life and can serve an adaptive function; however, when it reaches the level of symptomatology, it is more than a temporary worry.

According to the American Psychiatric Association (2013), anxiety is "the anticipation of future threat" and is associated with vigilance in preparation for future dangers and caution or avoidant behavior. Anxiety includes worry about various domains in one's life and can interfere with school, work performance, and relationships. Anxiety is difficult for the individual to control. It is a state of tension, dread, or fear of impending doom that results from external influences that threaten to overwhelm the individual (Marcus 2012).

Despite the uncomfortable feelings associated with anxiety, it does have a purpose. The purpose of anxiety is to warn the individual of impending threat, conflict, or danger. According to Zinbarg, Anand, Lee, Kendall, and Nunez (2015), anxiety is a future-oriented mood state associated with preparation for possible harm. This state can assist the individual in preparing a response to the threat and maintaining safety. Thus, anxiety is caused by concern about potential threats that the individual perceives as having no control over. Without intervention or symptom management, anxiety can become a cyclic and snowballing process. Financial stressors and concerns trigger fear and anxiety, which may trigger a lack of focus, which leads to self-doubt about job performance, which leads to more anxiety. And the cycle of anxiety begins.

Since the anxiety process is cyclic, intervention at any point can have beneficial results; that is, whether the intervention targets the source of the anxiety or targets the symptoms, the anxiety can be reduced. For example, the individual may eliminate the source of the concern by changing jobs or making different financial choices. In addition, they may implement coping mechanisms, which are methods used to control or manage anxiety. Examples include denial, humor, or displacement. A coping mechanism does not target the source of the anxiety; rather it focuses on reducing symptoms.

Humor is one example of a coping mechanism; laughing about a stressor makes the stressor less powerful. Denial is another coping mechanism that involves refusing to acknowledge the stressor. For example, an individual might deny their financial issues or the amount of debt that has accrued. Displacement transfers the feelings of anxiety to another person or another thing. For example, an individual might go to the gym to work off restlessness. For financial anxiety, because anxiety was found to be highly related to the way people handled their money, several studies support the use of financial therapy (Weisman 2002).

Financial therapy, we suggest, is the blending of the financial and psychological worlds, utilizing both therapeutic and fiscal competencies. Until recently, therapists focused on the emotional side of the problem without knowledge of finances or financial planners and spreadsheets focused on the numbers and without regard for the emotional response to money. The goal of financial therapy is to address financial challenges while at the same time assisting with related emotional, psychological, behavioral, and relational hurdles. Although combining financial and mental health therapy is a relatively new concept, undergraduate and graduate behavioral health curriculums are starting to include both areas in their programs. Individuals are obtaining dual education (e.g., a financial consultant who is also a licensed marriage and family therapist), or the service is delivered through a team where a financial planner partners with a therapist. Despite the limited data, anecdotal reports are positive.

Some Conventional Financial Wisdom—It's All About Time

One tool for managing financial stress is to build a basic understanding of common financial principles. For example, a recognition that "time" is a key factor in building wealth and managing money is essential. Quite simply, thoughtfully invested money grows over time (as does debt, if not properly managed). The "Rule of 72" provides a quick tool to calculate how quickly money can grow. Divide any annual interest rate into 72, and an investor can approximate when money will double. Using this rule of thumb, money earning an annual 7% interest rate will double in about 10 years. At a 2% annual interest rate, it will take approximately 36 years for money to double (Investopedia 2017). Clearly, time is a critical component of building savings, and one former financial executive counts "waiting to invest" as one of "7 money decisions you could regret forever" (Martin 2017).

Time is a factor for investments in the stock market too because generally, over time, stock market indexes rise and, in the event of market downturns, time is necessary for stocks to recover. But stock market "timing," that is, attempting to "buy low and sell high" by anticipating start market moves is generally considered a poor investment strategy and is likely anxiety-inducing. Warren Buffett, "the Oracle of Omaha," has stated that "...picking times to buy and sell [stocks] is a mistake of 99% of the population" (Serwer 2017). "Dollar cost averaging," another strategy requiring time, requires a consistent investment over time during up-and-down stock market cycles and has resulted in returns that have averaged approximately 10% over the past 50-plus years (McWhinney 2017).

Diversification of investments is key and helps to mitigate worries about risks in any given investment. For example, when interest rates rise, the prices of bonds go down, but the stock market and other investments will generally rise to off-set the downturn in bonds (SEC 2009).

"Paying yourself first" is another time-based and generally accepted money management principle. By using a "pay yourself first" strategy, the individual adopts a regular and systematic habit of saving that over time will be rewarding (Khalfani-Cox 2017).

Debt and tax management financial strategies are important and can be linked. For example, interest on debt attached to home ownership and some other debt attached to home ownership can be tax deductible. And every financial advisor will support the strategy of tax "avoidance," a strategy of minimizing federal and state tax liabilities (tax "evasion" is illegal) (Khalfani-Cox 2017).

Finally, time is necessary to smartly track and manage money. If the individual lacks time or expertise, financial advisors can offset both, contributing to less financial anxiety. Most experts agree that "fee-based financial advisors" are better than those advisors who are paid on commission. Fee-based advisors are generally considered more independent and free of conflict of interests that can be inherent in commission-based services (Quinn 2017).

Maximize Employer Benefits

Finding financial piece of mind starts with employment and the employer. In addition to a predictable annual compensation, vacation, and sick leave package, competitively positioned employers will offer a robust package of benefits, many of which are affordable and provide coverages that include:

- Group health, dental, and vision coverage
- Group life insurance and opportunities (sometimes) to buy more coverage
- Group disability insurance
- Flexible spending health and dependent care accounts
- Tuition reimbursement
- Retirement plans (e.g., 401(k), 403(b), 457(b) plans)

Each of these types of benefit offerings can minimize financial worry and mitigate risk. For example, another "money decision you could regret forever" is "skimping on insurance" (Martin 2017). Employers generally offer affordable group insurance products such as those listed above that can protect the individual and family members.

Flexible spending accounts offer opportunities to set aside income on a pre-tax basis (consistent with a tax avoidance strategy) to pay for eligible health and dependent care expenses. Regardless of an individual's tax bracket, setting aside pre-tax dollars can be very financially advantageous, allowing the individual to essentially pay for such expenses "on discount."

Maximal participation in employer's retirement plans, and steadily contributing to the plans each month, meets the principles of the time value of money and dollar cost averaging and helps to build wealth.

More recently, employers are offering innovative opportunities to purchase group legal and identify theft coverages. Both are new benefit tools that can help to mitigate financial anxiety.

Plan Early and Plan Ahead

Clearly, starting to save early captures the benefits of the time value of money. Saving small amounts early and consistently helps avoid the need to set aside much larger sums later in life.

Purchasing life and long-term care insurance early locks in premiums that would become much more expensive if such purchases were made later in life. In addition, as one ages, health events might occur that would make an individual ineligible for such coverage. It is better if coverage is purchased at a younger, healthier age.

Similarly, proactively setting up health-care powers of attorney, living wills, and last wills and testaments prepares individuals for events still yet unforeseen. As noted earlier, fear of the unknown greatly contributes to anxiety in general and financial anxiety in particular.

Identity Theft

According to the latest US Bureau of Justice data, "about 7 percent" of US residents ages 16 and older were victims of identity theft (BJS 2015). This increasing risk and prevalence of identity theft is evident by the multiple news stories about data breaches at retailers, incidences of skimming at ATMs, and theft. When identity theft occurs, the Federal Trade Commission estimates that it takes "an average of 6 months and 200 hours of work" to recover (IdentityHawk 2017).

Aside from the obvious benefits of avoiding identity theft and maintaining a solid history of "good credit management, good credit ratings, and good relationships with creditors," avoiding identity theft also helps avoid additional emotional distress. In fact, the Bureau of Justice reports that those individuals who spent considerable time restoring their identity also experienced more problems in the workplace, personal problems, and emotional distress (IdentityHawk 2017; BJS 2015).

Consequently, adopting good "identity protection" habits is the first step in protecting against identity theft, and, on the chance that it occurs anyway, taking advantage of employer-based identity theft coverage or purchasing such coverages in the private sector can be a prudent strategy.

Case Illustration 7.1: The Power of Time on Money

Upon graduating from medical school and completing his/her training at age 30, Physician A immediately begins saving $100/month by contributing into a retirement account with pre-tax dollars. If Physician A's tax bracket is 20%, then saving $100/month only costs Physician A $80/month because of the tax savings on the contribution. Over a 30-year period, this regular contribution will grow to approximately $58,419 at a 3% average annual interest rate. If the contribution were averaging a 6% annual interest rate, the account would grow to approximately $100,954. Over the same 30-year period and earning a 10% average annual interest rate, the account would grow to approximately $227,932. Three items are of note here:

1. The example uses a regular contribution over a 30-year period.
2. The monthly amount is relatively small at $100 and yet grows to substantial sums.
3. The average interest rate earned has a critical impact on the final value of the account at the end of 30 years.

In contrast, Physician B decides to initially forgo the contribution to the retirement fund, preferring to wait 20 years before contributions begin. First, Physician B pays more tax than Physician A. Then, if Physician B is seeking the same end results as Physician A, he/she would need to contribute over four times more per month than Physician A to reach the $58,000 total; at a 6% annual interest rate, Physician B would need to contribute over six times more than Physician A to reach $100,000; and at a 10% average annual interest rate, Physician B would need to contribute 11 times (or $1100/month) more than Physician A to reach $227,000.

In this example, the value of starting early with small sums of money becomes obvious. One can only imagine the financial piece of mind such planning and discipline brings.

Case Illustration 7.2: Financial Anxiety's Impact on Relationships

A young professional couple were looking forward to launching their careers and entering a time of financial stability. However, the salaries were not as competitive as they once hoped, and their debt was increasing. Financial anxiety began to soar. As a result, there were more frequent arguments about money, investments, and spending. The anxiety caused relationship issues, poor decision-making, and a lack of trust between the couple. This took a toll on the relationship. After more than a year of arguments and continued financial concerns, the couple separated and ultimately divorced. The divorce further complicated the financial status of both individuals due to dividing assets (including retirement accounts) and selling items such as their home at a loss.

In this scenario, financial anxiety is not the sole factor in the ultimate ending of the relationship—nothing is that simple. However, financial anxiety played a significant role in the destruction of the relationship and the ultimate harm to their financial situation. Some of the stress or the impact of the stress may have been mitigated if the couple would have utilized some of the strategies outlined in this chapter, such as seeking therapy, financial counseling, and/or using coping skills. The utilization of these techniques does not guarantee that the marriage would have remained intact, but it may have minimized the financial causes of the marital discord.

Case Illustration 7.3: Not All Online Financial Calculators Are Equal

Search the Internet for "online financial calculator" and over two million results will appear. Thus, readers might think that "an online calculator is an online calculator." However, in the calculations described in Case Illustration 7.1, using exactly the same interest inputs, that is, 3%, 6%, and 10%, and the same time periods, different results were obtained using an online calculator. At a 3% interest rate, the difference between the two results was small at less than 1%. At a 6% interest rate, the difference between the two results grew, and at a 10% interest rate, the difference between the two results varied by as much as 10%, $206,000 versus the $227,000 referenced in Case Illustration 7.1.

These variances occur because calculators can assume different compounding periods (e.g., daily, monthly, annually, etc.) and different timing of regular deposits (e.g., at the beginning of the month or the end of the month).

Consequently, the savvy money manager will read the fine print attached to calculators, test assumptions, and see if different calculators will return the same result. (The same should be done with financial advisors and other financial products.) While the differences can be small—as noted above—at low interest rates, at higher interests, and over longer periods of time, the differences can be meaningful. However, even with the variances noted, the principle of starting to save early and regularly still applies, resulting in a growth of significant savings and investments.

Conclusion

Based on all the information and data, financial anxiety is now a component of every middle-class American's consciousness (Derbyshire 1999). Given anxiety's effect on the body, finding and using every tool available to manage financial anxiety is essential to an individual's physical and mental wellbeing. In fact, a study published in the *British Medical Journal* found that survey participants with more anxiety were more likely to die prematurely (Goodman 2017). Understanding financial anxiety, recognizing the symptoms of anxiety, and taking steps to manage anxiety contributes to physical, emotional, and financial health. By developing an understanding of some general money management principles and leveraging some of the financial tools available, an individual can mitigate financial worry and its effects. Starting early, planning ahead, and protecting oneself from unforeseen events are critical steps to achieving financial peace of mind. In the case of financial anxiety, the informed physician has an opportunity to "financially heal thyself."

References

American Psychiatric Association (2013). *Diagnostic and statistical manual of mental disorders* (Fifth ed.) (pp. 189–234). American Psychiatry Publishing, Washington, DC

American Psychological Association (2015). American Psychological Association survey shows money stress weighing on Americans' Health Nationwide. Retrieved from http://www.apa.org/news/press/releases/2015/02/money-stress.aspx. Accessed 9 Apr 2017.

BJS (2015). 17.6 million U.S. residents experienced identity theft in 2014. Retrieved from https://www.bjs.gov/content/pub/press/vit14pr.cfm. Accessed 28 Apr 2017.

Brown R (2016). 8 ways to conquer anxiety about money. Retrieved from http://www.clark.com/ways-to-conquer-anxiety-about-money. Accessed 6 Mar 2017.

Derbyshire J. (1999). The anxious class. National Review April 19: 57–58.

Goodman B (2017). Even mild anxiety may shorten a person's life. Retrieved from http://www.webmd.com/mentalhealth/news//20120731/mild-anxiety-may-shorten-persons-life#1. Accessed 13 Apr 2017.

IdentityHawk (2017). How long does it take to recover from identity theft? Retrieved from http://www.identityhawk.com/identity-theft-recovery-time. Accessed 28 Apr 2017.

Investopedia (2017). Rule of 72. Retrieved from http://www.investo-pedia.com/terms/r/ruleof72.asp. Accessed 9 May 2017.

Khalfani-Cox L (2017). 6 money rules that take your finances to the next level. Retrieved from https://www.northwesternmutual.com/life-and-money/money-rules-that-take-your-finances-to-the-next-level/. Accessed 8 Mar 2017.

Marcus PE (2012). Anxiety and anxiety disorders. In: K.M. Fortinash and P.A. Holoday Worret (Eds), Psychiatric mental health nursing (pp. 184–203). 5th ed. Elsevier Mosby, St. Louis, MO

Martin E (2017). 7 money decisions you could regret forever. Retrieved from http://finance.yahoo.com/news/7-money-decisions-could-regret-143734334.html. Accessed 28 Apr 2017.

McWhinney J (2017). Dollar-cost averaging pays. Retrieved from http://www.investopedia.com/articles/mutualfund/05/071305/asp. Accessed 8 May 2017.

O'Neill B, Sorhaindo B, Xiao JJ, Garman ET (2005). Negative health effects of financial stress. Consumer Interests Annual 51: 260–262.

Peterson D, Strode R (2013). How to manage personal finances. In: Roberts L (ed) The Academic Medicine Handbook. Springer, New York, pp. 455–464.

Prawitz AD, Garman ET, Sorhaindo B, O'Neill B, Kim J, Drentea P. (2006). InCharge financial distress/financial well-being scale: Development, administration, and score interpretation. Financial Counseling and Planning 17(1): 34–50.

Quinn J B (2017). Managing your manager. AARP Bulletin, April 2017, p.12.

SEC (2009). Beginners guide to asset allocation, diversification, and rebalancing. Retrieved from https://www.sec.gov/reportspubs/investor-publications/investorpubassessallocationhtm.html. Accessed 8 May 2017.

Serwer A (2017). Here's the big mistake investors make. Retrieved from https://finance.yahoo.com/news/warren-buffett-heres-big-mistakes-investors-make-163820066.html. Accessed 3 May 2017.

Weisman R. (2002). Personal financial stress, depression, and workplace performance: Developing employer-credit union partnerships (pp. 51–66).: Filene Research Institute, Madison, WI

Wells C (2016). The biggest money mistakes we make-decade by decade. Retrieved from https://www.wsj.com/articles/the-biggest-money-mistakes-we-makedecade-by-decade-1477275181. Accessed 17 Mar 2017.

Wikipedia (2017). Great Recession. Retrieved from https:// en.wikipedia.org/wiki/Great_Recession. Accessed 20 Mar 2017.

Wood M (2015). 17 Statistics about medical school student debt. Retrieved from http://beckersasc.com/asc-turnarounds-ideas-to-improve-performance/17-statistics-about-medical-schoolstudent-debt. html. Accessed 10 Apr 2017.

Zinbarg RE, Anand D, Lee JK, Kendall AD, Nunez AM. (2015). Generalized anxiety disorder, panic disorders, social anxiety disorder, and specific phobias. In: Blaney PH, Krueger RF, Millon T (Eds). Oxford textbook of psychopathology. 3rd ed. Oxford University Press, New York, pp. 133–162.

Chapter 8
Legal Issues

Dana Welle

Physician wellness, or rather lack of wellness, can have significant implications on risk management and potential implications on individual and organizational medical-legal risk.
Neither of these two correlations have been studied in great
detail, but associations between physician wellness and risk
management can be drawn from current work on burnout and
professional fulfillment (Shanafelt et al. 2010). Additionally,
other ongoing research and work in areas related to medical-
legal risk might be ripe for the inclusion of physician wellness
in order to bring a more complete approach to these studies.

Legal action is not a good marker of patient safety or of
patient care outcomes, but it does have a succinct and
extremely personal impact on the physician providing care.
Physicians complete years of education and dedicate their
lives to the care of patients, often to the exclusion of other
pursuits, so when harm does come to one of their patients,
physicians feel personally responsible. Furthermore, when a
patient sues, it reflects a break in the bond held sacred, the
doctor-patient relationship.

Once an allegation of negligence is brought forth, the
patient takes on the role of adversarial plaintiff, requiring the

D. Welle (✉)
Stanford Hospital, Risk Management, Stanford, CA, USA
e-mail: dwelle@stanfordhealthcare.org

© Springer Nature Switzerland AG 2019   117
L. Weiss Roberts, M. Trockel (eds.),
The Art and Science of Physician Wellbeing,
https://doi.org/10.1007/978-3-319-42135-3_8

physician to defend his or her action or inaction. Not all patients who experience an unanticipated, preventable outcome seek legal action, and there are many factors to consider when evaluating why patients sue. In addition to individual patient characteristics, the legal climate, jurisdiction, and tort reform are just some of the external forces impacting the patient's decision to bring a legal action. Studies have also shown that once a physician is sued, it can affect ongoing medical care; for example, a physician may begin practicing defensive medicine which can lead to unnecessary testing and increased medical costs (Nahed et al. 2012). In other cases, being sued can cause physicians to change their scope of practice, where they practice, or cause physicians to leave the medical profession altogether (Nahed et al. 2012). Lawsuits can affect a physician's physical and emotional health and, in extreme instances, cause self-harm or suicide.

While this chapter is not meant to be a legal primer, it reviews the basic terminology and elements involved in medical malpractice or the more severe criminal accusations. This chapter also explores the perspective that physician wellness and risk management are congruent goals—a perspective that we hope will positively influence the legal climate within which a physician practices.

Legal Matters

Medical malpractice is ultimately a claim of negligence. Four essential elements are necessary for the patient-plaintiff to overcome the burden of proof of negligence by the physician: duty, breach, causation, and damages. Medical malpractice occurs when a negligent act or omission causes harm to a patient and the plaintiff must prove all four elements to "win" their case.

Duty relates to the physician-patient relationship and the requirement to treat the patient according to the standard of care. This relationship can be subjective and is often the easiest element to prove. The relationship is clear when a patient sees a physician in their professional environment such as a clinic or hospital. The relationship does not exist, for example, if a patient overhears a doctor giving medical advice at a social gathering. Questions related to the existence of the relationship arise frequently when a consulting physician does not directly treat the patient. Alternatively, a doctor traveling on an airplane has no duty to raise his or her hand to assist another passenger suffering from a medical emergency.

Breach and causation are the areas most contentious during a medical malpractice claim. Once the physician-patient relationship is established, the law acknowledges that there are certain medical standards that are professionally recognized as being acceptable medical treatment. Patients have the right to expect that their physician will care for them based on these standards. When the standard is breached, negligence may be established.

After establishing a relationship or duty to perform at the standard of care and a breach of that duty, the patient must prove the breach was the direct cause of harm. It is not enough to say that the physician violated the standard of care. The patient must prove the harm would not have occurred but for the negligence. If there is an injury without negligence, or negligence without injury, there is no case. Proving breach and causation results in the battle of the experts, with each side presenting testimony from other physicians who either support or repute the defending physician's care.

Finally, the patient must prove the negligence did indeed cause harm. Harm can take the form of death, disability, loss of income, unusual pain, suffering and hardship, or significant past and future medical bills. Depending on the jurisdiction, economic reward can be capped. For example, California has tort reform, or MICRA, which has mandated caps on damage awarded due to "pain and suffering."

Some examples of medical negligence that could lead to a lawsuit include failure to diagnose, surgical errors, improper medication, and poor follow-up or aftercare.

These four elements are argued once a suit is filed and then must be proved. However, the battle of proof can be onerous and often just being named in the suit can cause significant impact before any legal action begins.

Physicians who are sued for negligence naturally take the suit very personally. It is a direct attack on the physician's ability to care for a patient, the physician's training and expertise. The physician's breach of the standard of care is at issue, and while there are many reasons a patient may sue, for most physicians those underlying reasons don't matter when faced with a legal battle. The stress of being identified (singled out) as potentially negligently harming a patient greatly impacts physicians. Some have described a "Medical Malpractice Stress Syndrome" (MMSS) similar to PTSD.

Civil negligence is the most familiar and frequent type of legal action involving physicians; however, physicians have also been convicted of committing criminal acts against their patients. The most common cause of action is battery, also known as "unlawful touching," which happens most frequently when there is a breakdown in communication and informed consent. At the simplest level, if a surgeon operates on the wrong side or body part, that action may rise to the level of unconsented, unlawful touching, and the physician may be accused of committing battery against his or her patient rather than negligence. Communication and informed consent can be key in these matters.

Criminal acts can be more egregious and deliberate. Allan Zarkin, a New York gynecologist, was charged with first-degree assault for carving his initials into a patient. Michael Swango is serving three life sentences for poisoning three patients under his care (Jung 2006).

Case Illustration 8.1
Recently, a colleague was unable to control his drinking and arrived in an emergency department, intoxicated, to take care of a patient. Fortunately, the ED staff immediately recognized the physician's impaired state and removed him from the treating environment. The physician was investigated by the state medical board and

brought to trial where his license to practice medicine was revoked, pending a probationary period of 7 years during which the physician must adhere to strict guidelines, including random drug and alcohol testing, in order to continue practicing medicine. All off this very personal information is now available for public viewing on the state medical board website when you search for the physician's name.

In addition to the courtroom, physicians may be subject to investigation and disciplinary actions by their state medical board (see Case Illustration 8.1). State medical board contact information is given to patients in the hospital setting so patients may file complaints against their physicians. Other avenues available for patients are state health boards, insurance companies, and the Joint Commission. On a smaller scale, patient or staff complaints, including complaints about professionalism and practice standards, can also rise to the level of disciplinary review within the organization where the physician practices. Another vehicle for patients to voice their complaints, and one that is causing increasing distress among physicians, is social media.

This information is not to suggest that patients should not have an opportunity to voice any concerns about their care, including legal and disciplinary requests. It is meant to highlight the many channels within which a physician can be vulnerable to attacks on his or her expertise and character.

Risk Management

If legal and disciplinary actions are a defined endpoint, risk management strategies come into play as a means to reduce injury to patients, staff members, and visitors within an organization, thereby also preventing legal actions against a physician. Risk management is the proactive and sometimes reactive method to either prevent an incident or minimize the impact following an event. It is the identification, assessment, and prioritization of risk, followed by a collaborative, coordinated, and economical application of resources (Hubbard 2009). For example, after the Center for Disease Control (CDC) published research demonstrating prolonged urinary catheter use to be the leading risk factor for catheter-associated urinary tract infections, risk management plans at the University of Scranton were implemented requiring physicians to regularly evaluate catheters, with the end result being a decrease in patient risk (2015).

Most hospitals and malpractice insurance companies have risk managers to help physicians develop and implement risk mitigation strategies. Hospitals also have quality managers and patient safety managers collaborating with risk management, physicians, and staff to reduce patient harm. Some organizations may have one person in all roles while others may have a full staff in each separate department. Therefore, for purposes of this discussion, rather than separate patient safety and quality efforts uniquely, they will be combined under the category of risk management.

Case Illustration 8.2: One Case, Many Physician Wellness Issues

The following true story highlights many different physician wellness concerns as it relates to medical errors and the legal system.

A statewide risk management strategy was imposed in the state of New York in 1989 in response to the well-publicized death of 18-year-old Libby Zion in 1984. It wasn't only the medical cause of her death, but the conditions under which her physicians cared for her that played a huge role in new state regulations. Libby Zion was a previously healthy college freshman with a history of depression that presented to a Manhattan emergency room with fever, agitation, and strange jerking motions of her body. She subsequently died within 24 hours of her admission.

Ms. Zion was admitted from the Emergency Room for hydration and observation. Two residents evaluated Ms. Zion in consultation with the attending physician via phone. She was given a shot of meperidine, a painkiller, and sedative to control her shaking per phone guidance from the attending physician. The events of the next several hours aren't clear except that one of the residents left to care for approximately 40 other patients she was covering and the other resident left the ward to sleep but was available by pager. After they left, Ms. Zion became more agitated and the nurses paged the residents who gave orders for restraints and medication without further evaluating Ms. Zion. Ms. Zion eventually fell asleep, but her temperature became dangerously high and she suffered a cardiac arrest and died. A previously healthy young woman died of a mysterious infection.

Zion's father, an attorney and journalist, did not accept the doctors' assertion that they had done everything they could and began investigating his daughter's death, becoming convinced that staffing and workload played an important role in what he called his daughter's murder. As a columnist for the *New York Daily News*, he loudly vented his outrage about the state of medical education and overtime—the image of the bedraggled, unsupervised intern wreaking havoc in hospitals would be featured in the pages of the *Washington Post*, *The New York Times*, and *Newsweek*.

In May 1986, the grand jury considered murder charges against the physicians but did not indict. Instead, they issued a report strongly criticizing "the supervision of interns and junior residents at hospitals in New York County." In response, the New York State Health Commissioner created a panel to evaluate the training and supervision of doctors in the state, and in 1989 New York State adopted the panel's recommendations that residents could not work more than 80 hours per week or more than 24 consecutive hours and that senior physicians need to be present in the hospital at all times.

The Zion case did not conclude with reduced hours for trainees, and a civil suit was filed 10 years after her death. In the winter of 1994, the case, *Zion v. New York Hospital*, finally went to trial and was avidly covered by Court TV. The hospital claimed that Ms. Zion died as a result of cocaine ingestion that she concealed from her doctors; a claim not supported by toxicology and vigorously denied by the plaintiffs. The grand jury attributed responsibility to both the doctors and the patient and awarded the family $375,000, which Mr. Zion called a travesty of justice (Lerner 2006).

To the distress of the doctors, Mr. Sidney Zion referred to his daughter's death as a "murder". The Hearing Committee of the (New York) State Board of Professional Conduct conducted 30 hearings at which 33 witnesses testified between April 1987 and January 1989. At the end of the proceedings, the committee unanimously decided that none of the 38 charges against the 2 residents were supported by evidence. Its findings were accepted by the full board and by the state health commissioner, David Axelrod. However, under NY law the final decision rested with the Board of Regents, which was under no obligation to consider the committee's previous recommendations. The Board of Regents voted to "censure and reprimand" the residents for acts of gross negligence (Spritz 1991).

While the verdict against the two residents did not affect their right to practice, it was considered very surprising as it overruled the Commissioner's recommendations. However, in 1991, the state cleared the records of the two physicians of findings they had provided inadequate care to Zion.

The case above brings up several matters related to physician wellness. How did the death of Ms. Zion affect those caring for her? How did the state investigation and later the civil trial impact the physicians named in the suit? Has the risk management response to reduce work hours had the desired impact on patient safety? There are studies available investigating the work hours question. Unfortunately, not much has been written about the physicians involved in Ms. Zion's care, but there is a plethora of current literature discussing second victim syndrome and malpractice stress syndrome, and research is just beginning in the arena of the impact of physician wellness and patient outcomes.

Risk Management Strategy from Zion Case

In 2003, the Accrediting Council for Graduate Medical Education (ACGME) imposed the first national regulation of duty hours, which mirrored the first state-level regulations placed in New York in response to the Libby Zion case in 1989. Have these restrictions worked to address the concerns raised in the Zion case? Are work hours a successful risk intervention strategy? Does work hour restriction improve burnout measures? Several studies have investigated the link between work hour restrictions and patient safety. Fletcher et al. reviewed the literature on work hour restrictions and patient safety from 1966 to 2004 and found insufficient evidence to determine a causal relationship between reduced work hours and improved safety. The studies reviewed demonstrated variable interventions, suboptimal quality, and inconsistent results. Some studies showed improvement with work hour restriction, some showed no change, and some showed worsening safety parameters (Fletcher et al. 2005). This work was done only 1 year after the ACGME regulations were put in place, and in 2001, Fletcher synthesized the research evaluating the relationship pre and post ACGME residency hour restriction in relationship to patient and resident outcomes (Fletcher et al. 2011). Fletcher identified 5345 studies, with only 60 meeting his inclusion criteria. His meta-analysis suggested an improvement in mortality between pre and post ACGME work hour restrictions, but patient complication data were more nuanced—with some increasing and some decreasing. Resident wellbeing also improved as measured by the Maslach Burnout Inventory. Burnout most often improved as a result of a decrease in emotional exhaustion, and two studies found that a higher number of work hours were related to burnout. This study suggested that improvement in well-being may be one explanation for why some patient care parameters are improving in the post-2003 period as prior research has demonstrated links between resident well-being and quality of patient care (Fletcher et al. 2011).

In contrast, a 2013 *JAMA Surgery* article documented a high percentage of burnout after the implementation of work hour restrictions, with a high level of emotional exhaustion. The longitudinal study of 11 university-based general surgery residency programs of 213 surgical interns from July 11 to May 2012 found that suboptimal quality of life, burnout, and thoughts of giving up surgery were common, even under the new paradigm of reduced work hours. This same group of surgeons reported a decreased continuity with patients, decreased coordination of patient care, and less time spent in the operating room. Furthermore, suboptimal quality of life, burnout, and thoughts of giving up surgery were common even with reduced work hours (Antiel et al. 2013).

Evidence suggests that the first phase of duty hour restrictions implemented by the ACGME in 2003 only resulted in modest improvements in resident well-being and patient safety. The ACGME responded with a new risk management strategy and recommended a new set of duty hour restrictions in 2011. A longitudinal study of 2323 medical interns at 51 residency programs at 14 ACGME institutions looked at self-reported duty hours, hours of sleep, depressive symptoms, well-being, and medical errors at 3, 6, 9, and 12 months of the internship year. Despite the decrease in duty hours, there were no significant changes in hours slept, depressive symptoms, or well-being scores. With the new duty hour rules, the percentage of interns who reported making medical errors actually increased (Sen et al. 2013).

One could say "the jury is out" as it relates to improvement in physician wellness indicators with the new work hour restrictions, if this risk management strategy is the best option to respond to the issues raised in the Libby Zion case. We do know that work hours is only one predictor of physician wellness, so these mixed results may not be surprising.

Impact of Legal Events on Physician Wellness

Medical Malpractice Stress Syndrome (MMSS)

Not much has been written about the impact on the physicians involved in the Zion case. A search of their names reveals that only one of the physicians is still involved in patient care. While there may be a multitude of reasons why the other physicians may not be found using various search engines, the impact of the death of a patient on a young physician's life and subsequent legal and state action could play a role.

It is well known that some physicians who are named in malpractice litigation have left or contemplate leaving the profession of medicine, some have found solace in drugs and/ or alcohol, and in the extreme, some have committed suicide as a means of escape from the stress and isolation brought about by legal action. At their source, these actions are caused by the medical profession's failure in recognizing its own mental health and wellbeing needs.

We know that malpractice or litigation is at the top of the list of major stressors for most physicians. We also know that fear of potential litigation exists and, in some specialties, it can be a fear that changes the way the physician approaches their patients. A sobering figure reported in 2011 that 99% of physicians in high-risk specialties, such as emergency medicine, will be sued by age 65 (Jena et al. 2011).

Litigation as a stress factor for physicians was identified in the USA as early as the 1980s (Charles et al. 1988; Fileni et al. 2007). Psychiatry has classified disorders for the patient who suffers from psychological trauma. Society has come to understand the terminology of post-traumatic stress disorder (PTSD) as it occurs in people who have experienced trauma such as the devastation of September 11, the bombings of the Boston Marathon, or active combat. Witnessing natural disasters or experiencing serious accidents, personal assaults such as rape, or other life-threatening events can contribute to PTSD. It is a serious, potentially debilitating condition and the person experiencing PTSD can suffer from flashbacks, nightmares, or intrusive memories (2018).

Physicians can suffer similar symptoms from the traumatic event of being named in a suit for malpractice. Medical Malpractice Stress Syndrome (MMSS) describes the extreme stress that litigation can place on a physician with manifestations of isolation, negative self-image, and feelings of helplessness, hopelessness, and depression (Tunajek 2007). MMSS, like PTSD, does not limit itself to emotional or mental health symptoms, but can impact a physician's physical health as well. Litigation can be a lengthy process, as seen in the Zion case, with physicians suffering before the case, during the case, and after the case is over. The symptoms of MMSS wax and wane during the litigation process and can include feelings of intense shame, depression, guilt, and victimization. Physical symptoms can also plague the physician embattled in litigation, including fatigue, gastrointestinal symptoms, chest pain, and decreased concentration. The primary cause of these symptoms is the perception that the malpractice suit is an attack on the physician's integrity and intellect. The physician has studied for years to be the master of his or her craft and took an oath to "do no harm." The personal impact of MMSS occurs even if the legal action does not culminate in the courtroom and can begin with a formal complaint or investigation into the physician's care (Ansari-Winn 2014).

The stress of litigation is not without consequences. Professionally, the ultimate risk is the loss of the physician's career. Personally, a physician who suffers from MMSS as the result of legal action can experience significant behavior changes, impacting the safe practice of medicine and the physician's personal relationships (Reyes and Reyes 2017).

The severe impact that litigation can have on physician wellness was played out very publicly in Denver, Colorado in 2008 when a prominent business owner, Leslie Fishbein, suffered cardiac arrest and died after receiving trigger point injections with bupivacaine for chronic neck pain. She was a local celebrity for starring in her own TV commercials promoting her high-end furniture business. Her death drew tremendous attention and heavy scrutiny toward Dr. Daniel Brookhoff, Ms. Fishbein's treating physician.

Dr. Brookhoff was sued for wrongful death. Tragically, Dr. Brookhoff paid the ultimate price for the stress of his lawsuit. He was found locked inside a Toyota Camry under a comforter with his finger still on the trigger of a 0.38-caliber Smith & Wesson handgun (Felisa Cardona 2011). He committed suicide the day before the lawsuit filed against him was settled in court. Even after his death, Dr. Brookhoff was vilified as local papers reported his actions in the cause of Ms. Fishbein's death. Papers described Ms. Fishbein's early death as a tragedy with widespread ramifications, causing the closure of her furniture store and the loss of over 100 jobs. Papers did not mention the wife and children that Dr. Brookhoff left behind.

As mentioned previously, when a physician is sued, regardless of the merits of the allegations, it is perceived as a personal attack. Unfortunately, the odds of being sued are high; a study conducted by Anupam Jena and published in the New England Journal of Medicine in August 2011 determined that 7.4% of physicians are sued annually (Jena et al. 2011). The range varied across specialties, with 19.1% in neurosurgery, 18.9% in thoraciocardiovascular surgery, 15.3% in general surgery, 5.2% in family practice, 3.1% in pediatrics, and 2.6% in psychiatry. Specialties that were most likely to face indemnity claims were often not those with the highest average payments. For example, although neurosurgeons were sued most frequently, the average payment ($344,811) was less than the average payment for pediatricians ($520,924), who were sued less frequently. Even though neurosurgeons were several times more likely to face a claim, their average payouts were less. By age 45, 36% of physicians practicing in low-risk specialties will be sued. Frighteningly, 88% of physicians practicing in high-risk specialties will be subject to a malpractice claim by age 45. By age 65, the percentages increase to 75% and 99%, respectively, for physicians practicing in low- and high-risk specialties. This study also suggested that the fear of malpractice was not based on the amount of money being paid, but the actual suit, just being named as a defendant. Even though neurosurgeons may be paying less, the fact they are being sued more frequently can create a tangible fear. Not all suits end in payment. It is actually the risk of being sued, not the risk of losing a suit and paying money that may create malpractice stress. Insurance only pays the indemnity, or cost of losing a case. Even when a physician wins a case, there are defense costs that are never reimbursed by malpractice insurance, nor can a physician recover the indirect cost of time lost away from family and patients, added work related to preparing a defense, and reputational damage. It may not be the potential financial loss that creates stress during a lawsuit, but the act of being sued itself.

As previously mentioned, there are many reasons why patients sue. For example, a Harvard study of medical malpractice suggested that nearly 40% of claims were not associated with medical errors (Jena et al. 2011). So, by retirement age, at least three-fourths of physicians will have had to defend themselves in a court of law, many not even defending an error in their medical care.

Of additional interest, a recent study by David Studdert and Michelle Mello demonstrates that 1% of physicians account for 32% of law suits, and that as the number of claims increases over two, the risk of recurrent suits is exponential. Targeting these physicians for intervention could have a huge impact on their overall wellness and patient outcomes in addition to decreasing the impact of litigation stress on the organization in which they practice.

One might think that the commonality of the shared experience of being sued would lessen the blow when the process server comes to call, but this is not the case. Physicians are often instructed not to speak to anyone about the case, not even a spouse; physicians feel isolated and singled out, unaware that many of their colleagues walking the same halls are also undergoing similar stressors. If litigation is so common, and the impact so great, then developing means to support physicians through the stress of litigation is an essential risk management strategy.

Creating a formal structure to support physicians going through the stress of legal action is the first step to lessen the impact (Gallagher 2008). Support should be given by a peer who has gone through a similar process and is willing to provide emotional support to the physician involved. It is very important that the support not be confused with litigation coaching or strategy. No legal guidance or advice should be given by the supporting physician. Instead, the support structure should be one where colleagues are safely able to share how the legal event impacts them on a personal level and discuss opportunities to mitigate the stress.

Similarly, some legal support programs are led by trained professionals who counsel and support the physician. Again, these programs are not meant to provide legal guidance. When considering implementing a legal support program, it is important to consider the personal as well as the professional relationships of the physician involved. Legal actions can take months or years to resolve and can have a significant negative impact on personal relationships. Including the spouse or partner of the involved provider in support programs will also support the physician and could protect important relationships.

"Burnout may be what reinforces the connections between malpractice, defensive medicine and poor-quality of care" said Amitabh Chandra, a professor of public policy at the Harvard Kennedy School of Government and an economist who has written extensively on medical malpractice. "Ultimately, we are dealing with doctors who are working under enormous pressure," Dr. Chandra said. "For them, the emotional costs are colossal" (Chen 2011).

Medical Error: Second Victim

Legal action is a defined point, but what about errors that may or may not lead to patient harm or legal action? How do these events impact the physicians involved? The Institute of Medicine's report on medical mistakes, *To Err is Human*, described an alarming number of deaths related to preventable medical errors within healthcare systems (Institute of Medicine Committee on Quality of Health Care in, A 2000).

Patient harm, with or without medical error, greatly impacts physicians and the term "second victim" has been used to describe the often-silent sufferer in the patient care event. Physicians take an oath to "to do harm" so when harm does come to one of their patients, it can directly impact the physician. Additionally, when the outcome impacts an entire team of providers, the physician is often seen as the captain of the ship and takes on the role of addressing the team's concerns rather than his or her own.

While the first victims of medical errors are the patients who are harmed, the second victims are the caregivers and staff involved. Second victims are healthcare providers who are involved in an unanticipated adverse patient event, in a medical error, and/or in a patient-related injury. Providers become victims in the sense that they are traumatized by the event. Frequently, these individuals feel personally responsible for the patient outcome. Many feel as though they have failed the patient, second-guessing their clinical skills and knowledge base (Scott et al. 2009).

In 2011, a 50-year-old Cardiac Intensive Care nurse at Seattle Children's Hospital committed suicide just 7 months after making a mathematical error that led to an overdose of calcium chloride contributing to the death of a critically ill infant. Public investigation records showed it was the only serious medical mistake Kimberly Hiatt made in her 24 years of caring for patients. According to media reports, Kimberly was escorted from the hospital immediately after the mistake, put on administrative leave, and then hospital leaders terminated Kimberly's employment for undisclosed reasons. State licensing disciplinary actions required Kimberly to pay a fine and undergo a 4-year probation that included medication administration supervision at any future jobs. Her partner and co-parent, Lyn Hiatt, said Kimberly was "just devastated." Despite numerous efforts, she had no job offers, increasing her isolation and despair. Kimberly committed suicide on April 3 (Aleccia 2011; Grissinger 2014).

The problem is not rare—mistakes are made in medicine. According to Amy Waterman, an assistant professor of medicine at Washington University who studied the issue in a 2007 survey of more than 3100 practicing physicians, 92% of physicians surveyed said they'd experienced a near miss, a minor error, or a serious error, and 57% confessed to a serious mistake. After an error, doctors' confidence is often shaken and it affects their future ability. Of the physicians in Waterman's study, two-thirds reported anxiety about future errors, and half reported decreased job confidence and satisfaction (Aleccia 2011).

Burnout—whether associated with involvement in a recent medical error or excessive workload—may increase probability of subsequent errors. In a 2010 article from the Mayo Clinic, Shanafelt et al. found that 9% of surgeons reported concerns that they had made a major medical error in the past 3 months; burnout and depression were independent predictors of such errors in an analysis that controlled for other personal and professional factors (Shanafelt et al. 2010). In addition to medical error, literature supports that patient satisfaction and patient-reported recovery times are affected negatively the more burned out a physician becomes. This is particularly true when evaluating the depersonalization aspect of physician burnout (Halbesleben and Rathert 2008).

In a study of Italian radiologists, several factors were recognized as contributing to medical error. The radiologists surveyed reported excessive workload, insufficient time, lack of opportunity to consult with colleagues, poor work organization, tense and uncooperative work climate, obsolete equipment, inadequate continuing education, and imprecise requests from referring physicians. These stressors were inversely related to job satisfaction and the level of psychological and physical wellbeing. Increasing stress in the workplace is associated with low levels of job satisfaction and high levels of psychological distress (Fileni et al. 2007). This study also demonstrated that the experience of difficult working conditions and the discomfort, as well as increase in errors, that difficult working conditions cause, is at the basis of lower job satisfaction and excessive professional stress among radiologists, which lowers both psychological and physical wellbeing.

Error is inevitably present in all medical activity, and although everyone involved in patient care works hard, it is difficult to eliminate it entirely. However, its frequency and impact must be controlled and reduced. Once a medical error does occur, the uncontrollable variable is why a legal action is brought forth as a result of the error. The variable of physician burnout is one that can be measured and mitigation strategies adopted to improve medical error rates and the response to errors. Comprehensive efforts to improve physician burnout and professional fulfillment may improve patient satisfaction and overall quality of care.

Physicians do not tend to reach out for help and, when involved in a medical error, do not seek support from systems already in place, such as employee assistance programs (EAP) or faculty support resources. Many suffer in silence. A number of symptoms have been described related to the second victim syndrome, with an acute phase and a more chronic phase where the physician replays the event in his or her mind, looking for ways to change the outcome. "If only I had done.." becomes a destructive internal dialogue (see Chap. 3).

Creating a formalized program to support physicians involved in medical errors is an important step in mitigating the impact. Studies support the idea that physicians would rather receive support from peers, those who walk in similar shoes, than from any other source. Physician to physician peer support programs are being developed throughout the country, and though they may have individual nuances, the importance of having a trained peer supporter reaching out to a physician colleague is tantamount for any program to succeed.

Traditionally, risk managers record and investigate any patient care event causing patient harm or those events that could potentially rise to legal action. Additionally, risk management often serves as the first point of contact for legal activity. Many risk management activities don't formally address the potential impact these events have on those involved. With what we know about the relationships between errors, legal action, and burnout, a proactive risk manager is uniquely positioned to positively affect the impact these stressors have on providers and provide important insight to any organization's burnout mitigation efforts.

References

The Purpose of Risk Management in Healthcare (2015) The University of Scranton Online.

Posttraumatic Stress Disorder (PTSD) (2018) Anxiety and Depression Association of America, ADAA.

Aleccia J. (2011) Nurse's suicide highlights twin tragedies of medical errors. NBC News. http://www.nbcnews.com/id/43529641/ns/health-health_care/t/nurses-suicide-highlights-twin-tragedies-medical-errors/#.W6lLxXtKiUk

Ansari-Winn D (2014) 4 keys to manage medical malpractice stress syndrome. KevinMD.

Antiel RM, Reed DA, Van Arendonk KJ, Wightman SC, Hall DE, Porterfield JR, et al. (2013) Effects of duty hour restrictions on core competencies, education, quality of life, and burnout among general surgery interns. JAMA Surg,148: 448–55.

Charles SC, Pyskoty CE, Nelson A. (1988) Physicians on trialDOU-BLEHYPHENself-reported reactions to malpractice trials. Western Journal of Medicine 148: 358.

Chen P. (2011) When the Doctor Faces a Lawsuit. https://well.blogs.nytimes.com/2011/12/15/when-the-doctor-gets-sued-2/

Felisa Cardona HP. (2011) Fishbein's doctor kills himself on same day suit over her death is settled. The Denver Post.

Fileni A, Magnavita N, Mammi F, Mandoliti G, Lucà F, Magnavita G, et al. (2007) Malpractice stress syndrome in radiologists and radiotherapists: perceived causes and consequences. La Radiologia Medica, 112: 1069.

Fletcher KE, Reed DA, Arora VM (2011) Patient safety, resident education and resident well-being following implementation of the 2003 ACGME duty hour rules. J Gen Intern Med, 26: 907–19.

Fletcher KE, Underwood W, Davis SQ, Mangrulkar RS, McMahon LF, Saint S. (2005) Effects of work hour reduction on residents' lives: a systematic review. JAMA 294: 1088–1100.

Gallagher TH. (2008) Supporting health care workers after medical error: considerations for health care leaders. JCOM 15: 240–247.

Grissinger M. (2014) Too Many Abandon the "Second Victims" Of Medical Errors. Pharmacy and Therapeutics 39: 591–592.

Halbesleben JRB, Rathert C. (2008) Linking physician burnout and patient outcomes: Exploring the dyadic relationship between physicians and patients. Health Care Management Review, 33: 29–39.

Hubbard DW (April 6, 2009) The Failure of Risk Management: Why It's Broken and How to Fix It. Wiley, New York, p 304

Institute of Medicine Committee on Quality of Health Care in, A. (2000) To Err is Human: Building a Safer Health System. In: Kohn LT, Corrigan JM, Donaldson MS (eds.). National Academies Press, Washington, DC

Jena AB, Seabury S, Lakdawalla D, Chandra A (2011) Malpractice risk according to physician specialty. New England Journal of Medicine 365: 629–636.

Jung P, Lurie P, Wolf S (2006) Article in Health Matrix: U.S. Physicians Disciplined for Criminal Activity. Health Matrix: Journal of Law-Medicine 16:335.

Lerner B. (2006) A Case that Shook Medicine. The Washington Post.

Nahed BV, Babu MA, Smith TR, Heary RF (2012) Malpractice liability and defensive medicine: a national survey of neurosurgeons. PloS One 7: e39237.

Reyes R, Reyes C (2017) At Your Defense: Medical Malpractice Stress Syndrome Takes Its Toll. Emergency Medicine News 39: 19.

Scott SD, Hirschinger LE, Cox KR, McCoig M, Brandt J, Hall LW (2009) The natural history of recovery for the healthcare provider "second victim" after adverse patient events. Quality and Safety in Health Care 18: 325–330.

Sen S, Kranzler HR, Didwania AK, Schwartz AC, Amarnath S, Kolars JC, et al. (2013) Effects of the 2011 duty hour reforms on interns and their patients: a prospective longitudinal cohort study. JAMA Intern Med 173: 657–62; discussion 663.

Shanafelt TD, Balch CM, Bechamps G, Russell T, Dyrbye L, Satele D, et al. (2010) Burnout and medical errors among American surgeons. Ann Surg 251: 995–1000.

Spritz N. (1991) Oversight of physicians' conduct by state licensing agencies: lessons from New York's Libby Zion case. Ann Intern Med 115: 219–222.

Tunajek S (2007) Dealing with Litigation Stress Syndrome. American Association of Nurse Anesthetists News Bulletin

Chapter 9
Mental Illness

Kristin S. Raj

When considering impediments to wellness in physicians, untreated mental illness and its consequences must be addressed. Despite the aim of the profession to care for health concerns, physicians often neglect or intentionally ignore their own mental health. While physicians have lower mortality rates of heart disease and cancer than the population, physicians' rates of suicide are far higher. Whereas level of education is typically a protective factor against suicide, this does not hold true for the healing profession. Each year, the number of physicians who die by suicide is around 400, equivalent to at least one to four full classes of graduating medical students. A psychological autopsy of physician suicide was done with data from over 30,000 suicides between 2003 and 2008, obtained via the state-wide National Violent Death Reporting system from 16 states. Physicians were more likely to be older and married compared to the non-physicians who died by suicide. There was no difference in their mental health diagnosis or depressed mood at the time of death (Gold et al. 2013). Women physicians are particularly at risk; while women physicians attempt suicide less often than non-physician women (who overall attempt more than men by a factor of four, though complete less often than men),

K. S. Raj (✉)
Stanford School of Medicine, Department of Psychiatry
and Behavioral Sciences, Palo Alto, CA, USA
e-mail: kraj@stanford.edu

© Springer Nature Switzerland AG 2019   139
L. Weiss Roberts, M. Trockel (eds.),
The Art and Science of Physician Wellbeing,
https://doi.org/10.1007/978-3-319-42135-3_9

women physicians' rate of dying by suicide equals that of men. Women physicians are thus dying by suicide at a rate far above their non-physician counterparts (Center et al. 2003). Knowledge of the human body and medications is likely playing a role in contributing to these deaths. Indeed, poisoning is the second most common method of suicide for physicians, whereas suicide attempts via poisoning are less likely to result in death in the general population (Gold et al. 2013). Physician knowledge of effective mechanisms of poison and death is likely linked to their higher comparative rates of intentional overdose death. Given that the decision to commit suicide is often impulsive and most people regret the attempt after it occurs, the increased risk of fatality with physicians' attempts is of grave concern.

Physicians, just like others, suffer from a range of mental health issues. Depression is far more prevalent in medical students and resident physicians than in their age-matched counterparts in the population. The prevalence of depression in residents is 28%, ranging from 20.9% to 43.2% depending on the instrument used to detect this illness. Furthermore, the rates of depression in residents are increasing with each calendar year (Mata et al. 2015). Prevalence of bipolar disorder or treatment-resistant depression in physicians is not known but may be underappreciated, given evidence that physicians who complete suicide are more likely than non-physicians to have antipsychotics in their blood at the time of death (Gold et al. 2013). Physicians carry the same rate of substance abuse problems as the population, though they carry even higher risks of substance abuse issues with prescription medications (see Chap. 10). Their motivation is largely to alleviate emotional and physical pain rather than to get high, which speaks to the under-detection and treatment of primary mental illness and stressors (Merlo et al. 2013). Other mental health disorders, such as obsessive-compulsive disorder, eating disorders, and anxiety disorders, are also understudied in physicians.

Impacts on Patient Care

In addition to a need to improve physician mental illness care for the health of physicians, there is a need to improve their care for the health of patients. Residents who screened positive for depression, only a quarter of whom had a known diagnosis, made 6.2 times as many medical errors as their non-depressed counterparts. Burnout in and of itself was not associated with higher medication error rates (Fahrenkopf et al. 2008).

Issues Contributing to Undertreated Physician Mental Illness

The sometimes unspoken rub of this data is that given both their specific knowledge of health and knowledge of access to care, doctors should instead have the lowest rates of untreated mental illness and suicide. Systematic and cultural issues within medicine are contributing to these higher rates of untreated mental illness or suicide in doctors. As demonstrated in a prospective study over the course of internship, the prevalence of depression increased over 650% from prior to internship. Women and those with difficult early family life, a history of major depression, and neuroticism were at greater risk of developing depression, in addition to those with higher work hours and perceived medical errors and stressful life events. Specialty and age were not risk factors for development of depression (Sen et al. 2010). Regarding suicide specifically, a job problem contributing to suicide is more likely to occur in a physician than in a non-physician (Gold et al. 2013). In addition to the stresses of work in medicine, increased debt from medical school is associated with a higher risk of alcohol abuse and dependence (Jackson et al. 2016). There are thus clearly specifics currently inherent to the medical profession, rooted in unsolved and sometimes not even fully defined systemic dilemmas, that are contributing to physician mental illness. Work hours, educational debt, and management of acute job stressors are ripe areas for intervention to prevent or mitigate mental illness in physicians. Yet the greater barrier to overcome stigma remains.

Mental Illness Stigma Within Medicine

Existing mental illness stigma at multiple levels is preventing physicians from seeking and obtaining treatment (Fig. 9.1).

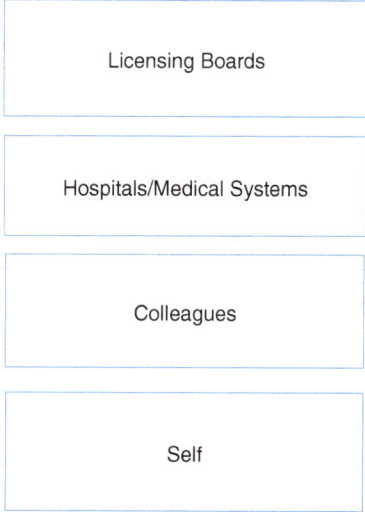

FIGURE 9.1 Levels at which physician mental illness stigmatization occur and thus potential areas for interventional impact to improve mental illness care

Within the medical field specifically, this stigma originates within the physicians suffering from mental illness themselves, as well as in colleagues, medical administrations, and medical licensing boards. The term stigma is so often used in mental health that we sometimes forget to really consider its meaning. Psychiatric illness stigma refers to a disapproval, discontent, or condescension toward those with such symptoms or diagnoses. These negative thoughts and feelings can exist within the stigmatizers and within the stigmatized. The very perception that one will be stereotyped or discriminated against presents a barrier to being open about suffering and to pursuing care. Historically, the culture of medicine has implicitly and at times explicitly valued infatigable, selfless, infallible physicians. Stigma about mental illness is pervasive in medicine and extends to impact even those who are earliest in entering the profession—medical students. Stigma is arguably more prevalent within medicine than external to it. Medical students already cite barriers to seeking mental health care as stigma, confidentiality concerns, and fear of documentation on their academic record; the latter two are additionally born out of a culture of stigma (Center et al. 2003). Less than half of medical students with suicidal ideation are seeking mental health care due to barriers (Center et al. 2003). Over half of interns in a prospective study who screened positive for depression cited confidentiality as a barrier to care as well (Guille et al. 2010).

In the prospective study of interns with a positive depression screen, over 90% noted a lack of time as a barrier to seeking care, a factor the medical students also listed (Center et al. 2003; Guille et al. 2010). Time to care for one's health must be emphasized in our medical system. This sense of lacking time for caring for one's mental health can originate from a devaluing of the medical importance of such care and from physicians' concerns (particularly among trainees) that colleagues then will have to cover for their absence in addition to maintaining their own duties and will resent this. It can also originate from a lack of professional infrastructure encouraging time for self-care as necessary and feasible. Indeed, physicians cite lack of convenient access to care. Many also describe a preference to self-manage their condition, potentially again speaking to fears about prejudice from their colleagues and even limited understanding of the nature of mental illness.

Stigma and a lack of understanding about mental health conditions also exist at the level of hospital systems. Due to fears of stigmatization from employers, in addition to the barriers described above, physicians delay seeking care, and sometimes push on with work until their condition has progressed to a point that it interferes with their work functioning. An optimal medical system would possess insight into those barriers to care and work internally to mitigate and remove them. The organization should work to understand the stigmatization pressures existing both in the minds of the impaired physicians as well as in their colleagues that systemically present major challenges to seeking timely care. However, many existing medical systems have yet to operate at this level. Frequently, physicians whose mental illness becomes apparent at work, even if not putting patients at risk, are sanctioned or put on probation.

Case Illustration 9.1

Sam is a 27-year-old unmarried man in his first year of internal medicine residency. He first developed depressive symptoms in his first year of medical school. He cites stress and unhappiness about attempting to memorize facts and uncertainty about a desire to pursue medicine. He had been a design major in college, but had felt family pressure to pursue medicine. He developed low mood and motivation, stopped attending class, and found himself pulling hairs from his beard which helped relieve some stress. He took several months off school and spent his days in bed with thoughts of wanting to be dead, but did not attempt suicide. He saw a psychologist and psychiatrist and began taking an antidepressant. These interventions helped enough with his mood for him to return to school. He discontinued the antidepressant after a year due to pressure from his parents to be off medications. He began clerkships and enjoyed his rotations, especially internal medicine, and performed very well. He remained depressed, especially when not participating in rotations, and had low motivation and interest in the evenings and on his days off. His mood improved briefly when he moved and began internal medicine residency, but his depression increased again with increasing stress and sleep deprivation during residency and the stress of his mother being diagnosed with lung cancer. His depressive symptoms were often masked during the day at work, and he also described that he worked to put forward an image of being "put-together" and high-achieving. When he returned home in the evenings, he had no energy, no motivation, an increase in hair pulling, and a sense of being overwhelmed and hopeless. Though he continued to work hard, once a month he would stop attending a biweekly afternoon outpatient clinic where he had been assigned to shadow an attending physician. He would find himself feeling overwhelmingly depressed and spent these afternoons in bed often. His attending did not comment on his absence for a few months, at which time she brought it to the attention of his program director. After a discussion with Sam, his program director encouraged him to seek psychiatric care and placed him on surveillance for "unprofessional behavior."

In the process of applying for his medical license, Sam received a letter from the state requesting an explanation for why he did not check "yes" to a question about if he had ever been diagnosed with an emotional or mental disorder that may impair his ability to practice medicine safely. The licensing board had received information from his program about his "unprofessional behavior." Sam was surprised as he did not think he had been impaired to practice medicine safely. His licensing process was prolonged.

This case highlights a physician who faced stigma about depression from first his family and then his professional environment. He had pushed himself to continue to perform strongly at work, though these attempts eventually fell short in an arena in which he didn't see his attendance as imperative for the care of patients. Stigma played a major role in preventing Sam from self-referral to treatment during his internship despite his severe suffering. Sam had stigmatized views of himself as being weak or incapable rather than suffering from an illness. His attending may have also been dealing with thoughts around stigma; she did not address concerns with Sam directly and instead ignored the problem of attendance until it reached a point that led her to first directly address it with his program director as a professional issue. While it is positive that his program finally encouraged him to seek mental health support, it was suboptimal that his absences were not noted and attended to more quickly. This may have helped him to see a need to seek care earlier, as well as to see the value his program placed on his health.

Additionally, this resident and his program would have benefitted had they taken a more nuanced approach to considering the conditions that led to his absences. Their broad determination that absences mean compromised patient safety led to major professional consequences.

Stigma and Medical Licensing Boards

The way many states' medical boards ask about mental illness is a major deterrent to physicians seeking assessment or treatment for themselves. Licensing and re-licensing questions in many states ask if someone has ever been diagnosed with a mental health issue. A study by Polfliet et al. in 2008 determined there had actually been an increase the prior decade in the number of questions about whether a physician has ever been diagnosed, despite ADA recommendations to assess only current functional impairment (Polfliet 2008). The APA also cites that "prior psychiatric history is, per se, not relevant to the question of current impairment" (Boyd et al. 2016). A system in which physicians are left with undiagnosed and untreated mental illness due to concerns that seeking care will impede their ability to practice is broken, and only serves to propagate potential harm to patients and physicians alike.

Neurobiology Education as a Method to Combat Mental Illness Stigma

Our collaborative medical system thus carries the responsibility to improve risk factors for mental illness within medical careers such as financial burden and residency stressors, to remove stigma, and to increase access to treatment for physicians. Mental health stigma in medicine may stem from a different origin than such stigma in the general public. Studies in the population surprisingly demonstrate that when people are educated that mental disorders have a genetic basis, they increased their social distance from those with illness and were more likely to assume dangerousness in them, in comparison to people who were told that the illnesses could be explained by social and environmental factors (Read et al. 2006). A potential explanation for this has been that the public ascribes a permanency and strong heritability when given genetic descriptions, which they may find fear-provoking. However, genetics is only a small part of the neurobiologic story of psychiatric conditions. As physicians are well-versed in the medical model of all other categories of conditions, education around the neurobiologic origin of all psychiatric conditions may prove to decrease stigmatization. While physical illness within the profession can still be stigmatized, it often meets greater acceptance than mental illness. This is perhaps due to its sometimes unavoidable visibility or to its greater rooting in understood biologic pathophysiology. When a psychiatric illness affects ones' ability to be "infatigable" and "selfless," those in medicine tend to attempt to "push through it" for fear of looking "incompetent" or "weak," which suggests a lagging understanding among many regarding the neurobiologic mechanisms of the conditions. As research progresses, the neurocircuitry, cellular, epigenetic, and genetic underpinnings of psychiatric issues continue to be elucidated, as well as how environment and social factors interact at each of those levels. However, few physicians have been educated in this. As we work to rewrite our educational curricula in medical school and residencies to reflect the neuroscience of mental illness, we may begin to see improvements in the specific mental illness stigma.

Case Illustration 9.2

A 34-year-old woman with a history of obsessive-compulsive disorder noticed worsening of her symptoms as she began her first radiology position after her fellowship. She described a significant increase in her checking behaviors, which at baseline on medication had been occupying

15 minutes a day. She found herself re-evaluating imaging at work for five to six times as long, and she began taking work home with her to do well into the night. She found herself losing sleep and lacking the time to make social connections at her new job. She knew that she was proficient at her job and that her checking was excessive, but she felt compelled to review the images to this extent. She feared that patients may be put at risk and potentially die if she did not. She questioned if she had picked the right field to go into because of this. Given the amount of time that she was working and not knowing the resources available at her new hospital, she did not seek care for over 6 months and her mood worsened. After hearing a noon conference talk on the mental health resources available at her institution, she sought treatment through this venue. Her checking began to improve with medication adjustment and therapy that implemented approaches around evaluating her thoughts and behaviors, as well as acceptance and meaning-making around having obsessive-compulsive disorder. She found self-acceptance and meaning after considering that a small level of checking her work helped her feel that radiology was a "good fit" for her. She became involved in physician wellness outreach at her institution.

This case illustrates one of many ways in which the position of being a physician can interact with psychiatric conditions. The specific duties of being a radiologist and the new independence of being an attending physician, along with the potential inherent risk to real lives at stake, served to acutely worsen this physician's symptoms of OCD. Sleep deprivation in medicine can worsen or instigate manic or depressive episodes, or it can trigger substance abuse in those predisposed. Limited time to eat or for self-care can worsen or lend to a relapse in eating disorders. Additionally, lack of time, lack of knowledge of resources, and limited access prolonged this physician's time to seeking care.

Approaches to Improving Physician Mental Health Care

A multi-prong approach to improving physician mental health should be undertaken. This would involve addressing issues at the level of the medical boards, hospital and health-care delivery systems, medical team culture, and physicians individually.

Physicians can individually evaluate the potential ways in which they inadvertently propagate mental health stigma in the culture of medicine, for their colleagues and within themselves. (See Table 9.1 for a list of potential thoughts that may clue one in to potential mental health stigma.) Physicians can work to increase access to resources for colleagues and take the time to access these resources themselves.

At the national level, the Accreditation Council for Graduate Medical Education (ACGME) now requires that programs have a commitment to physician wellbeing, a clear need for physicians at this level of training (Raj 2016). Programs are mandated to allow residents the opportunity to attend medical,

TABLE 9.1 Stigma thoughts

Here are some examples of thoughts that physicians may be having, yet not realize stem from a subconscious stigma about mental health. Recognizing these thoughts may help physicians notice ways in which stigma could be holding them back from seeking care

I should push through this

I'm just not cut out for this

I shouldn't need help with this

This will get better on its own

My colleagues are doing just fine with almost no sleep, so I should too

I must just be a weaker person than they are

Everyone is miserable, so what I'm feeling must be normal

mental health, and dental appointments even if during duty hours and are also required to provide access to mental health urgent and emergent care 24 hours a day, 7 days a week. The mandate also specifically describes that programs must have policies and procedures in place that ensure coverage of patient care in the event that a resident is unavailable and that these policies must be implemented without fear of negative consequences for the resident. Specific outlining of this from the ACGME is a positive step for physician mental health. The mandates fall short, though, in that they do not delineate needed restrictions on work hours beyond that of 80 hours per week averaged over a 4-week period. There are many programs that thus create rules that are detrimental to the mental health of their residents but follow the letter of the mandate, such as weeks in which residents are assigned to work 100 hours per week. There must be further regulation of aspects such as work hours or methods to ensure residents are allowed truly confidential methods of seeking mental health appointments. With regard to national licensing, it is imperative that licensing questions be rewritten for the sake of stigma reduction and fairness to physicians regarding private health information. These questions should only ascertain current impairments in work functioning due to "mental" and "physical" conditions alike rather than probe into any diagnosis or history of treatment.

At the organizational level, the University of California San Diego screens all medical students, resident physicians, and attending physicians for depression, following a US Preventive Task Force recommendation for all adults that seems particularly applicable to physicians. This example may be one to emulate, though would require careful steps to ensure confidentiality and faith on the part of physicians in order to do no harm. Given the demands of work hours and the desire for facilitated access, one method that some hospitals have employed is development of specific in-house physician mental health treatment. Flexible hours and priority, timely access to a provider are advertised. The availability of these providers in close proximity is often welcomed by busy physicians. For those whose confidentiality concerns cannot be assuaged, referrals to community providers can be facilitated by this mental health team. Administrations additionally would contribute positively by taking a nuanced and health-oriented approach to their physicians struggling with mental illness, especially given the substantial existing barriers these physicians encounter to obtaining care.

References

Boyd JE, Graunke B, Frese FJ, Jones JTR, Adkins JW, Bassman R. (2016) State psychology licensure questions about mental illness and compliance with the Americans with Disabilities Act. Am J Orthopsychiatry 86(6):620–631. https://doi.org/10.1037/ort0000177.

Center C, Davis M, Detre T, et al. (2003) Confronting depression and suicide in physicians: a consensus statement. JAMA 289(23):3161–3166. https://doi.org/10.1001/jama.289.23.3161.

Fahrenkopf AM, Sectish TC, Barger LK, et al. (2008) Rates of medication errors among depressed and burnt out residents: prospective cohort study. BMJ 336(7642):488–491. https://doi.org/10.1136/bmj.39469.763218.BE.

Gold KJ, Sen A, Schwenk TL. (2013) Details on suicide among US physicians: Data from the National Violent Death Reporting System. Gen Hosp Psychiatry 35(1):45–49. https://doi.org/10.1016/j.genhosppsych.2012.08.005.

Guille C, Speller H, Laff R, Epperson CN, Sen S. (2010) Utilization and Barriers to Mental Health Services Among Depressed Medical Interns: A Prospective Multisite Study. J Grad Med Educ 2(2):210–214. https://doi.org/10.4300/JGME-D-09-00086.1.

Jackson ER, Shanafelt TD, Hasan O, Satele DV, Dyrbye LN. (2016) Burnout and Alcohol Abuse/Dependence Among U.S. Medical Students. Acad Med 91(9):1251–1256. https://doi.org/10.1097/ACM.0000000000001138.

Mata DA, Ramos MA, Bansal N, et al. (2015) Prevalence of Depression and Depressive Symptoms Among Resident Physicians: A Systematic Review and Meta-analysis. JAMA 314(22):2373–2383. https://doi.org/10.1001/jama.2015.15845.

Merlo LJ, Singhakant S, Cummings SM, Cottler LB. (2013) Reasons for misuse of prescription medication among physicians undergoing monitoring by a physician health program. J Addict Med 7(5):349–353. https://doi.org/10.1097/ADM.0b013e31829da074.

Polfliet SJ. (2008) A national analysis of medical licensure applications. J Am Acad Psychiatry Law 36(3):369–374. http://www.ncbi.nlm.nih.gov/pubmed/18802186.

Raj KS.(2016) Well-Being in Residency: A Systematic Review. J Grad Med Educ 675–684. https://doi.org/10.4300/JGME-D-15-00764.1.

Read J, Haslam N, Sayce L, Davies E. (2006) Prejudice and schizophrenia: A review of the "mental illness is an illness like any other" approach. Acta Psychiatr Scand 114(5):303–318. https://doi.org/10.1111/j.1600-0447.2006.00824.x.

Sen S, Kranzler HR, Krystal JH, et al. (2010) A Prospective Cohort Study Investigating Factors Associated with Depression during Medical Internship. Arch Gen Psychiatry 67(6). https://doi.org/10.1001/archgenpsychiatry.2010.41.

Chapter 10
Substance Use Disorders

Chwen-Yuen Angie Chen and Tiffany I. Leung

I cannot help but believe that David's aloneness, his addiction, was worse for being in the medical profession—and not just because of ease of access, or stress, or long hours, but because of the way our profession fosters loneliness…There is a silent but terrible collusion to cover up pain, to cover up depression there is a fear of blushing, a machismo that destroys us. The citadel quality to medical training, where only the fittest survive, creates the paradox of the humane, empathetic physician like David, who shows little humanity to himself. The profession is full of 'dry drunks' physicians who use title, power, prestige and money just as David used drugs; physicians who are more comfortable with their work identity than with real intimacy. And so it is when one of our colleague is whisked away, to treatment, and the particulars emerge, the first response is 'I had no idea'. …It is not individual physicians who are at fault as much as it is the system we have created.

– The Tennis Partner, Abraham Verghese, MD

C.-Y. Angie Chen (✉)
Stanford University, Department of Primary Care
and Population Health, Palo Alto, CA, USA
e-mail: chchen@stanfordhealthcare.org

T. I. Leung
Maastricht University, Maastricht, The Netherlands

Maastricht University Medical Center+, Maastricht, The Netherlands

© Springer Nature Switzerland AG 2019   153
L. Weiss Roberts, M. Trockel (eds.),
The Art and Science of Physician Wellbeing,
https://doi.org/10.1007/978-3-319-42135-3_10

Overview: Recognizing Substance Use Among Physicians and Its Impact on the Practice of Medicine

Physicians, compared to the general population, tend to lead healthier lifestyles in terms of using less tobacco and adhering more often to preventive care guidelines. However, physicians experience comparable or even higher rates of substance use disorders (SUDs) than the general population (Earley 2014). Physician access and referral to treatment for substance use disorders should be no different than for any other professional or the general population, but, unlike many other professionals, physicians with active substance use disorders are a special population who pose a public health and safety risk similar to airline pilots (DuPont et al. 2009). It would stand to reason that the medical profession would be stalwart toward the research, education, and treatment of addictive disorders especially among its own, and yet acknowledging alcohol and drug use in the physician community seems even more challenging due to the stigma and risk of losing professional licensure. Despite the existence of state physician health programs (PHPs), which have proven to be the gold standard of addiction treatment, with better outcomes for the rehabilitation of impaired physicians than treatment as usual for the general public, sufficient access, resources, and successful re-integration into practice remain inconsistent for the addicted physician, as not all states have a PHP and each program may have a different relationship with the governing licensing board (DuPont et al. 2009).

The minimal recognition of substance use disorders among physicians likely begins with limited education and training in addiction medicine during medical school. This deficit is combined with a deeply ingrained culture of perfectionism and invincibility, coupled with social and professional stigma that tend toward penalizing and ostracizing physicians for mental health and substance use disorders. This scenario is a formidable foe to a vulnerable or impaired physician who desperately needs help. Perceived professional risk to the discovery of substance use disorders among physicians is underscored by state-to-state variations in the existence of physician health programs and standards set out by licensing bodies. There remain a few states, including California, where there is no formal physician health program at the time of this writing (Federation of State Physician Health Programs 2018).

Under-diagnosis and low rates of referral of addicted physicians to effective treatment create a dangerous ripple effect on patient care and safety, including increased medical errors, under-treatment of substance use disorders, and poor comorbid medical outcomes when impaired physicians continue to practice (DuPont et al. 2009; Pilowsky and Wu 2012; Yoast et al. 2008). In this chapter, the prevalence and characteristics of physicians suffering from substance use disorders, risks for developing these disorders, and the associated consequences of physician substance use disorder will be described across the life cycle of the medical profession, from physicians-in-training to the practicing physician. The culture of the profession and opportunities for improvement will be discussed, including how addiction among physicians has been handled through the various state physician health programs and how policies promoting standardization could be beneficial.

Epidemiology: Trends in Substance Use Among Physicians

Substance use disorders (SUDs) are defined along a spectrum of severity ranging from substance misuse, characterized as use for non-intended purposes, risky and hazardous use, to more significant substance dependence that is identified by tolerance, withdrawal, cravings, and a person's recurrent failure to meet home, work, school, or other responsibilities (U.S. Preventive Services Task Force 2013). Physician impairment, on the other hand, is defined as the inability or impending inability of a physician to practice his or her health profession in a manner that conforms to acceptable standards of practice (Baldisseri 2007). According to data collected by state physician health programs (McLellan et al. 2008), substance use disorders are the leading cause of physician impairment, although substance use disorders do not in all instances lead to impairment. Beyond substance use disorders, physician impairment can also be caused by maladaptive behaviors, process addictions, mental illness, or medical disability including that related to aging.

Approximately 10–12% of physicians develop a substance use disorder with a lifetime prevalence of 7.9%, which is close to the lifetime prevalence in the general population of 8–13%, although under-reporting may be a factor in the physician (Earley 2014). Alcohol is the most commonly misused substance among physicians and especially among those characterized under the physician health programs study by McClellan et al. (50.3%) (McLellan et al. 2008), and some surveys show a higher prevalence of alcohol overuse in surgical specialties (see below). Physicians also experience higher rates of unsupervised prescription drug use, particularly opioids and benzodiazepines. Suicide among physicians is also higher than the general population (Schernhammer and Colditz 2004; Lindeman et al. 1996; Center et al. 2003).

As in the general and physician population, there are more male physicians in treatment than women physicians, with a ratio of as high as seven-to-one, in some surveys (McGovern et al. 1998), likely mirroring the prevalence of addictive disorders in the physician community. However, despite not being in treatment, women physicians are more likely to report problematic drinking by the end of medical school and have substance use disorders later in their career compared to non-physicians (Flaherty and Richman 1993; Bissell and Jones 1976), but women make up only 13% of physicians in PHP treatment programs (DuPont et al. 2009).

Unique risk factors for physicians developing substance use disorders include easier drug access as a physician and the biological effect of the "drug of preference." As an example, opioid access and use can result in rapidly rising tolerance, leading to increasing opioid diversion, and, consequently, increasing risk of detection of SUD by a colleague (Earley 2014). Also, a physician's personality traits, such as perfectionist behavior and high-class ranking, are arguably a risk factor for SUD (Bissell and Jones 1976). Compulsive behaviors (Udel 1984) may also contribute to increased risk. The strongest predictor of SUD in physicians is genetic loading, or a family history of addiction, which is the same for the general population (Flaherty and Richman 1993).

Current evidence on physician impairment and physician substance use most frequently reports substance use disorder prevalence among medical specialties, with five specialties representing most of those with use disorders: anesthesiology, emergency medicine, psychiatry, family, and internal medicine (Earley 2014). Additional studies describe possible associations between specialty and the type of substance used, for example, higher than average risk of alcohol use disorders among dermatologists, surgical specialties, emergency medicine physicians, pathologists, anesthesiologists, family medicine doctors, radiologists, obstetric-gynecologists, and preventive and occupational medicine physicians (Oreskovich et al. 2015). There is a notably higher prevalence of benzodiazepine use among psychiatrists (Oreskovich et al. 2015). State physician health programs (PHPs) are uniquely positioned to be able to collect data on physician substance use disorders because such programs can closely follow physicians from treatment entry through substance monitoring and treatment completion (DuPont et al. 2009; McLellan et al. 2008).

Nonetheless, due to the sensitive nature of physician impairment and general stigma around substance use disorders, data collection and evidence-based studies on these topics are challenging. For example, limitations of studies assessing SUD prevalence among physicians of various medical specialties are primarily in their method of data collection, which frequently includes anonymous convenience sample self-reporting in questionnaires. This may result in a biased view of physician substance use disorders. Additionally, poor quality data and reporting and a lack of critical analysis of available data can lead to under-reporting of physician impairment and its potential causes. This can lead to reduced availability of confidential, compassionate treatment options, overall under-treatment, and insufficient policies toward successful rehabilitation and re-integration of physicians back into practice.

However, knowledge gaps remain, such as data on ethnic and cultural variation and extent and etiology of substance use disorders among doctors across the span of their careers, starting in medical school.

Culture of Substance Use in Medical Training

Substance use, particularly alcohol, among medical trainees is a frequent yet also under-reported occurrence, such that the actual prevalence of substance use meeting criteria for a substance use disorder diagnosis is unknown. One study surveyed approximately 5000 medical students from 16 medical schools in the USA, finding that about one-third of students engaged in excessive drinking and binge drinking (Frank et al. 2008).

In many ways, the process of medical training reflects the binging pattern and "use-despite-harm" characteristic of addiction. Binging is analogous to the unhealthy imbalance or integration of work and play: there is a lack of moderation in the way medicine is learned in medical school, where tremendous effort, time, and resources are expended to learn an enormous breadth of information in a limited amount of time. In residency, duty hours still well exceed normal working hours and conditions for the average laborer. As an occupation with high professional expectations, physicians-in-training and practicing physicians seek to prove competence, sometimes by overworking, attempting to meet super-human expectations, and subsequently developing maladaptive behaviors that habituate poor self-care and potential reliance on substances, such as alcohol or prescription drugs, to facilitate self-management. Typical warning signs of overwork, poor self-care, burnout, or substance use disorders, including changes in mood and judgment, may be ignored, despite the concerns of family, friends, or peers.

Case Illustration 10.1

A fourth-year neurology resident at Jackson Health System in Florida drew nationwide attention and outrage in January 2016 after a video was posted to YouTube.com, showing her assaulting an Uber driver while intoxicated with alcohol. She apologized later for her actions, noting that she had ended a 2-year relationship that day and her father had been hospitalized in the hours before the encounter occurred. Her residency was terminated in April 2016 (Alexander 2016; Goldstein 2016).

Discussion Questions:

- What contributing factors could have led to alcohol use for this resident as a measure to cope with the reported circumstances?
- What led to this physician's termination? What alternative, more compassionate options might be possible?
- What role does social media play as it increases potential for public scrutiny and judgment of physicians, their employers, and associated organizations?

In another survey of medical students, of 2046 senior students from 23 US medical schools who responded, 87.5% reported using alcohol in the past month, 10% used marijuana, 10% used tobacco, 2.8% used cocaine, and 2.3% used tranquilizers without a doctor "telling them to" (Baldwin et al. 1991). In the same survey, an additional 1.1% of students reported misusing an opioid other than heroin. The majority of these students reported first using substances, excluding cigarette smoking, either in high school or college. For cigarette smoking, 35.3% of respondents first started smoking during grade school or before and 44.5% started in high school. First use of alcohol or marijuana also usually occurs during high school. However, first use of tranquilizers occurred after starting medical school for 35.9% of seniors who used them.

In this same study, medical school seniors appeared to be more lenient in their attitudes toward colleagues who used alcohol and marijuana occasionally, compared to colleagues who used other drugs such as cocaine, tranquilizers, amphetamines, psychedelics, and opiates (Baldwin et al. 1991). However, students also tended to endorse harsher consequences, such as suspension or expulsion, instead of treatment or counseling if they perceived that their colleagues were impaired by such use.

Less is known about the use of substances, especially prescription stimulants, among medical students and residents with the intention of enhancing cognitive or academic performance. The use of stimulants, whether prescribed or misused, in this manner is a well-known and concerning phenomenon among undergraduate students, with past years' use prevalence rates of up to 2–11% (Ponnet et al. 2015). Medical students and residents train toward an occupation with high professional expectations and accompanying tendencies toward perfectionism; the use of performance-enhancing substances has an unknown effect on learning, development of new skills, and longer-term consequences, such as increasing risk for or enabling the use of other substances (Rose and Curry 2009).

The relative lack of attention to substance use disorders as part of the medical school curriculum also contributes to the problem of SUD among medical trainees. This also results in inadequate preparation of future physicians in diagnosing and treating substance use disorders. One paper reported that although 54% of first-year students surveyed thought it was highly relevant to screen for substance use disorders, by the time they graduated, only 46% thought it was highly relevant (Frank et al. 2008). Medical schools provide little in the form of education to inform students' attitudes and behaviors regarding the relevance of substance use disorder counseling and treatment (Frank et al. 2008). Unfortunately, another study done in Massachusetts found that even after students graduate from medical school and advance in their training, perceived preparedness and willingness to treat SUD only decrease (Back et al. 2018). This is a missed opportunity for teaching about a potentially high-impact public health topic that is also relevant to physicians' self-care and care of peers (Brown et al. 1995).

Along with public outcry in response to the opioid epidemic in the early 2000s, medical education has also developed a growing recognition and urgency to train physicians in addiction medicine. For example, the governor of Massachusetts launched a collaborative effort in 2015 with the Massachusetts Medical Society and the Massachusetts Department of Public Health to develop a series of ten core competencies relevant to prescription drug misuse that each of the state's 3000 medical students will learn (Governor's

Medical Education Working Group on Prescription Drug Misuse 2015; Antman et al. 2016). A group of the core clerkship directors in Massachusetts—including those in family medicine, medicine, obstetrics-gynecology, pediatrics, psychiatry, and surgery—have already begun to incorporate subsets of the competencies into their curricula.

In another example of medical education development in addiction medicine, the Warren Alpert Medical School of Brown University collaborated with the Rhode Island Department of Health to develop a 4-year integrated addiction medicine curriculum for medical students (McCance-Katz et al. 2017). In addition to at least 3 hours of didactics on SUD in the pre-clinical years, students must also perform a drug and alcohol screen on at least five patients per year for each of the 4 years of medical school. If the patients screen positive, they should then be able to perform brief intervention and referral to treatment (SBIRT) when appropriate. Additional case-based learning and clinical skills assessment are done in the clinical years.

To prevent the propagation of unhealthy lifestyles begun during medical training, dedicated curricula on addiction medicine, a growing number of addiction specialist role models, and even a change in how healthy behaviors are perceived for physicians-in-training are all necessary and in turn will improve patient care.

Addiction in Medical Practice: Affecting the Clinician and Affecting Care

Addressing substance use disorders in a routine outpatient visit can be challenging due to limited resources (Polydorou et al. 2008). Visit time is brief and a great deal of mandated screening questionnaires and related activities must occur in a short period of time. Physicians in clinical practice do not typically screen and counsel on substance use disorders as they do on tobacco (Pilowsky and Wu 2012). Additionally, there is a notable lack of insurance coverage to reimburse treating physicians for providing substance use screening and counseling, whether the patient is a physician or not.

Alcohol and drug screening in primary care is inconsistent. In a national survey conducted in 2000 by the National Center on Substance Abuse at Columbia University, of 648 primary care physicians and 510 adults receiving treatment for substance use in 10 treatment programs, a majority of patients (53.7%) reported that their primary care physician did nothing about their substance abuse; 43% reported that their physician never diagnosed it; and 10.7% believed their physician knew about their addiction and did nothing about it (National Center on Substance Abuse 2000). Only approximately 20% of primary care physicians considered themselves "very prepared to identify alcohol or drug dependence." In comparison, approximately 80% reported feeling very comfortable diagnosing hypertension and diabetes. Even though unhealthy alcohol use and follow-up are part of the Healthcare Effectiveness Data and Information Set (HEDIS) 2018 measures (National Committee for Quality Assurance 2018), alcohol and drug screening is done in only an estimated 14–43% of visits by family physicians or pediatricians (Millstein and Marcell 2003). Universal screening for risky alcohol use and other substance use, including cannabis and prescription drug misuse, is still not standard practice, despite a grade B recommendation from the US Preventive Services Task Force on alcohol screening and counseling (U.S. Preventive Services Task Force 2013) and a grade I recommendation for illicit drug use screening (U.S. Preventive Services Task Force 2014), which includes the non-medical use of prescription drugs.

In the special situation where the patient is a physician, honest and open substance use disorders screening may also be hampered by stigma associated with this condition in the medical profession. Substance use disorders pose a significant public health issue, and when occurring in a physician, there are added professional concerns. SUD screening is warranted in physicians with any active disease who would benefit from appropriate and confidential treatment.

In addition to practical limitations and cultural stigma of SUD in physicians, the treating physician's practice patterns can be influenced by personal beliefs and values, a phenomenon observed in other healthcare scenarios. If health experts, including physicians, engage in drinking behaviors similar to the populations they serve, this cognitive dissonance could contribute to a reduced sense of necessity to perform SUD screening and discuss the health risks of alcohol use. For example, only 13% of UK participants responded without prompting that there is a link between alcohol and cancer (Burki 2016), even though the association has been documented as early as 1903 (Newsholme 1903). With prompting, 50% of surveyed participants identified a link between alcohol and cancer (Burki 2016). In fact, women who drink between 70 and 140 g of alcohol per week (or approximately 7–14 drinks per week) have a 5% increase in risk of all cancers and a 13% increase in risk of breast cancer, compared with those drinking less than 20 g per week (or approximately two drinks per week). In addition to heightened cancer risks with higher alcohol use, suicide risk is significantly increased among people with mood disorders or schizophrenia and comorbid alcohol or substance use disorders.

As a profession, the American Board of Medical Specialties has only recently, in 2016, recognized addiction medicine as a board-certifiable clinical subspecialty. This represents a significant formal acknowledgment by the medical profession that addiction medicine is an important clinical and public health domain. Additionally, this presents greater opportunities to address training gaps and potentially complex cognitive scenarios in SUD screening and discussion.

Physician Suicide and Substance Use Disorders

Alcohol use and suicide have been extensively studied in the general population, with a strong association found between the two, especially as they relate to aggression and impulsivity (Sher 2006; Brady 2006). This association is especially concerning for physicians, as the logical conclusion might be that because physicians have higher rates of substance use disorders, particularly alcohol use, then they might also experience proportionally higher rates of suicide, although this has yet to be confirmed in observational studies of physician suicides. One paper published in 1986 performed a psychological autopsy, reconstructing risk factors for suicide as an investigative process in the setting of deaths due to suicide among US physicians, and concluded that mood and substance use disorders were among the key risk factors (Council on Scientific Affairs 1987). In McLellan et al., of 904 physicians enrolled in 16 state physician health programs, all had substance use disorders, and 22 had died as a result of failing to complete a monitoring contract; 6 of these deaths were due to suicide (McLellan et al. 2008).

Little is known regarding how substance use disorders contribute to physicians' plans, attempts, or death by suicide and whether substance use disorders are a major contributor at the time of death. An individual case study of a physician suicide describes 1 physician's career-long SUD patterns (Johnston 1979), and another case series describes the outcomes of 36 British physicians with alcoholism, which included 5 deaths by suicide (Murray 1976). However, such cases are not nearly enough to provide sufficient details of the complex relationship between SUD and suicide among physicians.

Individual physicians, advocates, and members of the academic community are calling attention to physician suicide independent of commonly published academic literature (Wible 2016; Myers 2017). Stigma associated with substance use disorders, especially among physicians, interferes with access to timely, non-judgmental, confidential, and rehabilitative treatment. Furthermore, reliable study of physician suicide events is hampered by numerous factors, including stigma, lack of standardized postvention processes (interventions conducted after a suicide largely supporting the bereaved family, friends, peers, and professionals), and lack of investigation as a public health imperative.

With further investigation and collection of supporting data, understanding the link between physician SUD and suicide would provide insights into impactful opportunities for intervention. Addiction is a treatable condition, and if physician suicide can be prevented with timely and effective addiction treatment, then further program funding and development could be justified in support of such effective interventions.

Helping the Addicted Physician: Fostering a Culture of Wellness

A culture of wellness is defined as "a set of normative values, attitudes, and behaviors that promote self-care, personal and professional growth, and compassion for colleagues, patients, and self" (Bohman et al. 2017). To fully embrace the concept of compassion for colleagues, the medical community, especially policy-making or professional organizations, as well as healthcare organizations who employ physicians, should foster a culture that destigmatizes addiction and mental health disorders, encourages help-seeking behaviors in times of acute stress, and enables the development of healthy and sustainable behaviors (see Chap. 2).

Fully embracing and developing a culture of wellness requires a multi-faceted approach that combines individual-level interventions with those implemented at the level of an institution or healthcare organization in education and policy reform. For example, an organization could implement peer support programs to support physicians and trainees after critical or traumatic events. Or, a residency program could implement a compassionate postvention program in the wake of a colleague's suicide (Center et al. 2003; American Foundation for Suicide Prevention 2018). Policymaking could include prohibiting degrading working conditions, such as excessive duty hours for residents, improving state licensing procedures to reduce the stigma of mental health conditions and substance use disorders, and increasing support for the compassionate, non-punitive rehabilitation and re-integration of physicians into the workforce.

Such reforms would create a cultural context that enables physicians-in-training and physicians in practice to readily seek guidance and treatment in any difficult circumstance, including those concerning substance use. Additionally, in earlier stages of the physician career pipeline, an emphasis on a healthy relationship with substances such as alcohol or prescription drugs should involve de-normalizing routine reliance on substances as stress reliever and avoiding a binge use pattern.

The hidden curriculum, the implicit positive and negative messages conveyed to learners through medical educators' actions and speech (Lehmann et al. 2018), may exacerbate stigmatization of substance use disorders. The manner in which we either normalize substance use or judge the difficulty of treating patients with addiction, for instance, may inadvertently influence whether a trainee or practicing physician feels safe from retribution or punishment when considering voluntary self-disclosure or even feeling willing to seek help. For example, if self-care is implicitly perceived as weakness, then the risk for burnout in a vulnerable physician may be high. An environment that is too rigid to allow for self-care, such as those where an organization's infrastructure is built upon a false culture of strength and peak performance, may even create sources of difficult-to-navigate stressors.

To reveal the hidden curriculum of any training institution, the American College of Physicians recommends the following (Lehmann et al. 2018): (1) allowing for time dedicated to guided reflection, (2) encouraging explicit conversations about uncomfortable or emotionally challenging experiences, and (3) using challenges as a way to continuously improve systems and culture. A culture of compassion and reflection that is integrated into the character and culture of an institution is essential to foster the necessary environment that would optimally support physician colleagues with a substance use disorder. Physicians would be proactively and positively encouraged to seek treatment and long-term counseling, as well as gradual re-integration into the workforce. Suspension or expulsion from training or practice (Baldwin et al. 1991) seems to be the antithesis of a compassionate culture of wellness.

Case Illustration 10.2

A former dean of the University of Southern California's Keck School of Medicine, who held that position for over a decade, resigned from the position 3 weeks after a female companion overdosed in March 2016. Investigative reporting by the *Los Angeles Times* revealed videos that suggested a long-standing pattern of behaviors consistent with substance abuse and addiction (Pringle et al. 2017). It was reported that in one video, for example, he is shown, dressed in a tuxedo, with an orange pill on his tongue and says "Thought I'd take an ecstasy before the ball." He then swallows the pill.

Discussion Questions:

- Was this physician impaired?
- What is the responsibility of peers and colleagues of the addicted physician? Professional organizations to which the physician belongs? A primary care provider for the addicted physician?
- What is the responsibility, if any, of the employer in this situation in facilitating rehabilitation? If none, why?
- Are SUD-associated behaviors the result of bad judgment?
- Should physicians with SUD be punished for their behavior? What role does termination as a form of punishment play?
- In resigning a position of authority after a sentinel event, does this indicate some level of individual recognition of the severity of SUD?
- How does media coverage contribute to a physician's public humiliation? Is such coverage warranted in response to such behaviors?

A culture of wellness regarding physician substance use disorders also must include educating the general public and policymakers regarding the need for SUD treatment among physicians. Otherwise, those outside the medical community may falsely continue to adopt policies that shame or criminalize physicians with SUD or otherwise discriminate against them for their condition. It is commonly forgotten that physicians are patients too. And while the safety and protection of their patients are also a priority, especially when physicians' licenses or credentials may be under surveillance during SUD treatment and rehabilitation, such protection should not also bluntly disregard the wellbeing, privacy, and life of the individual physician.

Prevention and Treatment for Physicians at All Stages

Early intervention is the most effective method to prevent the development of progressive substance use disorders among physicians throughout their careers. In medical school and residency, early intervention starts with de-normalizing alcohol as a tool to manage stress, mood, and sleep and as a socially acceptable and frequent activity for cultural assimilation into the medical trainee community. Health behavior change typically begins with awareness and pre-contemplation of changing behavior; however, failing to identify abnormal patterns of alcohol and substance usage early in medical training is problematic as a public health issue in the medical community. It seems that much of the experimentation and habituation to alcohol and cannabis use for medical students starts even earlier than medical school or undergraduate studies, and that initiation begins as early as high school (Baldwin et al. 1991); if this is the case for vulnerable matriculating medical students, then orientation provides one of the best times to educate an incoming class on the concepts of risky substance use along with reminders of self-care.

Comorbid conditions in physicians, including thought and mood disorders, post-traumatic stress disorder, and pain syndromes, can contribute to the development of addiction as well, similar to the general population (Earley 2014). In 2009, the University of California, San Diego School of Medicine, launched a Suicide Prevention and Depression Awareness Program that sought to broadly reach all levels of trainees and faculty, including pharmacy students, to anonymously and confidentially screen, assess, refer, and later educate on the topic of depression and suicide prevention (Moutier et al. 2012). Of the 374 respondents, 67% met criteria for moderate risk and 27% met criteria for high risk of suicide. Although the screening included a survey of drug and alcohol use, it is unclear from this 2009 publication how much emphasis or association was given to alcohol and drug use contributing to suicidal risk. What we can glean from this initiative is that it may be the first of its kind to perform such an intervention regarding physician suicide and similar programs could be tailored for substance use disorders.

A culture of wellness that is willing to recognize these vulnerabilities can potentially develop more compassionate assistance programs for physicians to seek guidance or referrals, accommodating the unique needs and traits of physicians with SUD. In undergraduate medical education, additional opportunities exist to incorporate educational activities for medical students about SUD and its physiological, clinical, and social consequences, as well as highlight uniquely vulnerable populations and associated ethical and legal issues, such as SUD among physicians. Such community introspection, folded into standard medical education, could provide an integrated educational and cultural framework for further prevention and management of physician SUD throughout the medical professional life cycle. As an example, basic sciences education on SUD could be emphasized during the first 2 years of medical school in core neurobiology and related coursework. Practical aspects of healthy substance use behaviors could be included as part of a student life handbook and orientation, which is a standard in college orientations as well. Subsequent curricula on student wellbeing can later reinforce concepts and incorporate clinical knowledge, behavior, and skills as part of psychiatry and primary care clerkships.

Finding Help: Physician Health Programs

The first state physician health program was established in New Jersey in 1982, responding to an initiative by the American Medical Association in 1973 to address specialty care and supervision over the addicted physician in need of help and to protect the public (Candilis 2016). Referrals to a state physician health program (PHP) comprised of self-referrals, clinical colleagues, state licensing boards, hospital medical staff, treatment providers, medical schools, law enforcement, family members, attorneys, and other PHPs. For example, physicians may voluntarily seek treatment if they find that their substance use has resulted negative consequences, and compensatory behaviors can no longer hide such consequences. In approximately 14% of cases, hospitals have well being committees that will refer to a state's PHP. Since the first New Jersey PHP established over 35 years ago, every state but four (California, Delaware, Nebraska, and Wisconsin) as of 2018 had some form of PHP that can refer a physician to treatment and be the clearing-house to monitor treatment adherence. The intention is that the PHP can serve as a neutral third party that evaluates and determines the readiness of a physician to safely re-integrate back into the clinical setting. The primary aim of the PHP is to ensure that the physician is not impaired and can return to work without compromising patient safety. PHPs do not themselves provide formal addiction treatment but act instead like case managers and monitors.

With that said, PHPs enter into a signed contract with a participating impaired physician and closely follow that physician from treatment entry at a specialty treatment site to treatment completion. Then, the PHP continues drug monitoring and relapse prevention evaluations for an average of 5 years before PHP oversight ends. Most PHPs provide general addiction education programs: they mandate some form of mutual help such as Alcoholics Anonymous, Narcotics Anonymous, or Caduceus Meetings; document drug monitoring results (urine toxicology, breathalyzer, hair follicle, etc.); document workplace surveillance; coordinate care with treatment facilities; and communicate with licensing boards, hospitals, and malpractice carriers.

PHPs can improve physician outcomes and successfully facilitate rehabilitation toward re-integration into the workforce. In a study by McLellan et al., of the 647 physicians from

16 PHPs who were monitored for 5 years, 81% had negative urine toxicology results throughout their monitoring, and 95% of the 515 who completed their monitoring contract had returned to either licensed clinical or non-clinical work (McLellan et al. 2008). This study found that PHPs can provide a safe, confidential, and effective role in helping rehabilitate addicted physicians while ensuring patient safety. However, this was a limited study that is not indicative of all national programs, as these programs are not standardized, and there is a paucity of evidence to describe which PHP monitoring and treatment components are effective. Such data would support the development of standardized, evidence-based program criteria. However, as it stands, PHPs are already unique in that their outcomes are vastly better than the substance use treatment provided to the general public, with some reported abstinence rates of 78% over 11 years (DuPont et al. 2009).

Physicians have much to lose in undergoing treatment and rehabilitation, and are therefore often highly adherent, driven by nature to perform well in an effort to regain work status or licensing. Therefore, it is unclear if physicians do better in any treatment modality, whether it is PHP monitoring or addiction treatment as usual, because stakes are higher.

As a medical community, it is imperative that we promote non-punitive, confidential, and nationally standardized PHPs where referral is robust and physicians can be assured that treatment is accessible long before patient harm and other similar consequences may force a physician to lose their license and career.

Key Points to Remember

1. A foundational understanding of the neurobiology of addiction as a core component of medical knowledge and clinical skills is necessary for physicians-in-training and practicing physicians to approach SUD as a pathophysiology, rather than as solely an error of poor judgment. Currently, there may be a fleeting acceptance

that addiction has a basis in a physiologic dysfunction, but there is still an overall lack of understanding and embrace in both personal practice and clinical practice with patients on how addiction affects us.

2. Knowledge of the diagnostic criteria for substance use disorder, which lies on a spectrum of disease from mild to severe, is important, as there are many junctures in which intervention may stave off worsening development of the disorder.

3. SUD is prevalent among physicians, who are not immune and may in fact be particularly vulnerable to addiction. Known prevalence may actually underestimate reality, but knowing true prevalence may keep the medical community vigilant in addressing the problem of SUD among physicians. However, we cannot know true prevalence until the risk for punitive action against physicians is removed, so that physicians can seek addiction treatment without stigma or fear of career-breaking consequences.

4. Physicians are uniquely vulnerable and at risk for SUD, and a thorough understanding of these risks and considerations would prepare each physician, as a treating physician or as teachers and role models for medical students, to be able to detect triggers for development of SUD. Physicians-in-training, including medical students and residents, as well as practicing physicians should have access to a safe haven to discuss SUD concerns.

5. Knowledge of the treatment and resources available are critical: cognitive behavioral, non-pharmacologic and medication assisted therapies to ameliorate withdrawal syndromes and facilitate relapse prevention should be taught and made accessible to physicians and the population at large.

6. Physician Health Programs should exist in all states as a confidential, non-punitive, and if possible standardized with an emphasis on healthy re-integration of the physician back into the work force.

References

Alexander B (2016). Doctor in Uber driver attack video fired from Miami hospital. USA Today. https://www.usatoday.com/story/news/nation/2016/04/23/doctor-uber-driver-attack-video-fired-miami-hospital/83432610/. Published April 23, 2016.

American Foundation for Suicide Prevention (2018). Healthcare Professional Burnout, Depression and Suicide Prevention. https://afsp.org/our-work/education/healthcare-professional-burnout-depression-suicide-prevention/. Accessed March 21, 2018.

Antman KH, Berman HA, Flotte TR, Flier J, Dimitri DM, Bharel M (2016). Developing Core Competencies for the Prevention and Management of Prescription Drug Misuse. Acad Med 91(10):1348–1351. https://doi.org/10.1097/ACM.0000000000001347.

Back DK, Tammaro E, Lim JK, et al. (2018) Massachusetts Medical Students Feel Unprepared to Treat Patients with Substance Use Disorder. J Gen Intern Med 1–2. https://doi.org/10.1007/s11606-017-4192-x.

Baldisseri MR (2007). Impaired healthcare professional. Crit Care Med 35(2 Suppl):S106–16. https://doi.org/10.1097/01.CCM.0000252918.87746.96.

Baldwin DC, Hughes PH, Conard SE, Storr CL, Sheehan D V (1991). Substance Use Among Senior Medical Students. JAMA 265(16):2074–2078. https://doi.org/10.1001/jama.1991.03460160052028.

Bissell L, Jones RW (1976). The alcoholic physician: a survey. Am J Psychiatry 133(10):1142–1146. https://doi.org/10.1176/ajp.133.10.1142.

Bohman B, Dyrbye L, Sinsky CA, et al. (2017) Physician Well-Being: The Reciprocity of Practice Efficiency, Culture of Wellness, and Personal Resilience. NEJM Catal. August 2017. https://catalyst.nejm.org/physician-well-being-efficiency-wellness-resilience/.

Brady J (2006). The Association Between Alcohol Misuse and Suicidal Behavior. Alcohol Alcohol 41(5):473–478. https://doi.org/10.1093/alcalc/agl060.

Brown RL, Edwards JA, Rounds LA (1995). Medical students' need of and support for substance-abuse prevention. Teach Learn Med 7(2):102–110. https://doi.org/10.1080/10401339509539722.

Burki TK (2016). Low public awareness of link between cancer and alcohol. Lancet Oncol 17(5):e184. https://doi.org/10.1016/S1470-2045(16)30045-6.

Candilis PJ (2016). Physician Health Programs and the Social Contract. AMA J Ethics 18(1):77–81. https://doi.org/10.1001/journalofethics.2016.18.1.corr1-1601.

Center C, Davis M, Detre T, et al. (2003) Confronting Depression and Suicide in Physicians. JAMA 289(23):3161. https://doi.org/10.1001/jama.289.23.3161.

Council on Scientific Affairs (1987). Results and implications of the AMA-APA Physician Mortality Project. Stage II (1987) JAMA 257(21):2949–2953. https://doi.org/10.1001/jama.1987.03390210097033.

DuPont RL, McLellan AT, Carr G, Gendel M, Skipper GE (2009). How are addicted physicians treated? A national survey of Physician Health Programs. J Subst Abuse Treat 37(1):1–7. https://doi.org/10.1016/j.jsat.2009.03.010.

Earley PH (2014). Physician Health Programs and Addiction among Physicians. In: Ries RK, Fiellin DA, Miller SC, Saitz R, eds. The ASAM Essentials of Addiction Medicine. 5th ed. Lippincott Williams &Wilkins, Philadelphia, p 602–621.

Federation of State Physician Health Programs (2018). State Programs. https://www.fsphp.org/state-programs. Published 2018. Accessed March 17, 2018.

Flaherty JA, Richman JA (1993). Substance use and addiction among medical students, residents, and physicians. Psychiatr Clin North Am 16(1):189–197. http://www.ncbi.nlm.nih.gov/pubmed/8456044.

Frank E, Elon L, Naimi T, Brewer R (2008). Alcohol consumption and alcohol counselling behaviour among US medical students: cohort study. BMJ 337:a2155. http://www.ncbi.nlm.nih.gov/pubmed/18996938.

Goldstein S (2016). Miami doctor who berated Uber driver in viral video is fired. New York Daily News. http://www.nydailynews.com/news/national/miami-doctor-berated-uber-driver-viral-video-fired-article-1.2611674. Published April 22, 2016.

Governor's Medical Education Working Group on Prescription Drug Misuse (2015). Medical Education Core Competencies for the Prevention and Management of Prescription Drug Misuse: Recommendations from the Governover's Medical Education Working Group on Prescription Drug Misuse. Massachusetts; 2015. http://www.mass.gov/eohhs/docs/dph/stop-addiction/governors-medical-education-working-group-core-competencies.pdf.

Johnston GP (1979). Dangers of Self-Prescription. J Indiana State Med Assoc. 72(8):570–572.

Lehmann LS, Sulmasy LS, Desai S (2018). Hidden Curricula, Ethics, and Professionalism: Optimizing Clinical Learning Environments in Becoming and Being a Physician: A Position Paper of the American College of Physicians. Ann Intern Med. (February 2017). https://doi.org/10.7326/M17-2058.

Lindeman S, Läärä E, Hakko H, Lönnqvist J. (1996) A systematic review on gender-specific suicide mortality in medical doctors. Br J Psychiatry 168(MAR.):274–279. https://doi.org/10.1192/bjp.168.3.274.

McCance-Katz EF, George P, Scott NA, Dollase R, Tunkel AR, McDonald J (2017). Access to treatment for opioid use disorders: Medical student preparation. Am J Addict 26(4):316–318. https://doi.org/10.1111/ajad.12550.

McGovern MP, Angres DH, Uziel-Miller ND, Leon S (1998). Female physicians and substance abuse. Comparisons with male physicians presenting for assessment. J Subst Abus Treat Abus Treat 15(6):525–533. http://www.ncbi.nlm.nih.gov/pubmed/9845866.

McLellan AT, Skipper GS, Campbell M, DuPont RL (2008). Five year outcomes in a cohort study of physicians treated for substance use disorders in the United States. BMJ 337:a2038. http://www.ncbi.nlm.nih.gov/pubmed/18984632.

Millstein SG, Marcell AV (2003). Screening and counseling for adolescent alcohol use among primary care physicians in the United States. Pediatrics 111(1):114–122. http://www.ncbi.nlm.nih.gov/pubmed/12509563.

Moutier C, Norcross W, Jong P, et al. (2012) The Suicide Prevention and Depression Awareness Program at the University of California, San Diego School of Medicine. Acad Med 87(3):320–326. https://doi.org/10.1097/ACM.0b013e31824451ad.

Murray RM (1976). Characteristics and prognosis of alcoholic doctors. Br Med J. Dec 25;2(6051):1537–9.

Myers M (2017). Why Physicians Die by Suicide: Lessons Learned from Their Families and Others Who Cared. Michael F. Myers, Brooklyn, NY, USA.

National Center on Substance Abuse (2000). Missed Opportunity: National Survey of Primary Care Physicians and Patients on Substance Abuse. New York, NY, USA. https://www.centeronaddiction.org/addiction-research/reports/national-survey-primary-care-physicians-patients-substance-abuse.

National Committee for Quality Assurance (2018). HEDIS 2018. HEDIS 2018. http://www.ncqa.org/hedis-quality-measurement/hedis-measures/hedis-2018%0A%0A. Published 2018. Accessed March 21, 2018.

Newsholme A (1903). The Possible Association of the Consumption of Alcohol with Excessive Mortality from Cancer. Br Med J 2(2241):1529–1531. http://www.ncbi.nlm.nih.gov/pubmed/20761240.

Oreskovich MR, Shanafelt T, Dyrbye LN, et al. (2015) The prevalence of substance use disorders in American physicians. Am J Addict 24(1):30–38. https://doi.org/10.1111/ajad.12173.

Pilowsky DJ, Wu L-T (2012). Screening for alcohol and drug use disorders among adults in primary care: a review. Subst Abuse Rehabil 3:25–34. https://doi.org/10.2147/SAR.S30057.

Polydorou S, Gunderson EW, Levin FR (2008). Training physicians to treat substance use disorders. Curr Psychiatry Rep 10(5):399–404. http://www.ncbi.nlm.nih.gov/pubmed/18803913.

Ponnet K, Wouters E, Walrave M, Heirman W, Van Hal G (2015). Predicting Students' Intention to use Stimulants for Academic Performance Enhancement. Subst Use Misuse 50(3):275–282. https://doi.org/10.3109/10826084.2014.952446.

Pringle P, Ryan H, Elmahrek M, Hamilton M, Parvini S (2017). An overdose, a young companion, drug-fueled parties: The secret life of USC med school dean. Los Angeles Times. http://www.latimes.com/local/california/la-me-usc-doctor-20170717-htmlstory.html. Published July 17, 2017.

Rose SH, Curry TB (2009). Fatigue, Countermeasures, and Performance Enhancement in Resident Physicians. Mayo Clin Proc. 2009;84(11):955–957. http://www.ncbi.nlm.nih.gov/pmc/articles/PMC2770906/.

Sher L (2006). Alcohol consumption and suicide. QJM An Int J Med 99(1):57–61. https://doi.org/10.1093/qjmed/hci146.

Schernhammer ES, Colditz GA (2004). Suicide rates among physicians: a quantitative and gender assessment (meta-analysis). Am J Psychiatry 161(12):2295–2302. https://doi.org/10.1176/appi.ajp.161.12.2295.

Udel MM (1984). Chemical abuse/dependence: physicians' occupational hazard. J Med Assoc Ga;73(11):775–778. http://www.ncbi.nlm.nih.gov/pubmed/6512428.

U.S. Preventive Services Task Force (2014). Final Recommendation Statement: Drug Use, Illicit: Screening. https://www.uspreventiveservicestaskforce.org/Page/Document/RecommendationStatementFinal/drug-use-illicit-screening. Published 2014. Accessed July 25, 2017.

U.S. Preventive Services Task Force (2013). Final Recommendation Statement: Alcohol Misuse: Screening and Behavioral Counseling Interventions in Primary Care. https://www.uspreventiveservices-taskforce.org/Page/Document/RecommendationStatementFinal/alcohol-misuse-screening-and-behavioral-counseling-interventions-in-primary-care. Accessed July 25, 2017.

Wible P (2016) Physician Suicide Letters Answered. 1st ed. Pamela Wible, M.D., Publishing, Eugene, OR, USA

Yoast RA, Wilford BB, Hayashi SW (2008). Encouraging Physicians to Screen for and Intervene in Substance Use Disorders: Obstacles and Strategies for Change. J Addict Dis 27(3):77–97. https://doi.org/10.1080/10550880802122687.

Part III
Fostering Physician Resilience

Chapter 11
Relationships

Christina Tara Khan

Introduction

Relationships are a cornerstone of the human experience. For most people, interactions with others can have a substantial effect on mood and wellbeing. Positive and supportive interactions are an important buffer for stress, while interpersonal conflict can introduce and exacerbate stress. For physicians, the demands of medicine can be so excessive that having a supportive home or personal environment is essential to navigating the training years and successfully managing the undue stress and workload that clinical practice presents. The intersection of medical postgraduate training with early adult development makes this a challenging time for physicians in training, who are learning to take on responsibility in their new careers while also navigating the roles and responsibilities of early-to-middle adulthood. Many physician trainees in their 20s and 30s, having devoted substantial time and

C. T. Khan (✉)
Stanford Health Care/Stanford Children's Health/Veterans Affairs
Palo Alto Health Care System, Department of Psychiatry and
Behavioral Sciences, Stanford, CA, USA
e-mail: ckhan@stanford.edu

© Springer Nature Switzerland AG 2019   181
L. Weiss Roberts, M. Trockel (eds.),
The Art and Science of Physician Wellbeing,
https://doi.org/10.1007/978-3-319-42135-3_11

resources to their career development, are now honing their social-emotional skills and learning to navigate relationships and conflict. This chapter is devoted to exploration of the role relationships may play in supporting physicians, particularly during the training years, and resources available to address interpersonal conflict.

Benefits of Social Support

A career as a physician requires daily interactions with other human beings. For many aspiring physicians, serving others is a primary reason for choosing a career in medicine. Regardless of preference, most physicians will be required to interact with other human beings in their daily work. This means daily frequent communication with a variety of team members and with patients and their families, as well as challenges in communication amidst difficult clinical encounters. As with any human services profession involving person-to-person contact, the potential for burnout is high, with more than half of practicing physicians in the United States reporting at least one symptom of burnout, representing an increase in recent years (Shanafelt et al. 2015).

The social support literature for physicians as a population is small. A systematic review of studies from 1970 through 2007 (Voltmer and Spahn 2009) showed that various sources of social support had distinct effects on physicians' health and the potential to contribute to prevention of burnout. This included social support from a variety of sources including colleagues and a professional network, a spouse, friends, and support groups. A more recent study of physicians in Israel (Russo et al. 2016) also highlighted the importance of both work and nonwork sources of support to facilitate work-life balance, which in turn augmented the likelihood of physicians having positive energy and psychological availability.

More broadly, the social support literature supports the importance of relationships for maintaining both physical and psychological health (Holt-Lunstad and Uchino 2015). Indicators of social isolation have been linked with depressive symptoms, and most researchers agree that social ties can have a significant protective effect on psychological wellbeing and depression (e.g., Kawachi and Berkman 2001; Gariépy et al. 2016). Accumulating evidence from the neurobiology literature suggests that social support confers resilience to stress, possibly through moderating genetic and environmental vulnerabilities (Ozbay et al. 2007). It is thus of value for physicians and physician trainees who are habitually confronted with excessive stress to strengthen and protect this important buffer.

Culture of Medicine

Culture can play an important role in perceived support. The culture of modern medicine has underpinnings in a military model and embodies characteristics of this culture that have persisted for decades. While some of these features, such as respect and accountability, may be beneficial to the efficiency of medical practice, others can be counterproductive and lessen a sense of perceived support for practicing physicians. For example, hierarchical structure within medical organizations and teams and a top-down approach to decision-making may discourage individuals in a more subordinate or less prestigious position to proactively engage in asserting their opinion or to engage in effective conflict resolution. Such a structural and cultural hierarchy can be oppressive and may have a deleterious effect on confidence and perhaps even on clinical decision-making (Srivastava 2013). Moreover, this aspect of medical culture may intersect with young physicians' developmental stage to create additional vulnerability. As many young physicians in training are developmentally emerging from a delayed adolescence, they are beginning to get to know themselves in relation to the world around them. A hierarchical culture in the work setting where they have invested much of their resources may compound a developing and tenuous sense of self. A culture that discourages self-advocacy may increase risk for burnout and psychological and physical impairment and may also have implications for patient care. Chapter 5 focuses on the psychological and physical risks of burnout to the physician.

The caretaker role can be a double-edged sword. Certain common personality characteristics of physicians such as a tendency toward perfectionism are imminently useful for overcoming the hurdles it takes to have a career in medicine. These characteristics can also help physicians to be highly effective scientists and healers. Nevertheless, the push to answer every question and leave no stone unturned can also drain emotional and intellectual resources and make it difficult for physicians to delegate tasks or to do "good enough." Over time, this intensity of caretaking increases risk for emotional exhaustion and eventually depersonalization, features of professional burnout. Medical culture promotes a myth of the strong and even invincible physician. While this illusion may be attractive to patients who want to see confidence in their healers, it can be of disservice to the physicians who are pressured to overlook their own humanity. Ultimately, physician burnout can have a multitude of negative effects on patient care and productivity (Dewa et al. 2014).

Another aspect of culture that is increasingly important is diversity on medical teams. Many institutions, including those that espouse attention to diversity and inclusion, struggle with institutional and implicit bias (Hannah and Carpenter-Song 2013). Microaggressions from those in leadership are common, and leaders are often not even aware of their own biases (Smedley et al. 2003; Staats et al. 2017). Individuals who are not members of the majority culture may find it especially challenging to navigate interpersonal dynamics in the face of implicit or unconscious bias, and this may have unfavorable effects on members of underrepresented groups in medicine (Allen and Garg 2016). For trainees and early-career physicians, bias and lack of diversity can have a profound impact on sense of community and belonging, at a time when they are just beginning their careers. Such challenges can have a negative impact on physicians' mental health and may also negatively impact retention rates for non-majority groups in medicine (Smedley et al. 2003; Carnes et al. 2008).

Navigating Relationship Conflicts

While a supportive work environment and supportive personal relationships can be protective, unfavorable workplace factors and strain in personal relationships can contribute to physician stress and burnout. Relationship conflict will inevitably surface; how physicians deal with conflict can determine the impact on their wellbeing.

In the professional domain, medical schools widely acknowledge that physicians need strong communication skills (Ha and Longnecker 2010). Decades of research demonstrates that good clinical communication is associated with many desirable outcomes, including patient satisfaction, adherence to treatment, health behavior and health status, and even costs of care (e.g., Joosten et al. 2008). However, many trainees report feeling unprepared to manage the breadth and volume of difficult patient interactions they encounter during their residency years. Challenging patient care scenarios can lead to increased stress and over time can have a negative effect on wellbeing and mental health. Studies have documented a decline in empathy during the medical school and residency years as trainees become increasingly involved in clinical care (Newton et al. 2008; Rosenthal et al. 2011). In response, there is currently momentum to include empathy and compassion training in medical education, with some empirical support from well-designed intervention trials (Kelm et al. 2014). In addition to empathy and compassion training, institutions may consider strategies to address communication needs in patient care for their students and physicians, including interventions focused on humanism, interpersonal effectiveness skills, and conflict resolution (West et al. 2016).

Conflict in interpersonal relationships at home may also present challenges. While these issues may be different from work-related challenges, the antecedents and consequences can be similar. Excessive stress, hardship, personality differences, and differences in communication style can all complicate otherwise straightforward conversations and lead to misunderstandings, disagreements, arguments, and tension. Depending on the quality of the relationship and the ability of those involved to work together, conflicts can escalate over time, creating more intense interpersonal distress that may become disruptive to a physician's wellbeing, creativity, or ability to engage in daily tasks. Resources for physicians vary depending on the nature of the relationship and the conflict and may range from peer or family support to self-help interventions or professional help or counseling. It is not uncommon for physicians in training to seek out couples therapy or marriage counseling for the first time during their training years. Both individual and couples therapy may be useful for addressing misunderstandings and teaching interpersonal effectiveness techniques that can be helpful in both the work and home settings.

Work-Home Integration

We hear much about "work-life balance" in an effort to improve the practice of medicine, not just for patients but also for providers. Some older professionals may scoff at this term, and there is a pervasive myth that younger physicians are "weak" or "entitled" for wanting to work shorter hours. Despite these criticisms, there have been advances in addressing concerns associated with overwork, including reduction of duty hours, hour limits to shifts for new physicians, and dedicated nonclinical time included in some training programs (Temple 2015). Nevertheless, the global impact of such changes requires more systematic study, and the culture of medicine has a long way to go in addressing the wellness of healers. Individual physicians must achieve their own personal balance between the stressors and resources of their individual circumstances.

Cultivating Personal Wellness

Physicians have numerous options available to them to cultivate personal wellness. Many have honed a variety of coping skills to manage stress throughout their studies and training years. Some continue to use these skills, while others start to lose their connections amidst an increasing burden of stress.

While physicians as a group are talented, many with significant accomplishments outside of medicine, it is not uncommon for physicians to lose touch with their prior interests and
activities upon starting residency training or upon starting
their practice. For many, this is a loss of an important potential buffer to work-related stress. Extracurricular and creative
interests may provide a locus of self-worth and control outside of the professional domain. Some physicians are able to
maintain engagement in activities by having a regular exercise or sport routine for stress management. Others stay
active by engaging in music or literature groups with their
peers, while many utilize travel as a means of stepping away
from the demands of the workplace. For those who are starting a family, focus on the home and family activities are a way
to cultivate meaning outside of the workplace.

Regardless of which, these activities are an important buffer to work-related stress and to the potential loss of meaning
in the face of limited control, particularly during the training
years. Diversifying one's sense of self into multiple domains
of human and social capital helps to manage and reduce the
risk posed by any one individual domain, not entirely dissimi-
lar to the strategy in financial investing. Interaction with supportive others is often an important part of these activities
and also helps to create meaning and a sense of belonging.
When schedules and lifestyles are aligned, cultivating personal wellness can become a shared activity. A strategic focus
on self-care and quality of living through attention to exercise
(see Chap. 13), nutrition (see Chap. 14), contemplation practices (see Chap. 12), and creative or extracurricular activities
may thus help with both perceived support and a sense of
control and balance. More detailed information on these topics is covered in other chapters.

Resources for Physicians

Hospital systems are increasingly recognizing the impact of
physician wellness on patient care and are putting in place
mechanisms of support for their medical professionals.

Peer Support

Peer support programs are growing as a means of supporting physicians who have experienced critical incidents, difficult patient care scenarios, and other stressful events. Some of the benefits of offering peer support include tapping into existing relationships and foregoing the need for more formal interventions that are more likely to require documentation. The literature on peer support among physicians is young, but discussion forums among physicians reveal the importance of physicians connecting with one another through peer support or supervision (Shapiro and Galowitz 2016).

Professional Support

With the increase in awareness of physician burnout, many health organizations are arranging to have on-site or easily accessible professional support available to their physicians. The variety of programs available is broad, ranging from wellness-focused resources to more intensive resources for physicians in crisis. Many programs have direct links to a mental health professional who can help direct physicians to available resources (e.g., Stanford WellConnect, https://med.stanford.edu/psychiatry/special-initiatives/wellconnect.html). There are some key barriers to utilization of professional support by physicians, such as finding time for appointments and concerns about having documentation of a mental health visit. Peer support can help circumvent some of these concerns. Nevertheless, physicians are equally if not more susceptible to mental illness than the general population and for many, access to a mental health professional will be important and necessary (See Chap. 9) (Goldman et al. 2015).

Personal Wellness

Hospital systems are increasingly offering wellbeing programs for their employees to support prevention-focused care and health maintenance. These may include access to fitness centers or classes covering a variety of topics such as contemplation, fitness, and nutrition; incentives to engage in health screenings and preventative care; coaches and trainers to support individualized wellness plans; communication coaches; and options to assist with work-life integration such as parental leave, child care assistance, and meal planning services, to name a few. Physicians are encouraged to find out what is available to them at their institutions, as many of these opportunities are underutilized.

Case Illustrations

Case 11.1 Cultural Factors

Personal wellness can be challenged when risk factors for burnout intersect and compound vulnerability for an individual physician. Shayna is a 27-year-old urology resident in her second year of training. Shayna was connected with the hospital's Confidential Peer Support Team following a critical incident where one of the postoperative patients she was caring for coded following a medical error. Shayna reveals to her peer supporter that she has felt burned out and demoralized almost every day since starting her internship. She is concerned this is affecting her ability to focus on patient care and may have contributed to the error she made; however, she has not discussed this with anyone. On further discussion, Shayna shares that she feels quite alone in her program, and as the only person of her particular cultural background, she often feels as if she does not "fit in." This makes it harder to develop relationships with her peers and attendings, many of whom are from the majority culture or male. She feels like a "black sheep" at times, as if everyone is waiting for her to "mess up." The hours are particularly challenging, and Shayna does not do well with less than 6 hours of sleep per night. She also has a harder time skipping meals than some of her peers, which seems to be the norm in the surgical culture. Following the critical incident, Shayna feels even more ostracized and concerned that everyone is blaming her for the adverse outcome. She has days where she feels hopeless, sometimes to the point that she wishes she wouldn't wake up the next day or wishes everything would just go away. She has not acted on these thoughts and feelings, nor has she shared them with anyone. The thoughts come and go and seem to be related to her level of stress and sleep deprivation.

Discussion Questions: What factors have contributed to Shayna's vulnerability in this scenario? What resources would you recommend for Shayna?

Case 11.2 Caretaker Role

Nicholas is a 38-year-old physician recently out of training who is coping with a divorce. Nicholas and his partner were married for 9 years, during which time Nicholas came to realize he had very little control within the relationship. While Nicholas was in charge of the finances, his spouse tended to make all other decisions. When they would get into a disagreement, the outcome would be driven by his partner's emotional state. Nicholas felt a strong need to take care of his partner and would do anything to keep his partner from getting angry. Meanwhile he tended to keep his own frustrations to himself and would cope by working out or going drinking with friends. His tolerance for alcohol has increased significantly, and he now finds himself drinking daily after work. After years of conflict with no lasting resolution, they tried to undergo marital counseling but ultimately opted for divorce. At work, Nicholas has also been dissatisfied and has many symptoms of burnout. First as a resident and now as a junior physician, he feels he is at the "bottom of the totem pole" and powerless to make meaningful change within the organization. He works late almost every day and feels he overextends himself more than his peers to try to address the complaints of dissatisfied patients. Nicholas is now dating again and finding he has a hard time expressing his needs within the relationship. He is noticing his tendency to avoid conflict and keep his frustrations to himself, as he did in his marriage. He would like to change this pattern and learn how to be more assertive about his feelings and needs.

Discussion Questions: What factors have contributed to Nicholas' burnout, and what are some of the consequences? What resources may be helpful for him?

Case 11.3 Nonphysician Partner

Mariana is in her third year of practice after residency in a multispecialty group and is now in a role where she is supervising new attendings. She recently took on an administrative role as lead practice pediatric hospitalist, where she is tasked with overseeing the team of colleagues at her site and managing their professional development. Mariana was excited to be given the opportunity to take on a leadership role but is finding it difficult to balance this new position with her ongoing patient load, particularly since the position is taking more time than she has been allotted. She has been working late hours almost daily and when she gets home she just wants to go to sleep. There have been multiple instances where she has had to cancel plans with her partner who is a business consultant with a very different work schedule. Mariana feels her partner has limited understanding of the structure and culture of medicine and of her everyday struggles. Her partner has expressed frustration that Mariana is unavailable to spend time together at home. Her partner usually ends up either going out with friends or staying in watching television alone. When Mariana tries to approach her partner to make plans, she often gets a pessimistic response that they cannot count on her to come through. Mariana sees the truth in this but also feels frustrated that her partner does not understand her situation. She feels her friends in medicine understand her situation better and have been more supportive. She is not sure what to do as she feels this is becoming a worrisome pattern in her relationship.

Discussion Questions: What can Mariana do to relieve some of the stress at work and at home? What resources might she consider?

Conclusion

Relationships and interpersonal communication are an important aspect of physicians' daily work. Positive relationships at work and at home can be protective for the stressors present in clinical medicine and the ever-present potential for professional burnout. Many physicians in training and in their early career are at a developmental stage in which they are learning about themselves in relationships and honing their interpersonal and conflict resolution skills. When stress becomes excessive and interpersonal communication breaks down, there are a variety of resources available for peer and professional help. Schools of medicine and hospital systems are increasingly recognizing the importance of physician wellness and burnout and are implementing novel programs to support medical staff. Physicians are encouraged to utilize these resources to help shape and maintain supportive relationships as they navigate the challenges of early career and clinical practice.

References

Allen BJ, Garg K (2016) Diversity Matters in Academic Radiology: Acknowledging and Addressing Unconscious Bias. J Am Coll Radiol 13:1426–1432. https://doi.org/10.1016/j.jacr.2016.08.016

Carnes M, Morrissey C, Geller SE (2008) Women's Health and Women's Leadership in Academic Medicine: Hitting the Same Glass Ceiling? J Women's Heal 17:1453–1462. https://doi.org/10.1089/jwh.2007.0688

Dewa CS, Loong D, Bonato S, et al (2014) How does burnout affect physician productivity? A systematic literature review. BMC Health Serv Res 14:1–10. https://doi.org/10.1186/1472-6963-14-325

Gariépy G, Honkaniemi H, Quesnel-Vallée A (2016) Social support and protection from depression: Systematic review of current findings in western countries. Br J Psychiatry 209:284–293. https://doi.org/10.1192/bjp.bp.115.169094

Goldman ML, Shah RN, Bernstein CA (2015) Depression and suicide among physician trainees: recommendations for a national response. JAMA Psychiatry 72:411–412. https://doi.org/10.1001/jamapsychiatry.2014.3050

Ha JF, Longnecker N (2010) Doctor-patient communication: a review. Ochsner J 10:38–43. https://doi.org/10.1043/toj-09-0040.1

Hannah SD, Carpenter-Song E (2013) Patrolling your blind spots: introspection and public catharsis in a medical school faculty development course to reduce unconscious bias in medicine. Cult Med Psychiatry 37:314–339. https://doi.org/10.1007/s11013-013-9320-4

Holt-Lunstad J, Uchino BN (2015) Social support and health. In: Health Behavior: Theory, Research, and Practice. John Wiley & Sons, New York, p 183

Joosten EAG, DeFuentes-Merillas L, de Weert GH, et al (2008) Systematic Review of the Effects of Shared Decision-Making on Patient Satisfaction, Treatment Adherence and Health Status. Psychother Psychosom 77:219–226. https://doi.org/10.1159/000126073

Kawachi I, Berkman LF (2001) Social ties and mental health. J Urban Heal 78:458–467. https://doi.org/10.1093/jurban/78.3.458

Kelm Z, Womer J, Walter JK, Feudtner C (2014) Interventions to cultivate physician empathy: A systematic review. BMC Med Educ 14:1–11. https://doi.org/10.1186/1472-6920-14-219

Newton BW, Barber L, Clardy J, et al (2008) Is there hardening of the heart during medical school? Acad Med 83:244–249. https://doi.org/10.1097/ACM.0b013e3181637837

Ozbay F, Johnson DC, Dimoulas E, et al (2007) Social support and resilience to stress: from neurobiology to clinical practice. Psychiatry (Edgmont) 4:35–40. doi: None

Rosenthal S, Howard B, Schlussel YR, et al (2011) Humanism at heart: Preserving empathy in third-year medical students. Acad Med 86:350–358. https://doi.org/10.1097/ACM.0b013e318209897f

Russo M, Shteigman A, Carmeli A (2016) Workplace and family support and work–life balance: Implications for individual psychological availability and energy at work. J Posit Psychol 11:173–188. https://doi.org/10.1080/17439760.2015.1025424

Shanafelt TD, Hasan O, Dyrbye LN, et al (2015) Changes in Burnout and Satisfaction with Work-Life Balance in Physicians and the General US Working Population between 2011 and 2014. Mayo Clin Proc 90:1600–1613. https://doi.org/10.1016/j.mayocp.2015.08.023

Shapiro J, Galowitz P. (2016) Peer Support for Clinicians: A Programmatic Approach. Acad Med 91(9):1200–1204. https://doi.org/10.1097/ACM.0000000000001297.

Smedley BD, Stith AY, Nelson AR (2003) Committee on Understanding and Eliminating Racial and Ethnic Disparities in Health Care. Unequal treatment: confronting racial and ethnic disparities in health care. National Academy of Science. p 191

Srivastava R (2013) Speaking upDOUBLEHYPHENwhen doctors navigate medical hierarchy. N Engl J Med 368:302–305. https://doi.org/10.1056/NEJMp1212410

Staats C, Capatosto K, Tenney L, Mamo S (2017) State of the Science: Implicit Bias Review 2017 edition. The Ohio State University, Kirwan Institute

Temple J (2015) Resident duty hours around the globe: Where are we now? BMC Med Educ 14:S8. https://doi.org/10.1186/1472-6920-14-S1-S8

Voltmer E, Spahn C (2009) [Social support and physicians' health]. Z Psychosom Med Psychother 55:51–69. https://doi.org/10.13109/zptm.2009.55.1.51

West CP, Dyrbye LN, Erwin PJ, Shanafelt TD (2016) Interventions to prevent and reduce physician burnout: a systematic review and meta-analysis. Lancet 388:2272–2281. https://doi.org/10.1016/S0140-6736(16)31279-X

Stanford WellConnect: https://med.stanford.edu/psychiatry/special-initiatives/wellconnect.html

Chapter 12
Mindfulness

Louise Wen and Mickey Trockel

Case Illustration

Angela is a married second-year resident in anesthesiology. She has no personal history of mental illness. She finds her residency experience both appropriately challenging and rewarding, and she is both enthusiastic and passionate about her training.

Over the course of a month, she experiences an intersection of multiple stressors. On a particularly high-acuity and high-intensity rotation, she and her colleagues repeatedly violate resident work-hour regulations and deliberate who to approach to help rectify the issue. She finds herself beginning to rapidly accumulate a sleep debt. Furthermore, they have a high-stakes boards exam at the end of the month. Residents who are unable to

L. Wen
Stanford University Hospital, Department of Anesthesiology, Stanford, CA, USA

M. Trockel (✉)
Stanford Hospital and Clinics, Department of Psychiatry and Behavior Science, Palo Alto, CA, USA

School of Medicine, Stanford University, Palo Alto, CA, USA
e-mail: trockel@stanford.edu

© Springer Nature Switzerland AG 2019   195
L. Weiss Roberts, M. Trockel (eds.),
The Art and Science of Physician Wellbeing,
https://doi.org/10.1007/978-3-319-42135-3_12

pass the exam after a limited number of attempts will be asked to leave the training program.

During one patient care encounter, she incurs a needle stick injury from a known HIV-positive patient and begins antiretroviral prophylactic therapy. She experiences the side effects of fatigue, nausea, and weight loss while on the medication. During a follow-up blood draw, she learns that she has developed acute kidney injury, also a known side effect of the medication.

She finds that her mood remains in an unusual, persistently negative state. She takes an online self-assessment for depression and scores moderately severe. When she confides in a fellow resident colleague of this finding, her colleague reassures her that a formal diagnosis of depression cannot be made when a person is in a state of unrelenting sleep deprivation. Angela agrees with her friend's assessment and feels that her mental state can be directly attributed to her current and temporary situation.

Angela does not have thoughts of self-harm or any passive or active suicidal ideations. However, she does consider quitting residency altogether and begins to explore the feasibility of pursuing options for an alternative career.

She shares her emotional distress with her aunt who knows that prior to residency training, Angela had a robust meditation practice. Angela's aunt advises her to revisit her meditation practice that evening. Furthermore, she advises Angela to seek a therapist in the morning if she continues to experience these negative emotions.

Angela takes her aunt's advice and does a simple 20-minute sitting meditation. After the meditation, she feels as if her brain has done a clean reboot and feels like she has discovered the reserve to push through. She continues a daily meditation practice. Over the next 2 weeks, Angela completes her clinical rotation, finishes her 4-week regimen of antiretroviral therapy, and passes her board exam. Angela and her colleagues work with the chief resident who mediates with the rotation course and residency program directors to rectify the work-hour situation for subsequent residents on that rotation. Meditation continues to be part of Angela's self-care routine and she successfully completes her residency training.

Introduction

Mindfulness is the practice of nonjudgmental awareness of the present moment (Fjorback et al. 2011). Through practice, individuals can learn to identify moments when the mind's attention strays from the present moment and volitionally maintain focus on the present moment. With practice, mindfulness trains the mind to be able to choose and release attachment to maladaptive emotional states, thus facilitating clarity of thought and emotional wellness (Ludwig and Kabat-Zinn 2008). This mental tool has historical origins in Buddhism and is practiced with the intention of mitigating suffering and promoting kindness. However, the practice of mindfulness does not require adherence to religious concepts (Ludwig and Kabat-Zinn 2008).

The study of the applications of mindfulness interventions has become increasingly common and have included populations as diverse as healthcare providers, patients, students, workers, military personnel, and prisoners (Creswell 2017). The efficacy of mindfulness applications in affecting specific clinical conditions has been studied, including for depression, drug addiction, and eating disorders (Creswell 2017).

In light of the toll of physician burnout for both physicians and their patients, mindfulness has been considered as a technique of interest in helping physicians build their resilience (Epstein and Krasner 2013). Resilience has been described as the ability to effectively respond to challenges while simultaneously preserving one's psychological and physical health and can be a protective factor against burnout. Burnout is a complex and critical issue in medicine today, meriting a multimodal and interdisciplinary approach, and meditation and mindfulness can be an important component of resilience-building strategies.

This chapter will review common mindfulness interventions and summarize the research on current mindfulness interventions. In bridging the application for physicians, the chapter will then briefly discuss the issue of physician burnout and then explore how mindfulness practices can have an impact not only on physicians themselves but also through them to affect their patients.

Mindfulness Interventions

One of the most recognized and studied mindfulness interventions in the scientific literature is the mindfulness-based stress reduction (MBSR) course, which is an 8-week program developed in the 1970s by Job Kabat-Zinn. In its full form, the program involves 2.5 hours of classes each week, home practice of 45 minutes a day, and a day-long silent retreat. The practice of MBSR has been associated with reductions in stress and improvements in wellbeing, including psychological health and empathy (Lamothe et al. 2016).

Given the barrier of the significant time commitment required for completing longer mindfulness courses, the efficacy of mindfulness interventions of varying durations of time has been studied   (Creswell 2017). One group of researchers has been testing interventions as short as 20 minutes of training for 3 days (Zeidan et al. 2010b). They found immediate benefits of participating in this short-term intervention, including reductions in fatigue, pain sensitivity, and anxiety and increases in mindfulness, working memory, and executive functioning (Zeidan et al. 2010a, b).

Another mindfulness intervention is Vipassana Meditation, which is taught in the form of a standardized 10-day silent retreat. Participants meditate up to 11 hours each day (Khoury et al. 2017). One group conducted a systematic review and meta-analysis of 20 studies that explored the effects of such meditation retreats and found that participation led to reductions in depression, anxiety, and stress (Khoury et al. 2017).

In recent years, public and academic interest in mindfulness practices have resulted in internet and smartphone-based mindfulness programming. The advantages of this model of delivery are that it is not only economical but also conveniently accessible. Initial studies do show benefits to this format (Creswell 2017). However, a disadvantage is lack of in-person access to a trained mindfulness instructor.

Some may wonder whether mindfulness practices meaningfully differ from relaxation or stress management practices. In a randomized controlled trial of nearly 100 patients who carried a diagnosis of generalized anxiety disorder, the intervention group received a 2-month mindfulness intervention, and the control group received stress management training of an equal duration of time (Hoge et al. 2013). The subjects who meditated had greater improvements in anxiety scores, including after being challenged with an experimental social stressor, compared to the subjects in the stress management group.

Other researchers have explored the differences in results between mindfulness meditation and sham meditation, where subjects are told that they are meditating but not actually guided to practice the core principles of mindfulness meditation (Zeidan 2010). Interestingly, only the subjects who were actually practicing mindfulness meditation experienced benefits, which included reductions in negative mood, depression, fatigue, confusion, and heart rate.

Overview of Research Studies on the Applications of Mindfulness

Research studies have explored the effects of mindfulness on both physical and mental health across various populations. Several studies have examined the relationship between mindfulness and immunology. Chronic stress is known to activate the production of inflammatory markers, which correlate with increased morbidity and mortality. Controlled studies have shown that participants in mindfulness intervention programs

have attenuated serum levels of known stress inflammatory markers including C-reactive protein and interleukin-6
(Creswell 2017). In patients with HIV infections, mindfulness
programs can be a protective factor against the development
of AIDS by maintaining or increasing the protective CD4+ T
lymphocyte counts (Creswell 2017). However, studies on the
effect of mindfulness exercises on antibody responses to vac-
cines are still inconclusive (Creswell 2017).

Researchers have examined the effect of mindfulness in
specific patient populations and have shown that quality of
life indices improve for patients with fibromyalgia, irritable
bowel syndrome, and breast cancer (Creswell 2017). Various
controlled studies have identified MBSR as a valid approach
in the treatment of chronic pain syndromes to reduce pain
symptomatology (Creswell 2017), including back pain and
rheumatoid arthritis.

In the workplace, mindfulness practices lead to reductions
in stress and improvements in job satisfaction (Creswell
2017). Soldiers practicing mindfulness are able to mollify the
adverse effects of experiencing periods of high stress (Creswell
2017). In classroom settings, mindfulness interventions in
children show preliminary results of reducing stress, rumination, and aggression, while improving cognition, mood, and
coping strategies (Creswell 2017).

Given the known detrimental effects of stress on lifestyle
factors such as nutrition and sleep, researchers have also
tested the effect of mindfulness in these domains. Controlled
studies have generated preliminary evidence supporting the
benefits of mindfulness interventions in reducing tobacco use,
reducing intake of foods high in sugar, and improving quality
of sleep (Creswell 2017).

Studies have also explored the effect of mindfulness on
emotional and mental health. Mindfulness interventions
train individuals to cultivate awareness of one's emotional
state and regulate adverse thought processes that contribute
to mental health issues. Patients who complete mindfulness interventions have increased resilience and decreased
subsequent episodes of major depression relapses (Creswell
2017). Preliminary data in controlled studies suggest that
mindfulness practices can potentially decrease the severity

of symptoms during a depressive episode (Creswell 2017). Individuals who suffer from anxiety and post-traumatic stress disorder also show improvement in severity of symptoms following mindfulness interventions (Creswell 2017). When women practice mindfulness during pregnancy, they report fewer symptoms of anxiety and depression both during and after their pregnancy (Creswell 2017).

Mindfulness has also shown potential applications for addictive states. By exercising mindfulness, individuals can learn to identify the early stages of urges of cravings and prevent impulsive behavior. After smokers participate in mindfulness programs, they report decreases in craving and improvements in smoking cessation. When individuals suffering from substance abuse engage in mindfulness interventions, they have reductions in drug use, legal issues, and relapse (Creswell 2017).

Recent research has explored the effects of mindfulness on cognitive performance and interpersonal dynamics in the general population. Individuals practicing mindfulness exhibit improvements in their capacities for sustaining attention, working memory, and problem-solving compared to their controlled counterparts (Creswell 2017). Mindfulness interventions facilitate improvements in interpersonal dynamics through dissipating stress and fostering flexibility and openness to mind-set changes. After mindfulness interventions, participants report improvements in relationship satisfaction, reductions in loneliness, and expansion of sense of compassion for self and others. Furthermore, controlled studies exploring the effects of mindfulness programs on behaviors show an increase in prosocial behaviors after the mindfulness intervention (Creswell 2017).

The Issue of Physician Burnout

The urgency of physician stress and burnout has been increasingly prioritized as a critical issue. Of particular concern is the negative repercussion of burnout not only on physician health and wellbeing but also on patient safety and patient care outcomes. The burnout syndrome is characterized by emotional exhaustion, depersonalization of patients, and a reduced sense of personal accomplishment (Maslach et al. 2001). Studies estimate that a range of 30–60% (Shanafelt et al. 2002; Shanafelt et al. 2003; Eisenach et al. 2014; Shanafelt et al. 2005; Spickard et al. 2002) of physicians suffer from burnout syndrome. Medical trainees manifesting with burnout syndrome are more likely to report reduced quality of life and suicidal ideation (van der Heijden et al. 2008). Burnout not only affects the health of physicians, but also the care they provide to their patients. This troubling effect on patient care has been described in the literature among surgeons (Balch et al. 2009), internal medicine physicians (Campbell et al. 2010), and anesthesiologists (Hyman et al. 2011). Specifically, when physicians suffer from either burnout or depression, they self-report higher rates of medical errors than their colleagues (Shanafelt et al. 2010; De Oliveira et al. 2013), their patients rate them lower on quality of care measures (Luken and Sammons 2016), and they report lower levels of productivity (Luken and Sammons 2016). Residency exposes trainees to particularly acute emotional and physical stressors, including decreased time with friends and family, significant clinical responsibility, limitations in personal and professional control, sleep deprivation, and nutritional imbalances (Thomas 2004; Lefebvre 2012). Within a year of starting residency, the prevalence of mood disorders increases among house staff to 30%, triple the rates found in the general public (Lefebvre 2012).

Relevance of Mindfulness for Physicians and Healthcare Professionals (Good for Doctors)

A body of research has been focused on measuring the effects of mindfulness practices on physicians. Recognizing that stress and burnout can often occur during graduate education and medical training, one group of researchers conducted a systematic review of 19 randomized and non-randomized controlled trails of studies in health professional students, which included 1815 participants (McConville et al. 2017). Ten of those studies had medical students as their primary participants. The spectrum of benefits included reductions in stress, anxiety, and depression, together with improvements in mindfulness, mood, self-efficacy, and empathy.

One group completed a systematic review of 39 interventional studies examining the effects of MBSR on healthcare professionals (Lamothe et al. 2016). They found that the practice of MBSR in healthcare providers correlated with reductions in their own levels of burnout, stress, anxiety, and depression. Practicing MBSR also positively affected mindfulness levels.

The following individual studies specifically explored the effects of mindfulness training in physician populations. A pilot study of 30 primary care physicians found that participation in an abbreviated MBSR course resulted in reductions of burnout, depression, anxiety and stress (Fortney et al. 2013). One randomized controlled trial of 42 physicians found that the physicians who completed the MBSR program exhibited significant improvements in mindfulness, positive emotions, and relaxation, as well as reductions in resting heart rate (Amutio et al. 2015). In an observational study, 70 primary care physicians completed an 8-week mindfulness training course closely modeled after the MBSR course format. The effects of the course on these physicians included improvements in mindfulness, burnout, empathy, and mood disturbance (Krasner et al. 2009).

Similarly, structured trials have focused on medical students. One study of 58 medical students found that those who completed the MBSR program experienced increases in self-compassion and reductions in perceived stress (Erogul et al. 2014). A separate study of over 300 medical students, half of whom completed a 10-week MBSR intervention, found reductions in mood disturbance, anxiety, and fatigue (Rosenzweig et al. 2003).

The acknowledgment that time and accessibility are barriers for physicians to commit to and participate in a full MBSR course has led to studies exploring shorter mindfulness interventions for physicians. One pilot study designed a remote mindfulness course which included three 90-minute in-person trainings, weekly video modules online, and weekly coaching calls (Pflugeisen et al. 2016). Of the 23 physicians enrolled, 19 completed the intervention. At the end of the program, the physician participants demonstrated reductions in stress and emotional exhaustion as well as increases in mindfulness skills.

Given the prevalence and convenience of smartphone-based apps, several groups have studied the effect of Headspace, a free self-directed mindfulness smartphone app. One pilot study of 43 resident physicians showed that participants improved both their mindfulness and their positive affect after using the Headspace app. A randomized controlled trial of 88 medical students exploring the effects of using the Headspace app found that the intervention group had decreased levels of perceived stress and improvements in general wellbeing.

Relevance of Mindfulness for Patient Care

A growing body of research has explored how levels of physician mindfulness might affect patients' health. The premise for this perspective is that mindfulness may enhance emotional competency in physicians. This emotional skill set can foster and cultivate a healthy physician-patient relationship, thus affecting patient care outcomes. Physicians who exhibit emotional competency positively affect their patient relationships, demonstrate stronger empathy and communication skills, and build protection against burnout (Lamothe et al. 2016). Since mindfulness directly cultivates an internal state of awareness, acceptance, and nonjudgment, it is thought to be another tool for physicians to build this emotional competency.

One study explored the patients of therapists and compared the mental health outcomes of patients between those treated by therapists who did practice meditation and those who did not. Therapists who meditated saw greater improvements in their patients. Patient symptom reduction was seen across scales that included somatization, insecurity in social contact, obsessiveness, anxiety, anger, hostility, phobic anxiety, paranoid thinking, and psychoticism (Grepmair et al. 2007).

In an observational study, researchers examined the impact of physician mindfulness on patient care by asking clinicians to complete the Mindful Attention Awareness Scale. Physicians with higher mindfulness scores exhibited favorable factors in their patient encounters. For example, more mindful physicians exhibited more effort in building rapport with their patients, carried a more positive emotional tone with patients, and were rated more favorably in the categories of communication and patient satisfaction (Beach et al. 2013).

A longitudinal cohort study of 27 clinicians explored the effect of an MBSR course on both the clinicians and their patient ratings (Dobkin et al. 2016). After the MBSR course, clinicians experienced improvements in mindfulness and decreases in stress and burnout. Their patients' ratings of their clinicians' communication reflected improvements as well, specifically in the areas of interest, understanding, and attention. Qualitatively, audio recordings of these patient encounters found that clinicians spoke less and allowed their patients to speak more. Furthermore, clinician-initiated communications had more agreement and encouragement.

Conclusion

A growing body of research has pointed out the benefits of mindfulness practices for the general population. Studies also show that even physicians who engage with these practices are not only able to enjoy the benefits of mindfulness, but also improve their communication with their patients. A mindfulness practice can be an important personal component to the multifaceted approach for physician wellness.

References

Amutio A, Martínez-Taboada C, Hermosilla D, Delgado LC (2015). Enhancing relaxation states and positive emotions in physicians through a mindfulness training program: A one-year study. Psychol Heal Med 20(6). https://doi.org/10.1080/13548506.2014.986143.

Balch CM, Freischlag JA, Shanafelt TD (2009). Stress and Burnout Among Surgeons. Arch Surg 144(4):371–376. https://doi.org/10.1001/archsurg.2008.575.

Beach MC, Roter D, Korthuis PT, et al. (2013) A multicenter study of physician mindfulness and health care quality. Ann Fam Med 11(5):421–428. https://doi.org/10.1370/afm.1507.

Campbell J, Prochazka AV, Yamashita T, Gopal R (2010). Predictors of persistent burnout in internal medicine residents: a prospective cohort study. Acad Med 85(10):1630–1634. https://doi.org/10.1097/ACM.0b013e3181f0c4e7.

Creswell JD (2017). Mindfulness Interventions. Annu Rev Psychol 68(1):491–516. https://doi.org/10.1146/annurev-psych-042716-051139.

De Oliveira GS, Chang R, Fitzgerald PC, et al. (2013) The prevalence of burnout and depression and their association with adherence to safety and practice standards: A survey of united states anesthesiology trainees. Anesth Analg 117(1):182–193. https://doi.org/10.1213/ANE.0b013e3182917da9.

Dobkin PL, Bernardi NF, Bagnis CI. (2016) Enhancing Clinicians' Well-Being and Patient- Centered Care Through Mindfulness. J Contin Educ Health Prof. 36(1):11–6. https://doi.org/10.1097/CEH.0000000000000021.

Eisenach JH, Sprung J, Clark MM, et al. (2014) The Psychological and Physiological Effects of Acute Occupational Stress in New Anesthesiology Residents: A Pilot Trial. Anesthesiology 121(4):878–893. https://doi.org/10.1097/ALN.0000000000000397.

Epstein RM, Krasner MS (2013). Physician Resilience. Acad Med 88(3):301–303. https://doi.org/10.1097/ACM.0b013e318280cff0.

Erogul M, Singer G, McIntyre T, Stefanov DG (2014). Abridged Mindfulness Intervention to Support Wellness in First-Year Medical Students. Teach Learn Med 26(4):350–356. https://doi.org/10.1080/10401334.2014.945025.

Fjorback LO, Arendt M, Ornbøl E, Fink P, Walach H (2011). Mindfulness-based stress reduction and mindfulness-based cognitive therapy: a systematic review of randomized controlled trials. Acta Psychiatr Scand 124(2):102–119. https://doi.org/10.1111/j.1600-0447.2011.01704.x.

Fortney L, Luchterhand C, Zakletskaia L, Zgierska A, Rakel D (2013). Abbreviated mindfulness intervention for job satisfaction. Ann Fam Med 11(5):412–420. https://doi.org/10.1370/afm.1511.

Grepmair L, Mitterlehner F, Loew T, Bachler E, Rother W, Nickel M. (2007) Promoting Mindfulness in Psychotherapists in Training

Influences the Treatment Results of Their Patients: A Randomized, Double-Blind, Controlled Study. Psychother Psychosom 76(6):332–338. https://doi.org/10.1159/000107560.

Hoge EA, Bui E, Marques L, et al. (2013) Randomized controlled trial of mindfulness meditation for generalized anxiety disorder: effects on anxiety and stress reactivity. J Clin Psychiatry 74(8):786–792. https://doi.org/10.4088/JCP.12m08083.

Hyman SA, Michaels DR, Berry JM, Schildcrout JS, Mercaldo ND, Weinger MB (2011). Risk of burnout in perioperative clinicians: a survey study and literature review. Anesthesiology 114(1):194–204. https://doi.org/10.1097/SA.0b013e31824bba7b.

Khoury B, Knäuper B, Schlosser M, Carrière K, Chiesa A (2017). Effectiveness of traditional meditation retreats: A systematic review and meta-analysis. 2017 Jan;92:16–25. https://doi.org/10.1016/j.jpsychores.2016.11.006.

Krasner MS, Epstein RM, Beckman H, et al. (2009) Association of an educational program in mindful communication with burnout, empathy, and attitudes among primary care physicians. JAMA 302(12):1284–1293. https://doi.org/10.1001/jama.2009.1384.

Lamothe M, Rondeau É, Malboeuf-Hurtubise C, Duval M, Sultan S (2016). Outcomes of MBSR or MBSR-based interventions in health care providers: A systematic review with a focus on empathy and emotional competencies. Complement Ther Med 24:19–28. https://doi.org/10.1016/J.CTIM.2015.11.001.

Lefebvre DC (2012). Perspective: Resident Physician Wellness: A New Hope. Acad Med Grad Med Educ 87(5). https://doi.org/10.1097/ACM.0b013e31824d47ff.

Ludwig DS, Kabat-Zinn J (2008). {MIndfulness} in medicine. JAMA 300(11):1350–1352. https://doi.org/10.1001/jama.300.11.1350.

Luken M, Sammons A (2016). Systematic Review of Mindfulness Practice for Reducing Job Burnout. Am J Occup Ther 70(2):7002250020p1. https://doi.org/10.5014/ajot.2016.016956.

McConville J, McAleer R, Hahne A (2017). Mindfulness Training for Health Profession Students-The Effect of Mindfulness Training on Psychological Well-Being, Learning and Clinical Performance of Health Professional Students: A Systematic Review of Randomized and Non-randomized Controlled Trials. Explor J Sci Heal 13:26–45. https://doi.org/10.1016/j.explore.2016.10.002.

Maslach C, Schaufeli WB, Leiter MP (2001). Job Burnout. Annu Rev Psychol 52:397–422. https://doi.org/10.1146/annurev.psych.52.1.397.

Pflugeisen BM, Drummond D, Ebersole D, Mundell K, Chen D (2016) Brief Video-Module Administered Mindfulness Program for Physicians: A Pilot Study. Explor J Sci Heal 12(1). https://doi.org/10.1016/j.explore.2015.10.005.

Rosenzweig S, Reibel DK, Greeson JM, Brainard GC (2003). Mindfulness-Based Stress Reduction Lowers Psychological Distress In Medical Students. Teach Learn Med 15(2):88–92. https://doi.org/10.1207/S15328015TLM1502_03.

Shanafelt TD, Balch CM, Bechamps G, et al (2010). Burnout and medical errors among American surgeons. Ann Surg 251(6):995–1000. https://doi.org/10.1097/SLA.0b013e3181bfdab3.

Shanafelt TD, Novotny P, Johnson ME, et al. (2005) The well-being and personal wellness promotion strategies of medical oncologists in the North Central Cancer Treatment Group. Oncology 68(1):23–32. https://doi.org/10.1159/000084519.

Shanafelt TD, Sloan JA, Habermann TM (2003). The well-being of physicians. Am J Med. 114(6):513–519. https://doi.org/10.1016/s0002-9343(03)00117-7.

Shanafelt TD, Bradley KA, Wipf JE, Back AL (2002). Burnout and self-reported patient care in an internal medicine residency program. Ann Intern Med 136(5):358–367. https://doi.org/10.7326/0003-4819-136-5-200203050-00008.

Spickard A, Gabbe SG, Christensen JF (2002). Mid-career burnout in generalist and specialist physicians. JAMA 288(12):1447–1450. https://doi.org/10.1001/jama.288.12.1447.

Thomas NK (2004). Resident burnout. JAMA 292(23):2880–2889. https://doi.org/10.1097/01.sa.0000171433.45854.d1.

van der Heijden F, Dillingh G, Bakker A, Prins J (2008). Suicidal Thoughts Among Medical Residents with Burnout. Arch Suicide Res 12(4):344–346. https://doi.org/10.1080/13811110802325349.

Zeidan F (2010). Effects of Brief and Sham Mindfulness Meditation. J Altern Complement Med 16(8):867–873. https://doi.org/10.1089/acm.2009.0321.

Zeidan F, Gordon NS, Merchant J, Goolkasian P (2010a). The Effects of Brief Mindfulness Meditation Training on Experimentally Induced Pain. J Pain 2010;11(3):199–209. https://doi.org/10.1016/j.jpain.2009.07.015.

Zeidan F, Johnson SK, Diamond BJ, David Z, Goolkasian P (2010b). Mindfulness meditation improves cognition: Evidence of brief mental training. Conscious Cogn 19(2):597–605. https://doi.org/10.1016/j.concog.2010.03.014.

Chapter 13
Exercise

Erica Frank and Debora R. Holmes

North American physicians tend to live longer than their peers, and we do so because we engage in healthier habits. Such preventive habits matter not just to us and our personal health but also to the health of our patients; those of us with the healthiest habits are the most likely to advise our patients about related preventive habits—and this is particularly true for exercise. A "Healthy Doc = Healthy Patient" relationship (Frank et al., 2005b) encourages prevention-oriented health-care systems in order to better support and evaluate these positive effects on patients.

The foundation of the Healthy Doc = Healthy Patient principles is as follows:

- North American physicians tend to live longer than their peers
- Physicians live longer because they have healthier habits (including as medical students) than their contemporaries

E. Frank (✉)
Faculty of Medicine, School of Population and Public Health, University of British Columbia, Vancouver, BC, Canada
e-mail: Erica.frank@ubc.ca

D. R. Holmes
NextGenU.org, Clear Lake, WA, USA

© Springer Nature Switzerland AG 2019
L. Weiss Roberts, M. Trockel (eds.),
The Art and Science of Physician Wellbeing,
https://doi.org/10.1007/978-3-319-42135-3_13

- North Americans' poor behavioral choices regarding diet, exercise, alcohol, and tobacco account for substantial mortality rates—for instance, taken together, these four behaviors account for about 40% of US mortality (Mokdad et al. 2004)
- Physicians and medical students with the healthiest habits are more likely to advise their patients about related preventive habits
- Appropriate physician self-disclosure about healthy personal habits can make physicians more believable and motivating to patients
- Physicians do not perform prevention counseling at very high rates (Lobelo et al. 2009)
- When medical schools encourage students to be healthy, it positively and significantly influences the students' patient counseling frequency ($p = 0.002$) and their perceived relevance ($p = 0.0007$) of such counseling
- Counseling patients makes a difference in their habits and their health

Physicians Tend to Live Longer than Their Peers Due to Better-than-Average Health Habits

Good exercise behaviors are strongly normative among North American physicians, both those in training and those in practice. Research has shown that, for instance, Canadian physicians, US women physicians, and US medical students typically exercise more than do their same-age, same-gender peers in the general population (Frank 1995; Frank et al. 2003; Frank et al. 2004; Frank et al. 2006; Frank and Segura 2009). No large, representative study of US male physicians and exercise habits exists; however, Frank and Segura found in their 2009 study on Canadian physicians' health practices ($n = 3213$) that the surveyed male physicians reported an average of 295 total (mild + moderate + vigorous) min of exercise per week versus 255 total min reported by female physicians, a trend that is contrary to some findings regarding amounts of exercise of women versus men in the general population.

One study surrounding US medical students found they possess behavioral characteristics that are quite positive overall. In particular, regarding exercise, students reported a median of 4 hours of exercise on average per week, with strenuous exercise preferred (Frank et al. 2006). Similarly, Canadian physicians were found to have exercised a mean of 4.7 hours per week (Frank and Segura 2009).

Table 13.1 data, originating from the Frank, Bhat-Schelbert, and Elon (2003) study, exhibit the highly significant ($p < 0.001$) relationship between compliance with American College of Sports Medicine (ACSM) exercise recommendations—which include at least 150 minutes of moderate-intensity exercise each week (met through 30–60 minutes of moderate-intensity exercise 5 days a week or 20–60 minutes of vigorous-intensity exercise 3 days a week)—and US women physicians' self-reported general health status, along with a significant relationship between ACSM compliance and the number of bad physical health days and bad mental health days per month. Table 13.2 shows the highly significant

TABLE 13.1 US women physicians' physical and mental health characteristics and their compliance with American College of Sports Medicine exercise recommendations

		Compliance	
	n	**% (SE)**	**p value**
General health status			
Excellent/very good	2940	51.9 (1.1)	<0.001
Good	49	36.5 (2.3)	
Fair/poor	189	30.7 (4.3)	
Bad physical health days/month			
0	2069	51.1 (1.4)	0.006
≥1	1778	45.5 (1.5)	
Bad mental health days/month			
0	1912	50.7 (1.5)	0.04
≥1	1907	46.6 (1.4)	

TABLE 13.2 US women physicians' work stress and home stress levels and their compliance with American College of Sports Medicine exercise recommendations

		Compliance	
	n	% (SE)	*p* value
Work stress			
Severe	471	45.1 (2.8)	0.003
Moderate	2507	47.3 (1.2)	
Light	798	55.5 (2.3)	
Home stress			
Severe	178	30.6 (3.9)	<0.001
Moderate	1451	44.0 (1.6)	
Light	2198	54.0 (1.4)	

($p < 0.001$) relationship between ACSM exercise recommendations and home stress and the significant relationship between ACSM compliance and amount of work stress. Although Tables 13.1 and 13.2 data do not reveal the directions of causality, exercise was consistently correlated with healthier practices and outcomes (Frank et al. 2003).

Our first case illustrates the real-life story of a medical intern who experienced firsthand—and continues to experience—the benefits of exercise in stressful times.

Case Illustration 13.1: Verena
When I completed the first half of my medical internship in the oncology department of a large community hospital, I had a very hard time leaving behind the suffering and strokes of fate that my patients had to endure when stepping through the hospital's exit door each night. In addition, I lived in staff housing in very close proximity to the hospital—my living room faced the windows of the ward I worked in. I just couldn't seem to get away.

That's when I took up running. Every day after work, I would exchange my scrubs for running tights and a t-shirt and just take off into the close-by forest. Sometimes I would listen to music, podcasts, or audiobooks; sometimes my brain needed the peace and quiet and I would just run and become one with the beautiful nature around me.

After an hour or so, I would get home—drenched in sweat but with a peaceful mind. I was able to create the much-needed distance and larger perspective that would allow me to continue working in this profession without sacrificing my own wellbeing over it. Because what good can an unhealthy, unhappy, depressed, cynical physician do?

Now, 6 years later, I'm still running. In fact, I've completed several half-marathons, a marathon, and a half-ironman distance triathlon. The sport has given me joy and a healthy body, and, most of all, it is my most important outlet for stress. Thanks to running, I go to sleep happy and content every single night.

Physicians and Medical Students with Healthiest Habits Are More Likely to Advise Patients on Related Preventive Habits

Generally finding that healthier doctors influence patients in positive health-care practices, many researchers have assessed physician activity levels and physical activity counseling practices of doctors in training and in practice (Orleans et al. 1985; Lewis et al. 1986; Wells et al. 1986; Lewis et al. 1991; Reed et al. 1991; Schwartz et al. 1991; Konen and Fromm 1992; Williford et al. 1992; Crapse et al. 1993; Sherman and Hershman 1993; Najem et al. 1995; Delnevo et al. 1996; Kamien and Power 1996; Kreuter et al. 1997; Podl et al. 1999; Walsh et al. 1999; Wee et al. 1999; Glasgow et al. 2001; Easton et al. 2001; Frank et al. 2002; Peterson et al. 2003; Clair et al. 2004; Rogers et al. 2005; van der Ploeg et al. 2007; Buffart et al. 2009); additional research of note is summarized later. Physical activity counseling varies by practice setting and specialty; however, it can be generally concluded that such counseling is still suboptimal and may experience numerous barriers (Burack 1989; Garry et al. 2002).

The US Women Physicians' Health Study was a national survey conducted in 1993 investigating 4501 women physicians' personal health habits and their clinical health-promotion practices (Frank 1995). The sampling scheme was stratified according to decade of graduation (1950–1989) on the basis of the American Medical Association's Masterfile, with oversampling of earlier decades (response rate 59%). Just under half (46.1%) of the women physicians complying with Centers for Disease Control and Prevention (CDC) exercise recommendations (which recommend adults perform at least 150 minutes a week of moderate-intensity or 75 minutes a week of vigorous-intensity aerobic activity, or an equivalent combination of moderate- and vigorous-intensity aerobic activity) counseled on exercise at least once a year, compared to 39.6% of those with lower exercise levels counseling at the same frequency ($p < 0.01$) (Frank et al. 2000b).

Abramson, Stein, Schaufele, Frates, & Logan (2000) surveyed a random sample of 298 primary care physicians (84 family practitioners, 79 pediatricians, 58 geriatricians, and 77 internists), with the following findings:

- Physicians who perform aerobic exercise regularly are more likely to counsel their patients on the benefits of these exercises, as are physicians who perform strength training.
- Pediatricians and geriatricians counsel fewer patients about aerobic exercise than do family practitioners and internists.
- Counseling regarding strength (versus aerobic) training is less common in all physician groups surveyed, and lowest among pediatricians, of whom 50% did not advise these exercises for any of their patients.
- Inadequate time was noted by 61% and inadequate knowledge and/or experience by 16% of respondents as the major barriers to counseling regarding aerobic exercise.

Frank, Bhat-Schelbert, & Elon (2003) reported data from Women Physicians' Health Study respondents to determine compliance with ACSM recommendations. Although 96% of the women physicians reported exercising, only 41% exercised enough to meet the ACSM recommendations. Of those complying with the ACSM recommendations, 22.8% discussed exercise with patients every visit, and 23.3% discussed no more than once a year. In comparison, of those not complying with ACSM recommendations, only 16.4% discussed exercise with patients at every visit and 23.2% counseled no more than once a year. Physicians complying with ACSM recommendations were more likely to counsel patients on exercise (see Table 13.3, $p = 0.004$).

Livaudais et al. (2005) assessed physicians' performance of breast cancer risk reduction practices alongside counseling related to physical activity and other healthy behaviors and personal health practices. This study randomly selected 2002 California physicians in the year 2001, of whom 822 (50.0% of 1647 eligible physicians) responded. Among the physicians, 56% reported counseling at least 75% of their patients about physical activity. Sedentary, moderately active, and active physicians were, dose-wise, less likely to counsel their patients about physical activity compared to the very active physicians, indicating that the physicians' own level of physical activity was a predictor of counseling about physical activity.

Note that these findings, particularly those regarding barriers, suggest strategies that might increase physician exercise counseling behavior.

Appropriate Physician Revelation of Healthy Personal Habits Can Make Physicians More Believable

When physicians "walk the walk," patients very well may listen. Exercise and creativity meet in our second case illustration, which describes the perspective of the doctor behind the small but telling study that follows afterward.

TABLE 13.3 Relationship between compliance with American College of Sports Medicine exercise recommendations and counseling patients on exercise among women physicians

Complies with ACSM recommendations	Discusses exercise % (SE)			Perceived relevance to practice % (SE)		Confidence in counseling % (SE)		Training in counseling % (SE)	
	Every visit	≤1/ year	Other	High	Other	High	Other	Extensive	Other
Yes	22.8 (1.5)	23.3 (1.5)	53.9 (1.8)	40.7 (1.8)	59.3 (1.8)	50.9 (1.9)	49.1 (1.9)	22.7 (1.6)	77.3 (1.6)
No	16.4 (1.3)	23.2 (1.5)	60.4 (1.7)	38.4 (1.8)	61.6 (1.8)	38.5 (1.9)	61.5 (1.8)	13.7 (1.2)	86.3 (1.2)
p value	0.004			0.4		<0.001		<0.001	

Case Illustration 13.2: Erica

Pragmatism has led to a certain look (see Fig. 13.1) being my choice on most at-home mornings since I started medical school. Before laptop computers emerged on the scene, I read journals and books that were not too heavy to hold while I pedaled. But once I had ridden a few miles with a laptop secured to the front of my bike, I knew that I had found my preferred regular exercise modality. Here was a health-promotion activity that satisfied so many criteria simultaneously! I neither feel remorse that I'm wasting time getting a special outfit on for exercise, getting to my place of exercise, or even doing my exercise, feeling that my brain and hands and quadriceps should have higher purposes, nor that I must stew in boredom while exercising (a serious previous impediment to regular exercise for me).

In the thousands of miles that I have ridden since that day, I have learned to bike and simultaneously read, write, and even chair conference calls, although usually with the video function turned off.

And when I leave home, I also get to do fun, multitasking exercise. When I was an assistant professor, I would usually commute to work on my bicycle, about 20 minutes to Emory or to Grady Memorial Hospital from our home each way—a lovely way to begin and end each day. Likewise, it's often an educational and cardiovascular treat to walk around a new urban or biologically rich environment, en route to a task. Walking while talking with friends can be fruitful too, whether with a buddy in person or on the phone, a child in a stroller, or as a stroll with a significant other that pays attention to the light, weather, and your shared ecosystem. My favorite efficient travel exercise is swimming, and I have developed a set of (apparently humorous) truncated crawl and backstroke-like moves that work well in the constrained environment of a hotel swimming pool.

And how do I judge the efficacy of my activities? At 56, I retain a normal BMI, blood pressure, and lipids without medication, am able to accomplish without pain any physical feats needed or desired, and sporadically participate in triathlons without special preparation before or any pain after, although always (and contentedly) at the very back of the pack.

FIGURE 13.1 An image of author Dr. Frank at her usual (for more than 20 years) morning exercise—exercycle plus working on her laptop (pre-laptops, it was reading a medical journal while exercycling). What you do for your exercise seems to matter much less than just making sure you do SOME modestly aerobic activity that isn't too onerous or dull to do it often!

Photo credit: Kevin Bradley

Appropriate physician disclosure concerning healthy personal exercise and dietary habits can make doctors more believable and motivating to patients. And patients care about our encouragement surrounding exercise and other preventive practices. Several years ago, we conducted a small study ($n = 130$) in an Emory University general medical clinic waiting room (Frank et al. 2000a). We randomized individuals to watch either a standard 2-minute video from me (EF) on healthy diet and exercise habits or the standard video plus an extra 30 seconds divulging my own (as a doctor) personal health habits regarding diet and exercise. A Likert scale was used, with 1 representing the lowest value and 10 the highest. Patients found me, in the "physician-disclosure" video, to seem generally significantly healthier ($p = 0.004$), also finding me more believable and more motivating overall. More specifically, when patients were asked the questions, "How much did you believe what the doctor told you about [diet] [exercise] in the video?", patients found the extra 30 seconds made me more believable on both diet and exercise ($p = 0.006$ and $p = 0.002$, respectively). When asked the questions, "How much did the doctor in the video motivate or encourage you to [have a healthy diet] [exercise]?", patients also found me more motivating, on both counts ($p = 0.006$ and $p = 0.004$, respectively).

Medical School's Encouragement of Student Health Positively Influences the Student's Patient Counseling Frequency and Perceived Relevance

During medical school, encouragement of student health positively and significantly influences the amount students counsel their patients, along with the students' perceived relevance of such counseling. Medical students who exercise more are somewhat more likely to respond that counseling their future patients about exercise would be highly relevant (Frank et al.

2004); furthermore, in their clinical practice, such higher-activity senior medical students were more likely to actually counsel their patients about exercise (Frank et al. 2007).

In this same national US study, medical students were able to appropriately assess their exercise habits and need for improvement (Frank et al. 2007). The results may be seen in Table 13.4 (note, again, that for substantial health benefits, the CDC recommends adults perform at least 150 minutes a week of moderate-intensity or 75 minutes a week of vigorous-intensity aerobic activity, or an equivalent combination of moderate- and vigorous-intensity aerobic activity). At all three points in time (freshman year, entry to wards, and senior year), medical students' personal exercise habits and their understanding of the sufficiency of those habits seem tightly aligned (Frank et al. 2008).

In further strategically good news and as seen in Table 13.5, medical school deans and medical students alike are enthusiastic about the value and appropriateness of encouraging positive health behaviors among medical students and in medical schools more generally (Frank et al. 2005a). Taken from the Healthy Doc = Healthy Patient questionnaire survey and scored from 1 (strongly agree) to 5 (strongly disagree), both medical students and deans were likely to agree with the following statement: "Medical school faculty members should set a good example for medical students by practicing a healthy lifestyle" (1.4 for deans and 2.1 for medical students). A statement that medical schools should encourage their students and residents to practice healthy lifestyles garnered 1.3 on the scale from deans and 1.9 from students, and a statement that "in order to effectively encourage patient adherence to a healthy lifestyle, a physician must adhere to one him/herself" scored 2.1 and 2.2, respectively, from deans and students.

Compton, Carrera, and Frank (2008) found in their study that at freshman orientation, entry to wards, and senior year, a consistent, inverse, dose-responsive relationship existed between medical students' stress—as assessed from data obtained via student questionnaires at each of these points in time (including number of days of bad mental health in the past month, stress experienced in the past 12 months, and

TABLE 13.4 Medical students and exercise: student responses to the statement "I currently exercise enough"

	Freshman year (n = 1846)		Entry to wards (n = 1630)		Senior year (n = 1469)	
	Comply with CDC % (SE)	Median exercise score	Comply with CDC % (SE)	Median exercise score	Comply with CDC % (SE)	Median exercise score
Strongly agree	97 (1)	62	92 (2)	55	95 (2)	61
Agree	91 (1)	53	88 (2)	50	88 (2)	52
Neutral	67 (4)	41	64 (3)	41	70 (3)	43
Disagree	42 (3)	33	34 (2)	28	41 (2)	31
Strongly disagree	9 (2)	16	11 (3)	14	15 (3)	14

CDC = Centers for Disease Control and Prevention
Bivariate regression (dependent variable = exercise variable)
Comply with CDC exercise recommendations — Logistic p value = <0.0001
Raw exercise score (Godin-Shephard Leisure-Time Physical Activity Questionnaire) — Linear p value = <0.0001

TABLE 13.5 Healthy Doc = Healthy Patient principles: dean and student opinions

	Average of deans (*n* = 17)	Average of students (*n* = 1336)
Medical school faculty members should set a good example for medical students by practicing a healthy lifestyle	1.4	2.1
Medical schools should encourage their students and residents to practice healthy lifestyles	1.3	1.9
In order to effectively encourage patient adherence to a healthy lifestyle, a physician must adhere to one him/herself	2.1	2.2

Scale = 1 (strongly agree) to 5 (strongly disagree)

perceptions about the medical school's system for coping) — and exercise levels in the past 2 weeks (Table 13.6) and the past year (Table 13.7).

As seen in Table 13.8, a consistent, dose-responsive, and positive relationship also exists between medical students' prior month's exercise habits and their mental health.

In addition to the observational, national medical student study, Frank and colleagues developed, implemented, and tested a 4-year curricular and extracurricular intervention to promote healthy behaviors among students in the Class of 2003 attending Emory University School of Medicine in Atlanta, Georgia (Frank et al. 2005b; Frank et al. 2007). The objective of this intervention was to test whether the promotion of medical student health would efficiently improve patient counseling, using the Class of 2002 as controls. In general, students receiving the intervention perceived the medical school as a healthier environment than did the control students, reporting significantly more agreement with school-controlled items such as curricular encouragement of physical activity, emphasis on preventive medicine, provision

TABLE 13.6 Medical student stress in the last 2 weeks versus compliance with CDC exercise recommendations and median exercise score

	Freshman year (n = 1846)		Entry to wards (n = 1630)		Senior year (n = 1469)	
	Comply with CDC % (SE)	Median exercise score	Comply with CDC % (SE)	Median exercise score	Comply with CDC % (SE)	Median exercise score
Almost none	68 (3)	44	72 (4)	44	82 (3)	52
Relatively little	65 (2)	44	59 (3)	37	67 (3)	43
Moderate	64 (2)	43	53 (2)	36	58 (2)	40
A lot	58 (3)	38	49 (2)	35	59 (2)	36

CDC = Centers for Disease Control and Prevention
Bivariate regression (dependent variable = exercise variable)
Comply with CDC exercise recommendations—Logistic p value = 0.0001
Raw exercise score (Godin-Shephard Leisure-Time Physical Activity Questionnaire)—Linear p value = 0.0006

TABLE 13.7 Medical student stress in the last 12 months versus compliance with CDC exercise recommendations and median exercise score

	Freshman year (n = 1846)		Entry to wards (n = 1630)		Senior year (n = 1469)	
	Comply with CDC % (SE)	Median exercise score	Comply with CDC % (SE)	Median exercise score	Comply with CDC % (SE)	Median exercise score
Almost none	65 (7)	50	73 (12)	52	80 (7)	58
Relatively little	66 (2)	43	62 (4)	40	65 (4)	43
Moderate	63 (2)	42	57 (3)	40	63 (2)	42
A lot	63 (4)	42	54 (2)	35	59 (2)	38

CDC = Centers for Disease Control and Prevention

Bivariate regression (dependent variable = exercise variable)

Comply with CDC exercise recommendations—Logistic p value = <0.0001

Raw exercise score (Godin-Shephard Leisure-Time Physical Activity Questionnaire)—Linear p value = 0.0009

TABLE 13.8 Number of bad mental health days in last 30 days versus medical student compliance with CDC exercise recommendations and median exercise score

	Freshman year (n = 1846)		Entry to wards (n = 1630)		Senior year (n = 1469)	
	Comply with CDC % (SE)	Median exercise score	Comply with CDC % (SE)	Median exercise score	Comply with CDC % (SE)	Median exercise score
None	66 (2)	44	61 (3)	39	69 (3)	43
1–2 days	64 (3)	42	57 (3)	38	62 (2)	41
3–7 days	63 (3)	40	55 (3)	37	56 (2)	39
8–29 days	50 (5)	36	46 (3)	33	56 (4)	38
30 days	55 (14)	36	38 (9)	28	50 (12)	37

CDC = Centers for Disease Control and Prevention

Bivariate regression (dependent variable = exercise variable)

Comply with CDC exercise recommendations — Logistic p value = <0.0001

Raw exercise score (Godin–Shephard Leisure-Time Physical Activity Questionnaire) — Linear p value = 0.0009

of extracurricular activities (such as physical activity classes/ sessions), and even encouragement of exercising by class- mates. Significantly, students in the intervention group had approximately 50% greater odds of providing extensive counseling on exercise (p = 0.03) during their standardized patient encounters than did the control students; in other words, their prevention-related attitudes and counseling prac- tices (along with their personal physical activity) were posi- tively influenced by the intervention (Frank et al. 2007).

The Healthy Doc = Healthy Patient principles were pos- tulated to be applicable to medical students and doctors in developing countries, so Duperly et al. (2008a) decided to test these principles in Colombia, initially collecting data during 2006 from first- and fifth-year students attending eight medi- cal schools in Bogotá, Colombia (and more recently expand- ing that data collection to a nationally representative sample of 24 medical schools). Bogotá phase analyses (n = 661) confirmed the US findings of a strong association between personal health habits (including physical activity) and atti- tudes toward related preventive counseling (Duperly et al. 2008a, b). The study found lower rates of compliance with international physical activity recommendations (i.e., at least 150 minutes per week of moderate-to-vigorous physical activ- ity) among Colombian students than among US medical students (50% versus 61%); these rates were still better than those of age-matched peers in the Colombian general popu- lation. The Colombian Healthy Doc = Healthy Patient study provides further evidence of the strong, consistent, and gen- eralizable association between personal health practices and preventive counseling attitudes among doctors in training.

Counseling Patients Makes a Difference in Their Habits and Their Health

Even though we know that counseling patients makes a dif- ference in their habits and their health and that North Americans' poor behavioral choices regarding diet, exercise, alcohol, and tobacco account for substantial mortality rates—as stated earlier, approximately 40% of US mortality (Mokdad et al. 2004) —physicians do not perform prevention counseling at very high rates (Lobelo et al. 2009).

We have known for some time that physician advice on both diet and exercise can make a difference in encouraging patients to improve their own health-related practices. A 1997 CDC study of 20,847 adult Americans showed that when these patients had been given advice from their physicians to exercise, 74.7% of them were found to be exercising more, and without such advice, only 50.5% were found to be exercising more at follow-up (Centers for Disease Control and Prevention 1999).

Data such as these offer compelling reasons to encourage improved exercise (and nutrition and other health) habits among physicians, starting with medical students. Multiple studies have demonstrated that our own physical activity can significantly improve the likelihood that we will counsel our patients about diet and exercise (Lobelo et al. 2009).

Another study involving medical students, this time senior medical students, and 800 standardized patients (Frank et al. 2005b; Frank et al. 2007) indicated that students who had been exposed to a personal health promotion curriculum on exercise and diet during their medical school curriculum were more likely to counsel their patients about exercise/diet than were the control students. The intervention positively affected these medical students' perceptions of their school health-promotion environment and reduced tobacco use among male students; the exposed students were 65% more likely to counsel their patients about exercise and 49% more likely to counsel regarding diet.

A critical reason for encouraging sufficient medical student and physician exercise practices is that this manifestation of the Healthy Doc = Healthy Patient principle makes a significant difference with patient health. As shown in Table 13.9, senior medical students are significantly more likely to discuss exercise with patients if they are exercise-compliant themselves, and the previously cited CDC data show that it makes a difference if doctors discuss exercise (Centers for Disease

TABLE 13.9 Frequency of senior-year US medical students' counseling of patients on exercise versus compliance with CDC exercise recommendations and median exercise score

| | Senior year (n = 1469) | |
	Comply with CDC % (SE)	Median exercise score
Frequency of counseling patients on exercise		
Never/rarely	55 (3)	37
Sometimes	60 (2)	41
Usually/always	68 (3)	43

CDC = Centers for Disease Control and Prevention
Bivariate regression (dependent variable = exercise variable)
Comply with CDC exercise recommendations—Logistic p value = 0.003
Raw exercise score (Godin–Shephard Leisure-Time Physical Activity Questionnaire)—Linear p value = 0.01

Control and Prevention 1999); our Emory University clinic data show that it further helps our credibility and ability to motivate patients if we let patients know that we exercise and eat healthily ourselves (Frank et al. 2000a).

This manifestation of the Healthy Doc = Healthy Patient principle makes a significant difference with patient health … senior medical students are significantly more likely to discuss exercise with patients if they are exercise-compliant themselves, and the previously cited CDC data show that it makes a difference if doctors discuss exercise; our Emory University clinic data show that it further helps our credibility and ability to motivate patients if we let patients know that we exercise and eat healthily ourselves.

A similar relationship between US women doctors and their patients exists: those who comply with ACSM recommendations discuss exercise with their patients significantly more frequently and, in addition, are significantly (highly so) more likely to have confidence in their counseling and training surrounding exercise (Lobelo et al. 2009).

Conclusion

We already know (from large national samples with good response rates) the following:

1. There is a strong and consistent relationship between doctors' and medical students' increased exercise and their increased counseling of patients about exercise.
2. It is already normative for physicians/medical students to exercise more than the general population—an element of self-care correlating to better personal mental and physical health—and they are aware if they don't exercise enough.
3. With appropriate dissemination of and action on these findings, we can—and should—encourage exercise counseling by increasing physicians' personal exercise.

Collectively, evidence indicates a robust association between personal physical activity behaviors and clinical physical activity counseling practices in both practicing doctors and medical students. We already know how to positively intervene when it comes to exercise and medical students: medical schools and their students are willing to encourage more exercise, and when they do, that correlates with medical students exercising more and telling their patients to do likewise and, ultimately, more positive personal health outcomes. As physicians, we must take care of ourselves as well as our patients: exercising more helps us do a better job at both those tasks.

References

Abramson S, Stein J, Schaufele M, Frates E, Rogan S (2000) Personal exercise habits and counseling practices of primary care physicians: A national survey. Clin J Sport Med 10:40–48.

Buffart LM, van der Ploeg HP, Smith BJ, Kurko J, King LA, Bauman AE (2009) General practitioners' perceptions and practices of physical activity counselling: Changes over the past 10 years. Br J Sports Med 43(14):1149–53.

Burack RC (1989) Barriers to clinical preventive medicine. Prim Care 16:245–250.

Centers for Disease Control and Prevention (1999, February 5) Physician advice and individual behaviors about cardiovascular disease risk reduction—Seven states and Puerto Rico, 1997. MMWR 48(4):74–77. https://biotech.law.lsu.edu/blaw/bt/mm4804.pdf.

Clair JH, Wilson DB, Clore JN (2004) Assessing the health of future physicians: An opportunity for preventive education. J Contin Educ Health Prof 24:82–89.

Compton M, Carrera JS, Frank E (2008) Stress and depressive symptoms/dysphoria among U.S. medical students: Results from a large, nationally representative survey. J Nerv Ment Dis 196:891–897.

Crapse FJ Jr, Hudgins PM, Baker HH (1993) Lifestyle changes associated with osteopathic medical education. J Am Osteopath Assoc 93:1051–1054.

Delnevo CD, Abatemarco DJ, Gotsch AR (1996) Health behaviors and health promotion: Disease prevention perceptions of medical students. Am J Prev Med 12: 38–43.

Duperly J, Lobelo F, Segura C, Herrera D, Sarmiento F, Sarmiento OL, Frank E (2008a) Personal habits are independently associated with a positive attitude towards healthy lifestyle counseling among Colombian medical students. Circulation 117:198–291.

Duperly J, Segura C, Herrera DM, Sarmiento OL, Lobelo F (2008b) Medical student's knowledge on physical activity counseling is associated with their physical activity levels. Med Sci Sports Exerc 40(5):S251. https://doi.org/10.1249/01.mss.0000322570.29186.ae.

Easton A, Husten C, Malarcher A, et al. (2001) Smoking cessation counseling by primary care women physicians: Women Physicians' Health Study. Women Health 32:77–91.

Frank E (1995) The Women Physicians' Health Study: Background, objectives, and methods. J Am Med Womens Assoc 50:64–66.

Frank E, Bhat-Schelbert K, Elon LK (2003) Exercise counseling and personal exercise habits of U.S. women physicians. J Am Med Womens Assoc 58:178–184.

Frank E, Breyan J, Elon LK (2000a) Physician disclosure of healthy personal behaviors improves credibility and ability to motivate. Arch Fam Med 9(3):287–290. https://doi.org/10.1001/archfami.9.3.287.

Frank E, Carrera JS, Elon L, Hertzberg VS (2006) Basic demographics, health practices, and health status of U.S. medical students. Am J Prev Med 31(6):499–505. https://doi.org/10.1016/j.amepre.2006.08.009.

Frank E, Elon L, Hertzberg V (2007) Quantitative assessment of a 4-year intervention that improved patient counseling through improving medical student health. Med Gen Med 9(2):58. http://www.medscape.com/viewarticle/557088.

Frank E, Galuska DA, Elon LK, Wright EH (2004) Personal and clinical exercise-related attitudes and behaviors of freshmen U.S. medical students. Res Q Exerc Sport 75:112–121. https://doi.org/10.1080/02701367.2004.10609142.

Frank E, Hedgecock J, Elon LK (2005a) Personal health promotion at U.S. medical schools: A quantitative study and qualitative description of deans' and students' perceptions. BMC Med Educ. http://www.medscape.com/medline/abstract/15581424.

Frank E, Rothenberg R, Lewis C, Belodoff BF (2000b) Correlates of physicians' prevention-related practices. Findings from the Women's Physicians Health Study. Arch Fam Med 9:359–367.

Frank E, Segura C (2009) Health practices of Canadian physicians. Canadian Family Physician; 55(8):810–811. http://www.cfp.ca/cgi/reprint/55/8/810.

Frank E, Smith D, Fitzmaurice D (2005b) A description and qualitative assessment of a 4-year intervention to improve medical student health. Med Gen Med 7(2):4. http://www.medscape.com/viewarticle/501770.

Frank E, Tong E, Lobelo F, Carrera J, Duperly J (2008). Physical activity levels and counseling practices of U.S. medical students. Med Sci Sports Exerc 40(3):413–421. https://doi.org/10.1249/MSS.0b013e31815ff399.

Frank E, Wright EH, Serdula MK, Elon LK, Baldwin G (2002) Personal and professional nutrition-related practices of U.S. female physicians. Am J Clin Nutr 75:326–332.

Garry JP, Diamond JJ, Whitley TW (2002) Physical activity curricula in medical schools. Acad Med 77:818–820.

Glasgow RE, Eakin EG, Fisher EB, Bacak SJ, Brownson RC (2001) Physician advice and support for physical activity: Results from a national survey. Am J Prev Med 21:189–196.

Kamien M, Power R (1996) Lifestyle and health habits of fourth year medical students at the University of Western Australia. Aust Fam Physician, Suppl 1:S26–S29.

Konen JC, Fromm BS (1992) Changes in personal health behaviors of medical students. Med Teach 14:321–325.

Kreuter MW, Scharff DP, Brennan LK, Lukwago SN (1997) Physician recommendations for diet and physical activity: Which patients get advised to change? Prev Med 26:825–833.

Lewis CE, Clancy C, Leake B, Schwartz JS (1991) The counseling practices of internists. Ann Intern Med 114:54–58.

Lewis CE, Wells KB, Ware J (1986) A model for predicting the counseling practices of physicians. J Gen Intern Med 1:14–19.

Livaudais JC, Kaplan CP, Haas JS, Perez-Stable EJ, Stewart S, Des Jarlais G (2005) Lifestyle behavior counseling for women patients among a sample of California physicians. J Womens Health (Larchmt) 14(6):485–495. https://doi.org/10.1089/jwh.2005.14.485.

Lobelo F, Duperly J, Frank E (2009) Physical activity habits of doctors and medical students influence their counseling practices. Br J Sports Med. https://doi.org/10.1136/bjsm.2008.055426.

Mokdad AH, Marks JS, Stroup DF, Gerberding JL (2004): Actual causes of death in the United States, 2000. JAMA 291(10):1238–1245.

Najem GR, Passannante MR, Foster JD (1995) Health risk factors and health promoting behavior of medical, dental and nursing students. J Clin Epidemiol 48:841–849.

Orleans CT, George LK, Houpt JL, Brodie KH (1985) Health promotion in primary care: A survey of U.S. family practitioners. Prev Med 14:636–647.

Peterson DF, Degenhardt BF, Smith CM (2003) Correlation between prior exercise and present health and fitness status of entering medical students. J Am Osteopath Assoc 103:361–366.

Podl TR, Goodwin MA, Kikano GE, Stange KC (1999) Direct observation of exercise counseling in community family practice. Am J Prev Med 17:207–210.

Reed BD, Jensen JD, Gorenflo DW (1991) Physicians and exercise promotion. Am J Prev Med 7:410–415.

Rogers LQ, Gutin B, Humphries MC, et al. (2005) A physician fitness program: Enhancing the physician as an "exercise" role model for patients. Teach Learn Med 17:27–35.

Schwartz JS, Lewis CE, Clancy C, Kinosian MS, Radany MN, Koplan JP (1991) Internists' practices in health promotion and disease prevention: A survey. Ann Intern Med 114:46–53.

Sherman SE, Hershman WY (1993) Exercise counseling: How do general internists do? J Gen Intern Med 8:243–248.

van der Ploeg HP, Smith BJ, Stubbs T, Vita P, Holford R, Bauman AE (2007) Physical activity promotion: Are GPs getting the message? Aust Fam Physician 36:871–874.

Walsh JM, Swangard DM, Davis T, McPhee SJ (1999) Exercise counseling by primary care physicians in the era of managed care. Am J Prev Med 16:307–313.

Wee CC, McCarthy EP, Davis RB, Phillips RS (1999) Physician counseling about exercise. JAMA 282:1583–1588.

Wells KB, Lewis CE, Leake B, Schleiter MK, Brook RH (1986) The practices of general and subspecialty internists in counseling about smoking and exercise. Am J Public Health 76:1009–1013.

Williford HN, Barfield BR, Lazenby RB, Olson MS (1992) A survey of physicians' attitudes and practices related to exercise promotion. Prev Med 21:630–636.

Chapter 14
Nutrition

Maryam Sarah Hamidi

Introduction

Physicians are required to be alert and attentive and have impeccable judgment and decision-making abilities, often in fast-paced and high-stress settings. All of these abilities can be compromised by hunger, dehydration, sleepiness, and fatigue (Danziger et al. 2011; Neely et al. 2004; Symmonds et al. 2010). In two studies by Lemaire et al., physicians working at an urban teaching hospital in Canada reported that inadequate nutrition at work negatively impacted their work performance due to irritability, frustration, light-headedness, tremor, nausea, difficulty concentrating, and decision-making (Lemaire et al. 2010; Lemaire et al. 2011). In addition to direct physiological adverse effects, limited or lack of access to regular meals and adequate nutrition at workplaces can indirectly contribute to poor mental health. For example, uncertainty over the ability to access food in the future can provoke a stress response that may contribute to worry and

M. S. Hamidi (✉)
Stanford Medicine WellMD Center,
Department of Psychiatry and Behavioral Sciences,
Stanford, CA, USA
e-mail: Maryam.Hamidi@Stanford.edu

© Springer Nature Switzerland AG 2019
L. Weiss Roberts, M. Trockel (eds.),
The Art and Science of Physician Wellbeing,
https://doi.org/10.1007/978-3-319-42135-3_14

235

anxiety (Jones 2017). Eating meals in ways one perceives as socially unacceptable can induce feelings of alienation, powerlessness, shame, and guilt (Jones 2017). These factors may in particular affect house staff who often find themselves scavenging for food within healthcare institutions during night shifts.

Dehydration, also a common experience among physicians (Alomar et al. 2013; El-Sharkawy et al. 2016; Lemaire et al. 2011; Solomon et al. 2010), can increase fatigue and sleepiness; impair mood, ability to concentrate, short- and long-term memory, and motor coordination; and slow reflexes and visual perceptual abilities (Armstrong et al. 2012; Ganio et al. 2011; Houssein et al. 2016; Lindseth et al. 2013; Masento et al. 2014). The good news is that adequate workplace nutrition and hydration can improve physician cognition and wellbeing (Kassam et al. 2015; Lemaire et al. 2010). The following are some recommendations for improving physicians' nutrition and hydration status.

Organizational Strategies

The majority of physicians are dedicated to providing quality care to their patients even at the expense of their own personal wellness. This, combined with a pervasive culture in medicine that solely focuses on improving patient outcomes and neglects physicians' wellbeing, results in the degradation of physicians' health and increased rates of burnout. In such a culture, physicians often skip meals to attend to patients, teach their students, and help their teams and avoid having food or fluids in presence of patients in order to maintain a professional image. Interestingly, results of a recent survey in the UK suggest that a majority of patients, visitors, and staff from medical and surgical wards did not mind if healthcare professionals drank or ate in presence of patients (Wade 2012). Therefore, promoting a culture that values self-care may be one of the first important steps that healthcare organizations can take to improve physicians' nutrition and hydration status. Skipping meals, sleep deprivation, and resulting sleep-related impairment combined with chronic occupational stress and burnout increase the risk of emotional and uncontrolled eating behaviors and preferences for energy-dense foods (Nevanpera et al. 2012; Pardi et al. 2017; Tryon et al. 2013; Wansink et al. 2012; Yaroch and Pinard 2012). In addition, there is evidence that after a period of food deprivation, study participants were more likely to consume more of high carbohydrate-rich foods compared to vegetables or high protein foods (Wansink et al. 2012). The combination of these factors and availability of unhealthy food options at work negatively impacts physician's wellbeing. To counterbalance this, workplace cafeterias could improve physician wellness by making healthier food and beverage choices—such as fresh vegetables, salads, fruit, water, tea, and coffee—more accessible, affordable, visible, and enticing than options that are high in fat, added sugars, and sodium.

Furthermore, organizations can improve physicians' wellbeing and work performance by addressing main barriers to healthy eating for physicians in the workplace. Some examples are providing healthy food choices; creating policies to allow regular nutrition, hydration, and bathroom breaks; providing healthy and free snacks; and increasing awareness of the links between optimal nutrition and work performance (Hamidi et al. 2016; Leedo et al. 2017; Lemaire et al. 2010; Lemaire et al. 2011; Lesser et al. 2012; Pressel 2014). Other strategies include extending food service hours to midnight; offering healthy snacks and drinks to nighttime staff; and improving access to drinking water, food storage, and eating areas near operating rooms, in-patient areas, and staff workrooms (Hamidi et al. 2016; Lemaire et al. 2010; Lemaire et al. 2011; Lesser et al. 2012). A randomized controlled trial has shown that providing a 500 ml bottle of water to university hospital shift workers improved their hydration status and had beneficial effects on their energy levels and mood (Leedo et al. 2017).

Organizations can also improve and promote a sense of collegiality and community by providing spaces where physicians can share mealtimes. It has been shown that consumption of regular meals and eating together can promote mental health among employees and enhance team performance at workplaces (Kniffin et al. 2015). Creating spaces for commensality may be one of the many potential mechanisms that enhances healthcare organizations' performance.

Personal

The human brain is more sensitive to changes in concentration of nutrients compared to other organs and tissues (Pauling 1968). Strategies to optimize timing and composition of meals, hydration status, strategic use of caffeine, and daily nutrient intakes that can acutely affect mood and cognitive performance are discussed below.

Meal Composition

It has been proposed that the ratio of carbohydrate to protein in meals can acutely affect postprandial cognitive performance through altering brain levels of tryptamines and catecholamines (St-Onge et al. 2016), with ratios of 3 or less resulting in better overall cognitive performance (Fischer et al. 2002; Lindseth et al. 2011; Paz and Berry 1997). In addition to the amount of carbohydrates, the quality of carbohydrates can also affect post-meal sleepiness. For example, a high glycemic index (GI) carbohydrate-rich meal, compared to a low GI carbohydrate-rich meal, is associated with higher self-reported sleepiness (Afaghi et al. 2007). High-fat meals can also increase postprandial fatigue (Badawy et al. 1984; Kwan et al. 1986; St-Onge et al. 2016). Similar to carbohydrates, the quality and type of fat is important in brain health. It has been shown that higher intake ratio of polyunsaturated fatty acids (PUFA) to saturated fatty acids (SFA) is associated with better memory function and a reduced risk of memory impairment (Beilharz et al. 2015). In addition, higher intake ratio of omega-3 PUFA compared to omega-6 PUFA is associated with a lower risk of cognitive decline (Beilharz et al. 2015).

Large meals that are high in both fat and carbohydrates may slow down reaction times and result in higher self-reported fatigue and sleepiness (Cunliffe et al. 1997; Lloyd et al. 1994; Muller et al. 2013; Reyner et al. 2012; Wells et al. 1997). Age is also an important factor in response to meal composition. For example, consuming a high-carbohydrate and low-protein lunch was associated with reduced concentration and higher lapses of attention among those aged 40 years and over but not in those who were below the age of 40 (Spring et al. 1982). One suggestion for a balanced meal is to include 20–30 g of protein, 40–60 g of complex carbohydrates, and 20–30 g of fat with less than 7 g of saturated fat.

High fat and sugar intake are also associated with impairments in memory tasks that were sensitive to hippocampal function. The hippocampus has a role in episodic memory such as remembering recent food intake and regulating responsiveness to internal hunger and satiety cues (Beilharz et al. 2015). In one study, subjects with high fat and sugar intake were less accurate at recalling their prior food intake and were less sensitive to internal signals of hunger and satiety (Francis and Stevenson 2011). On the other hand, low sugar intake from sweetened food and beverages has been associated with better psychological health independent of other lifestyle behaviors, sociodemographic status, adiposity, and other medical conditions, and elimination of added sugar from the diet of depressed individuals results in reduction of depressive symptoms (Christensen 2001; Knuppel et al. 2017).

It has been shown that after a period of food deprivation, foods that are eaten first, usually starchy foods, and are available in larger quantities are the foods eaten most for the rest of the meal (Wansink et al. 2012). Therefore, it is optimal to start a meal with vegetables or a source of protein instead of foods high in sugar, fat, or carbohydrates.

Chronic stress and sleep deprivation may induce changes in the brain that promote habitual, emotionally rewarding behaviors and emotional eating, and limit goal-directed decisions about making healthy food choices (Hendy 2012; Nedeltcheva et al. 2009; Pardi et al. 2017; Scherr et al. 2017).

Protein has been shown to be effective in reducing reward mechanisms in the brain, self-reported hunger, and prospective food intake; increasing feelings of fullness and satiety; and decreasing cravings for savory, salty, and fatty foods (Casperson et al. 2017; Journel et al. 2012). On the contrary, highly palatable foods – rich in calories, carbohydrates, fat, and sodium- can improve mood for a few minutes and result in negative mood a couple of days later (Hendy 2012).

Diets high in unprocessed grains, legumes, fruits, vegetables, nuts, olive oil, seeds, and fish have been linked to a reduced rate of age-related cognitive decline, improved mood, and reduced depressive symptoms (Berendsen et al. 2017; Jacka et al. 2017; Morris et al. 2015; Opie et al. 2017; Sarris et al. 2015). In a clinical trial, addition of one fruit and one vegetable to the baseline diet of healthy study participants for 2 weeks was associated with improved psychological wellbeing including feeling more motivated (Conner et al. 2017). Multiple studies suggest that consuming 3–4 servings of vegetables per day (including at least 1 serving of green vegetables) and at least 2 servings of fruit is associated with better mood, cognitive performance, and reduced age-related cognitive decline (Jacka et al. 2017; Kang et al. 2005; Morris et al. 2018; Nguyen et al. 2017).

Even though there is some evidence of the beneficial effects of ketogenic diets on cognitive function of individuals with Alzheimer's disease and mild cognitive impairment (Cunnane et al. 2016), among healthy individuals, ketogenic diets can result in increased reaction times and reduced speed of memory and mental processing, flexibility, and impaired attention and mood (Edwards et al. 2011; Holloway et al. 2011; Wing et al. 1995).

Meal Timing

Late-night eating, in particular between hours of 24:00 and 06:00, when the circadian rhythm promotes sleep, may decrease alertness and impair cognitive performance

(Grant et al. 2017; Gupta et al. 2017), resulting in weight gain and increasing the risk of metabolic disorders (St-Onge et al. 2017; St-Onge et al. 2016), as observed in a study of resident physicians (Mota et al. 2013). Eating at night may increase work errors, delay response time, and increase lapses in attention (Grant et al. 2017). On the contrary, breakfast consumption can improve memory, attention, and motor and executive function in the morning (Benau et al. 2014; Galioto and Spitznagel 2016). Certain behaviors can help with synchronizing the circadian rhythm. These include consuming meals and snacks over a period of 8–12 hours in a day, eating meals and snacks at set times, and abstaining from eating outside of those set times (McHill et al. 2017; St-Onge et al. 2017). Several studies suggest chewing gum can be used to increase alertness and improve work performance during stressful events, and therefore, chewing gum may be a useful strategy during night shifts (Allen and Smith 2015; Sketchley-Kaye et al. 2011).

Effects of Diet on Sleep

Diet can also be used to promote and improve sleep quality. For example, a study has shown a low-fat and protein and high-glycemic-index carbohydrate meal (mostly composed of rice with 8% energy as protein, 1.6% as fat, and 90.4% as carbohydrate) 4 hours before bedtime significantly reduced sleep-onset latency (Afaghi et al. 2007). This meal was more effective in reducing sleep-onset latency when it was consumed 4 hours before bedtime compared to when it was consumed 1 hour before bedtime (Afaghi et al. 2007). A majority of studies suggest that feelings of sleepiness and fatigue occur around 2–4 hours after ingestion of a meal (Afaghi et al. 2007; Lowden et al. 2004; Wells et al. 1997). The general recommendation is to consume meals at least 4 hours before bedtime to avoid sleep disturbance. While having high carbohydrate meals before bedtime may help with sleep, to attain optimal sleep quality, it is important to ensure adequate intake of protein (1 to 1.5 g of protein per kg of body weight per day) and calories throughout the day (Zhou et al. 2016). Meals high in saturated fat and sugar can impair sleep quality and are associated with a lighter, less restorative sleep with more arousals and higher daytime sleepiness (St-Onge et al. 2016), as well as disruption of circadian rhythm, which can exacerbate sleep-impairment issues present in physicians during shift work (Grandner et al. 2010; Oosterman et al. 2015; Panossian and Veasey 2012). A recent study suggests that diets that contain at least three servings of fruits and vegetables per day are associated with better sleep duration (Noorwali et al. 2018). Certain fruits may also promote healthier sleep patterns. For example, consumption of two kiwifruits 1 hour before bedtime was associated with better sleep outcomes among people experiencing sleep disturbances (Lin et al. 2011). Consumption of 8 oz of tart cherry juice, high in antioxidants and melatonin, in the morning and evening has also been associated with better sleep outcomes (Howatson et al. 2012; Pigeon et al. 2010).

Nutrients

Many nutrients are not synthesized in humans de novo and need to be acquired from food and, when this is not possible, through dietary supplement sources (e.g., minerals, some vitamins, essential amino acids, and essential fatty acids).

Mental symptoms of inadequate nutrient intakes are often manifested long before physical symptoms (Pauling 1968). For example, non-anemic iron deficiency (defined as ferritin levels <50 ng/mL) might be an underlying reason for unexplained fatigue and reduced cognitive function in premenopausal women (Vaucher et al. 2012). Risk factors for deficiency include being a premenopausal woman, intense aerobic exercise, vegan diet, high tea or coffee intake especially with meals, low vitamin C intake, and genetic predisposition (McClung et al. 2009; O'Connor et al. 2016). Premenopausal women who are at high risk for iron deficiency should be screened by measuring both hemoglobin and serum ferritin. Daily iron supplementation in iron-deficient women improves cognitive performance and reduces symptomatic fatigue (Lomagno et al. 2014). Intermittent iron supplementation can be used in settings where daily supplementation is likely to be unsuccessful or not possible (Fernandez-Gaxiola and De-Regil 2011). It has been shown that 25-OH-Vitamin D concentrations <20 ng/mL are associated with sleep impairment and nonspecific pain (Beydoun et al. 2014; McCarty 2010; McCarty et al. 2013; McCarty et al. 2012). A few studies have shown that better vitamin D status is associated with better efficiency and sleep quality (St-Onge et al. 2016). A number of studies suggest that broad-spectrum micronutrient supplements are effective in reducing perceived stress, fatigue, mild psychiatric symptoms, and improving mood in healthy individuals (Long and Benton 2013; Popper 2014). Using a high-quality, broad-spectrum micronutrient supplement two to three times a week, in particular, during periods of high stress, may be beneficial.

Caffeine

Tea, coffee, and caffeinated drinks are commonly used by physicians to reduce sleepiness and fatigue and to cope with long working hours. It has been shown that caffeine can improve work performance in shift workers, reduce reaction times and error rates, increase alertness, and improve mood during periods of circadian rhythm misalignment and nighttime sleep deprivation (McHill et al. 2014; Wilhelmus et al. 2017). Coffee and tea are both natural sources of caffeine that contain other beneficial phytonutrients (Bhatti et al. 2013; Grosso et al. 2016) which make them superior sources of caffeine compared to colas. The effective dose of caffeine for alertness, with minimal side effects, varies between individuals and can range from 40 to 400 mg (Ruxton 2008). The caffeine content of a cup (250 ml) of tea, instant coffee, or can of cola beverage can range from 15 to 70 mg and for a cup of coffee range from 90 to 200 mg. After consuming caffeine, it takes 15–30 minutes for it to enter the bloodstream and another 60–90 minutes for it to reach peak plasma concentrations. Therefore, it is best to consume caffeine when feeling slightly sleepy or tired or right before taking a short nap (cafnap) for optimal effectiveness (Horne et al. 2008; Reyner and Horne 1997; Schweitzer et al. 2006). During night shifts, caffeine (especially in the form of tea or coffee) can be used to increase core body temperature and reduce sleepiness (McHill et al. 2014).

The half-life of caffeine ranges from 2.5 to 6 hours with individual differences, and the consumption of caffeine within its half-life prior to sleep can impair the quality of daytime recovery sleep after shift work (McHill et al. 2014; Ruxton 2008). Green tea is traditionally used to improve cognitive performance while maintaining a calm and relaxed state. In addition to caffeine, green tea contains L-theanine and epigallocatechin gallate G, with evidence of beneficial effects on mood and cognitive performance (Dietz and Dekker 2017). Due to the relaxation effects of L-theanine, coffee might be a better choice for tasks that require attention-switching and short-term alertness, whereas green tea can be used in situations where sustained attention, memory, and suppression of distraction are required (Dietz and Dekker 2017).

Hydration

Given the prevalence of dehydration in physicians and the importance of hydration in cognitive performance as described earlier, maintaining adequate hydration is both challenging and crucial for physicians. Drinking water when there is a loss of <1% body mass (levels that occur during everyday living) is associated with improved memory and focused attention and higher subjective energy (Benton et al. 2016). Fluid requirements vary greatly between individuals. In general, a urine output that is less than 30 mL/h for extended periods indicates that the person is dehydrated (Institute of Medicine 2005). Other common early signs of dehydration in adults include dark-colored urine, fatigue, headache, light headedness, dry mouth and skin, and constipation. In 2000, Casa et al. developed a urine color chart to be used as an educational tool for dehydration for athletes (Casa et al. 2000). Urine color can only be used as a crude indicator of hydration status in healthy individuals as other factors such as certain foods, medications, and vitamin supplement can affect its color. Therefore, this tool can be used as a reminder of hydration status for physicians. Drinking small amounts of fluids, using oral hydration salts to increase hydration, and consuming fruits and vegetables on a regular basis can help overcome dehydration without significantly increasing the frequency of visits to restrooms. Daily intake of at least five servings of fruits and vegetables not only improves hydration status but also provides fiber, carbohydrates, protein, and numerous vitamins, minerals, antioxidants, and other beneficial phytonutrients.

Case Illustration

Jamie is a healthy 36-year-old neurologist. She follows a vegan diet, and there is no cafeteria in her building. For lunch, she often grabs either a granola bar, potato chips, or dark chocolate bars from the lobby vending machine. She drinks a cup of coffee in the morning and a can of regular cola at work. She is often very hungry when she gets home at 6 pm and cannot stop eating until she goes to bed. Jamie often feels tired and down. She also has a hard time staying awake in the afternoon.

Question: What countermeasures could Jamie incorporate into her daily routine to help her feel less fatigued during the day, less sleepy in the afternoon, and improve her mood?

Conclusion

Improving physicians' nutritional status, in relation to their work performance, takes more than just individual physician's efforts, choices, and behaviors. Organizational policies that promote and facilitate healthy behaviors are vital to promotion and maintenance of physicians' work performance via optimizing their nutrition and hydration status. This can partly be achieved by brining into light the links between diet and physician's wellbeing among administrators, all healthcare providers, and patients and their families. Organizations that address barriers to physicians' nutrition at the individual, professional, and organizational levels, in addition to other strategies mentioned in this book, would be most successful in improving their healthcare quality and organizational performance.

References

Afaghi A, O'Connor H, Chow CM (2007). High-glycemic-index carbohydrate meals shorten sleep onset. Am J Clin Nutr 85(2):426–30.

Allen AP, Smith AP. (2015) Chewing gum: cognitive performance, mood, well-being, and associated physiology. Biomed Res Int 2015:654806.

Alomar MZ, Akkam A, Alashqar S, Eldali A (2013). Decreased hydration status of emergency department physicians and nurses by the end of their shift. Int J Emerg Med 6(1):27.

Armstrong LE, Ganio MS, Casa DJ, Lee EC, McDermott BP, Klau JF, et al.(2012) Mild dehydration affects mood in healthy young women. J Nutr 142(2):382–8.

Badawy AA, Morgan CJ, Davis NR, Dacey A (1984). High-fat diets increase tryptophan availability to the brain: importance of choice of the control diet. Biochem J 217(3):863–4.

Beilharz JE, Maniam J, Morris MJ (2015). Diet-Induced Cognitive Deficits: The Role of Fat and Sugar, Potential Mechanisms and Nutritional Interventions. Nutrients 7(8):6719–38.

Benau EM, Orloff NC, Janke EA, Serpell L, Timko CA (2014). A systematic review of the effects of experimental fasting on cognition. Appetite 77:52–61.

Benton D, Jenkins KT, Watkins HT, Young HA. (2016) Minor degree of hypohydration adversely influences cognition: a mediator analysis. Am J Clin Nutr 104(3):603–12.

Berendsen AA, Kang JH, van de Rest O, Jankovic N, Kampman E, Kiefte-de Jong JC, et al. (2017) Association of Adherence to a Healthy Diet with Cognitive Decline in European and American Older Adults: A Meta-Analysis within the CHANCES Consortium. Dement Geriatr Cogn Disord.43(3-4):215–27.

Beydoun MA, Gamaldo AA, Canas JA, Beydoun HA, Shah MT, McNeely JM, et al. (2014) Serum nutritional biomarkers and their associations with sleep among US adults in recent national surveys. Plos One 9(8):e103490.

Bhatti SK, O'Keefe JH, Lavie CJ. (2013) Coffee and tea: perks for health and longevity? Curr Opin Clin Nutr Metab Care. 16(6):688–97.

Casa DJ, Armstrong LE, Hillman SK, Montain SJ, Reiff RV, Rich BS, et al. (2000) National athletic trainers' association position statement: fluid replacement for athletes. J Athl Train 35(2):212–24.

Casperson SL, Hall C, Roemmich JN (2017). Postprandial energy metabolism and substrate oxidation in response to the inclusion of a sugar- or non-nutritive sweetened beverage with meals differing in protein content. BMC Nutr 3(1):49.

Christensen L (2001). The effect of food intake on mood. Clin Nutr 20:161–6.

Conner TS, Brookie KL, Carr AC, Mainvil LA, Vissers MC. (2017) Let them eat fruit! The effect of fruit and vegetable consumption on psychological well-being in young adults: A randomized controlled trial. PloS One 12(2):e0171206.

Cunliffe A, Obeid OA, Powell-Tuck J (1997). Post-prandial changes in measures of fatigue: effect of a mixed or a pure carbohydrate or pure fat meal. Eur J Clin Nutr 51(12):831–8.

Cunnane SC, Courchesne-Loyer A, Vandenberghe C, St-Pierre V, Fortier M, Hennebelle M, et al. (2016) Can Ketones Help Rescue Brain Fuel Supply in Later Life? Implications for Cognitive Health during Aging and the Treatment of Alzheimer's Disease. Front Mol Neurosci 9:53.

Danziger S, Levav J, Avnaim-Pesso L (2011). Extraneous factors in judicial decisions. Proc Natl Acad Sci 108(17):6889–92.

Dietz C, Dekker M. (2017) Effect of Green Tea Phytochemicals on Mood and Cognition. Curr Pharm Des. 23(19):2876–2905.

Edwards LM, Murray AJ, Holloway CJ, Carter EE, Kemp GJ, Codreanu I, et al. (2011) Short-term consumption of a high-fat diet impairs whole-body efficiency and cognitive function in sedentary men. FASEB J 25(3):1088–96.

El-Sharkawy AM, Bragg D, Watson P, Neal K, Sahota O, Maughan RJ, et al. (2016) Hydration amongst nurses and doctors on-call (the HANDS on prospective cohort study). Clin Nutr (Edinburgh, Scotland);35(4):935–42.

Fernandez-Gaxiola AC, De-Regil LM. (2011) Intermittent iron supplementation for reducing anaemia and its associated impairments in menstruating women. Cochrane Database Syst Rev (12):Cd009218.

Fischer K, Colombani PC, Langhans W, Wenk C. (2002) Carbohydrate to protein ratio in food and cognitive performance in the morning. Physiol Behavior 75(3):411–23.

Francis HM, Stevenson RJ (2011). Higher reported saturated fat and refined sugar intake is associated with reduced hippocampal-dependent memory and sensitivity to interoceptive signals. Behavioral Neurosci 125(6):943–55.

Galioto R, Spitznagel MB (2016). The Effects of Breakfast and Breakfast Composition on Cognition in Adults. Adv Nutr (Bethesda, MD);7(3):576s–89s.

Ganio MS, Armstrong LE, Casa DJ, McDermott BP, Lee EC, Yamamoto LM, et al. (2011) Mild dehydration impairs cognitive performance and mood of men. Br J Nutr 106(10):1535–43.

Grandner MA, Kripke DF, Naidoo N, Langer RD. (2010) Relationships among dietary nutrients and subjective sleep, objective sleep, and napping in women. Sleep Med 11(2):180–4.

Grant CL, Dorrian J, Coates AM, Pajcin M, Kennaway DJ, Wittert GA, et al. (2017) The impact of meal timing on performance, sleepiness, gastric upset, and hunger during simulated night shift. Ind Health 55(5):423–36.

Grosso G, Micek A, Castellano S, Pajak A, Galvano F. (2016) Coffee, tea, caffeine and risk of depression: A systematic review and dose-response meta-analysis of observational studies. Mol Nutr Food Res 60(1):223–34.

Gupta CC, Dorrian J, Grant CL, Pajcin M, Coates AM, Kennaway DJ, et al. (2017) It's not just what you eat but when: The impact of eating a meal during simulated shift work on driving performance. Chronobiol Intl 34(1):66–77.

Hamidi MS, Boggild MK, Cheung AM (2016). Running on empty: a review of nutrition and physicians' well-being. Postgrad Med J 92(1090):478–81.

Hendy HM (2012). Which comes first in food-mood relationships, foods or moods? Appetite 58(2):771–5.

Holloway CJ, Cochlin LE, Emmanuel Y, Murray A, Codreanu I, Edwards LM, et al. (2011) A high-fat diet impairs cardiac high-energy phosphate metabolism and cognitive function in healthy human subjects. Am J Clin Nutr 93(4):748–55.

Horne J, Anderson C, Platten C. (2008) Sleep extension versus nap or coffee, within the context of 'sleep debt'. J Sleep Res 17(4): 432–6.

Houssein M, Lopes P, Fagnoni B, Ahmaidi S, Yonis SM, Lepretre PM (2016). Hydration: The New FIFA World Cup's Challenge for Referee Decision Making? J Athl Train 51(3):264–6.

Howatson G, Bell PG, Tallent J, Middleton B, McHugh MP, Ellis J. (2012) Effect of tart cherry juice (Prunus cerasus) on melatonin levels and enhanced sleep quality. Eur J Nutr 51(8):909–16.

Institute of Medicine. (2005) Water. Dietary Reference Intakes for Water, Potassium, Sodium, Chloride, and Sulfate. The National Academies Press, Washington, DC

Jacka FN, O'Neil A, Opie R, Itsiopoulos C, Cotton S, Mohebbi M, et al. (2017) A randomised controlled trial of dietary improvement for adults with major depression (the 'SMILES' trial). BMC Med 15(1):23.

Jones AD (2017). Food Insecurity and Mental Health Status: A Global Analysis of 149 Countries. Am J Prev Med 53(2):264–273.

Journel M, Chaumontet C, Darcel N, Fromentin G, Tome D (2012). Brain responses to high-protein diets. Adv Nutr (Bethesda, MD);3(3):322–9.

Kang JH, Ascherio A, Grodstein F. (2005) Fruit and vegetable consumption and cognitive decline in aging women. Ann Neurol 57(5):713–20.

Kassam A, Horton J, Shoimer I, Patten S (2015). Predictors of Well-Being in Resident Physicians: A Descriptive and Psychometric Study. J Grad Med Educ 7(1):70–4.

Kniffin KM, Wansink B, Devine CM, Sobal J (2015). Eating Together at the Firehouse: How Workplace Commensality Relates to the Performance of Firefighters. Human Performance 28(4):281–306.

Knuppel A, Shipley MJ, Llewellyn CH, Brunner EJ (2017). Sugar intake from sweet food and beverages, common mental disorder and depression: prospective findings from the Whitehall II study. Sci Rep 7(1):6287.

Kwan RM, Thomas S, Mir MA (1986). Effects of a low carbohydrate isoenergetic diet on sleep behavior and pulmonary functions in healthy female adult humans. J Nutr 116(12):2393–402.

Leedo E, Beck AM, Astrup A, Lassen AD (2017). The effectiveness of healthy meals at work on reaction time, mood and dietary intake: a randomised cross-over study in daytime and shift workers at an university hospital. Br J Nutr 118(2):121–9.

Lemaire JB, Wallace JE, Dinsmore K, Lewin AM, Ghali WA, Roberts D (2010). Physician nutrition and cognition during work hours: effect of a nutrition based intervention. BMC Health Serv Res 10:241.

Lemaire JB, Wallace JE, Dinsmore K, Roberts D (2011). Food for thought: an exploratory study of how physicians experience poor workplace nutrition. Nutr J 10(1):18.

Lesser LI, Cohen DA, Brook RH (2012). Changing eating habits for the medical profession. JAMA 308(10):983–4.

Lin HH, Tsai PS, Fang SC, Liu JF. (2011) Effect of kiwifruit consumption on sleep quality in adults with sleep problems. Asia Pacific J Clin Nutr 20(2):169–74.

Lindseth GN, Lindseth PD, Jensen WC, Petros TV, Helland BD, Fossum DL (2011). Dietary Effects on Cognition and Pilots' Flight Performance. The International Journal of Aviation Psychology 21(3):269–82.

Lindseth PD, Lindseth GN, Petros TV, Jensen WC, Caspers J (2013). Effects of hydration on cognitive function of pilots. Military Medicine 178(7):792–8.

Lloyd HM, Green MW, Rogers PJ (1994). Mood and cognitive performance effects of isocaloric lunches differing in fat and carbohydrate content. Physiol Behav 56(1):51–7.

Lomagno KA, Hu F, Riddell LJ, Booth AO, Szymlek-Gay EA, Nowson CA, et al. (2014) Increasing iron and zinc in pre-menopausal women and its effects on mood and cognition: a systematic review. Nutrients 6(11):5117–41.

Long SJ, Benton D. (2013) Effects of vitamin and mineral supplementation on stress, mild psychiatric symptoms, and mood in non-clinical samples: a meta-analysis. Psychosomat Med 75(2):144–53.

Lowden A, Holmback U, Akerstedt T, Forslund J, Lennernas M, Forslund A (2004). Performance and sleepiness during a 24 h wake in constant conditions are affected by diet. Biol Psychol 65(3):251–63.

McCarty DE. (2010) Resolution of hypersomnia following identification and treatment of vitamin d deficiency. J Clin Sleep Med 6(6):605–8.

McCarty DE, Reddy A, Keigley Q, Kim PY, Cohen S, Marino AA. (2013) Nonspecific pain is a marker for hypovitaminosis D in patients undergoing evaluation for sleep disorders: a pilot study. Nat Sci Sleep 5:37–42.

McCarty DE, Reddy A, Keigley Q, Kim PY, Marino AA. (2012) Vitamin D, race, and excessive daytime sleepiness. J Clin Sleep Med 8(6):693–7.

McClung JP, Karl JP, Cable SJ, Williams KW, Young AJ, Lieberman HR. (2009) Longitudinal decrements in iron status during military training in female soldiers. Br J Nutr 102(4):605–9.

McHill AW, Phillips AJ, Czeisler CA, Keating L, Yee K, Barger LK, et al. (2017) Later circadian timing of food intake is associated with increased body fat. Am J Clin Nutr. 2017 Nov;106(5):1213–1219.

McHill AW, Smith BJ, Wright KP, Jr. (2014) Effects of caffeine on skin and core temperatures, alertness, and recovery sleep during circadian misalignment. Journal of Biological Rhythms 29(2):131–43.

Masento NA, Golightly M, Field DT, Butler LT, van Reekum CM (2014). Effects of hydration status on cognitive performance and mood. Br J Nutr 111(10):1841–52.

Morris MC, Tangney CC, Wang Y, Sacks FM, Barnes LL, Bennett DA, et al. (2015) MIND diet slows cognitive decline with aging. Alzheimer's & Dementia 11(9):1015–22.

Morris MC, Wang Y, Barnes LL, Bennett DA, Dawson-Hughes B, Booth SL. (2018) Nutrients and bioactives in green leafy vegetables and cognitive decline: Prospective study. Neurology. Jan 16;90(3):e214–e222.

Mota MC, De-Souza DA, Rossato LT, Silva CM, Araujo MB, Tufik S, et al. (2013) Dietary patterns, metabolic markers and subjective sleep measures in resident physicians. Chronobiology International 30(8):1032–41.

Muller K, Libuda L, Terschlusen AM, Kersting M (2013). A review of the effects of lunch on adults' short-term cognitive functioning. Can J Diet Pract Res 74(4):181–8.

Nedeltcheva AV, Kilkus JM, Imperial J, Kasza K, Schoeller DA, Penev PD (2009). Sleep curtailment is accompanied by increased intake of calories from snacks. Am J Clin Nutr 89(1):126–33.

Neely G, Landstrom U, Bystrom M, Junberger ML (2004). Missing a meal: effects on alertness during sedentary work. Nutr Health 18(1):37–47.

Nevanpera NJ, Hopsu L, Kuosma E, Ukkola O, Uitti J, Laitinen JH (2012). Occupational burnout, eating behavior, and weight among working women. Am J Clin Nutr 95(4):934–43.

Nguyen B, Ding D, Mihrshahi S. (2017) Fruit and vegetable consumption and psychological distress: cross-sectional and longitudinal analyses based on a large Australian sample. BMJ Open 7(3):e014201.

Noorwali EA, Cade JE, Burley VJ, Hardie LJ. (2018) The relationship between sleep duration and fruit/vegetable intakes in UK adults: a cross-sectional study from the National Diet and Nutrition Survey. BMJ Open 8(4):e020810.

O'Connor DL, Blake J, Bell R, Bowen A, Callum J, Fenton S, et al. (2016) Canadian Consensus on Female Nutrition: Adolescence, Reproduction, Menopause, and Beyond. J Obstet Gynaecol Can 38(6):508–54.e18.

Oosterman JE, Kalsbeek A, la Fleur SE, Belsham DD. (2015) Impact of nutrients on circadian rhythmicity. American Journal of Physiology Regulatory, Integrative and Comparative Physiology 308(5):R337–50.

Opie RS, Itsiopoulos C, Parletta N, Sanchez-Villegas A, Akbaraly TN, Ruusunen A, et al. (2017) Dietary recommendations for the prevention of depression. Nutr Neurosci Apr;20(3):161–71.

Panossian LA, Veasey SC. (2012) Daytime sleepiness in obesity: mechanisms beyond obstructive sleep apneaDOUBLEHYPHENa review. Sleep 35(5):605–15.

Pardi D, Buman M, Black J, Lammers GJ, Zeitzer JM (2017) Eating Decisions Based on Alertness Levels After a Single Night of Sleep Manipulation: A Randomized Clinical Trial. Sleep 40(2).

Pauling L (1968). Orthomolecular psychiatry. Varying the concentrations of substances normally present in the human body may control mental disease. Science (New York, NY) 160(3825):265–71.

Paz A, Berry EM (1997). Effect of meal composition on alertness and performance of hospital night-shift workers. Do mood and performance have different determinants? Ann Nutr Metab 41(5):291–8.

Pigeon WR, Carr M, Gorman C, Perlis ML. (2010) Effects of a tart cherry juice beverage on the sleep of older adults with insomnia: a pilot study. Journal of Medicinal Food 13(3):579–83.

Popper CW. (2014) Single-micronutrient and broad-spectrum micronutrient approaches for treating mood disorders in youth and adults. Child Adolesc Psychiatr Clin N Am 23(3):591–672.

Pressel DM (2014). Theory and practice of free food in hospitals: a guide for the hungry hospitalist. Hosp Pediatr 4(5):328–30.

Reyner LA, Horne JA (1997). Suppression of sleepiness in drivers: combination of caffeine with a short nap. Psychophysiology 34(6):721–5.

Reyner LA, Wells SJ, Mortlock V, Horne JA (2012). 'Post-lunch' sleepiness during prolonged, monotonous driving - effects of meal size. Physiol Behav 105(4):1088–91.

Ruxton CHS. (2008) The impact of caffeine on mood, cognitive function, performance and hydration: a review of benefits and risks. Nutr Bull 33(1):15–25.

St-Onge MP, Ard J, Baskin ML, Chiuve SE, Johnson HM, Kris-Etherton P, et al. (2017) Meal Timing and Frequency: Implications for Cardiovascular Disease Prevention: A Scientific Statement From the American Heart Association. Circulation 135(9):e96–e121.

St-Onge MP, Mikic A, Pietrolungo CE (2016). Effects of Diet on Sleep Quality. Adv Nutr (Bethesda, MD);7(5):938–49.

Sarris J, Logan AC, Akbaraly TN, Amminger GP, Balanza-Martinez V, Freeman MP, et al. (2015) Nutritional medicine as mainstream in psychiatry. Lancet Psychiatry 2(3):271–4.

Scherr RE, Laugero KD, Graham DJ, Cunningham BT, Jahns L, Lora KR, et al. (2017) Innovative Techniques for Evaluating Behavioral Nutrition Interventions. Adv Nutr (Bethesda, MD);8(1):113–25.

Sketchley-Kaye K, Jenks R, Miles C, Johnson AJ. (2011) Chewing gum modifies state anxiety and alertness under conditions of social stress. Nutr Neurosci 14(6):237–42.

Schweitzer PK, Randazzo AC, Stone K, Erman M, Walsh JK. (2006) Laboratory and field studies of naps and caffeine as practical countermeasures for sleep-wake problems associated with night work. Sleep 29(1):39–50.

Solomon AW, Kirwan CJ, Alexander ND, Nimako K, Jurukov A, Forth RJ, et al. (2010) Urine output on an intensive care unit: case-control study. BMJ (Clin Res Ed);341:c6761.

Spring B, Maller O, Wurtman J, Digman L, Cozolino L (1982). Effects of protein and carbohydrate meals on mood and performance: interactions with sex and age. J Psychiatric Res 17(2):155–67.

Symmonds M, Emmanuel JJ, Drew ME, Batterham RL, Dolan RJ (2010). Metabolic state alters economic decision making under risk in humans. PloS One 5(6):e11090.

Tryon MS, Carter CS, Decant R, Laugero KD (2013). Chronic stress exposure may affect the brain's response to high calorie food cues and predispose to obesogenic eating habits. Physiol Behav 2013;120:233–42.

Vaucher P, Druais PL, Waldvogel S, Favrat B. (2012) Effect of iron supplementation on fatigue in nonanemic menstruating women with low ferritin: a randomized controlled trial. CMAJ 184(11):1247–54.

Wade R (2012). Title: Everyone Needs Fluids, In response to: Urine output on an intensive care unit: case-control study

2012. Available from: http://www.bmj.com/content/341/bmj.c6761/rapid-responses.

Wansink B, Tal A, Shimizu M (2012). First foods most: after 18-hour fast, people drawn to starches first and vegetables last. Arch Inter Med 172(12):961–3.

Wells AS, Read NW, Uvnas-Moberg K, Alster P (1997). Influences of fat and carbohydrate on postprandial sleepiness, mood, and hormones. Physiol Behav 61(5):679–86.

Wilhelmus MM, Hay JL, Zuiker RG, Okkerse P, Perdrieu C, Sauser J, et al. (2017) Effects of a single, oral 60 mg caffeine dose on attention in healthy adult subjects. J Psychopharmacol (Oxford, England);31(2):222–32.

Wing RR, Vazquez JA, Ryan CM. (1995) Cognitive effects of ketogenic weight-reducing diets. Int J Obes Relat Metab Disord 19(11):811–6.

Yaroch AL, Pinard CA (2012). Are the hungry more at risk for eating calorie-dense nutrient-poor foods? Arch Intern Med 172(12):963–4.

Zhou J, Kim JE, Armstrong CL, Chen N, Campbell WW. (2016) Higher-protein diets improve indexes of sleep in energy-restricted overweight and obese adults: results from 2 randomized controlled trials. Am J Clin Nutr 103(3):766–74.

Chapter 15
Sleep

Caroline Uchechi Okorie

Sleep Physiology

Not too long ago, scientists thought sleep to be a passive state, reflecting only the absence of wakefulness. However, sleep is now known to be a dynamic collection of physiologic processes under neurobiological regulation. These processes play a role in different aspects of human health and functioning, including growing, healing, and learning (Carskadon and Dement 2005; Grandner 2017; Luyster et al. 2012). Normal sleep is made of two main types: non-rapid eye movement (NREM) and rapid eye movement (REM) sleep. In a well-rested, healthy adult, NREM and REM sleep alternate throughout the night in an approximate 90-minute cycle, about 4–6 times per night (Carskadon and Dement 2005; Luyster et al. 2012). NREM sleep is now divided into three stages: N1, N2, and N3 or slow-wave sleep (Carskadon and Dement 2005). N1 and N2 sleep consist of lighter sleep with

C. U. Okorie (✉)
Lucile Packard Children's Hospital and Stanford Children's Health, Department of Pediatrics, Division of Pulmonary, Asthma and Sleep Medicine, Palo Alto, CA, USA

© Springer Nature Switzerland AG 2019   255
L. Weiss Roberts, M. Trockel (eds.),
The Art and Science of Physician Wellbeing,
https://doi.org/10.1007/978-3-319-42135-3_15

low arousal thresholds, while N3 sleep is characterized by a deep sleep with marked reductions in sympathetic activity resulting in decreased heart rate, blood pressure, and slower, stable breathing (Luyster et al. 2012). Slow-wave sleep is considered important to the restorative process of sleep and in memory consolidation. Low amounts of N3 sleep have been associated with increased cardiovascular disease risk (Fung et al. 2011). REM sleep is characterized by atonic muscles with occasional twitching, cardiorespiratory irregularities and most notably, dreaming (Carskadon and Dement 2005; Luyster et al. 2012).

There are several factors that modify sleep stage distribution, including age, prior sleep history, circadian rhythms, temperature, medications, pathology, sleep-disordered breathing, and sleep fragmentation. It is normal to have multiple brief arousals during sleep (up to 5% of the total night). These are often too short for a person to remember and tend to happen at the time of REM sleep transitions. These arousals increase in frequency as we age while our total sleep needs tend to decrease. While babies sleep for the majority of the day, young and middle-aged adults typically require 7–9 hours of sleep a day (Carskadon and Dement 2005; Hirshkowitz et al. 2015; Mathur and Douglas 1995). In adults, both short sleep (<6 hours per day) and long sleep (>9 hours per day) are associated with negative health consequences (Centers for Disease Control and Prevention (CDC) 2011; Kalmbach et al. 2017; Luyster et al. 2012).

Table 15.1 represents the recommended sleep hours over a 24-hour period by age, as recommended by the National Sleep Foundation. The last column represents the hours that may still be appropriate

Regulation of Sleep

Much like the body works to regulate core body temperature, there is a homeostatic process that regulates sleep. The strength of this process is dependent upon the amount of time between the last sleep period. The pressure to sleep increases as the person remains awake. With prolonged sleep

TABLE 15.1 Sleep duration recommendations (in a 24-hour period)

Age	Recommended hours (hours)	May still be appropriate (hours)
Newborn (0–3 months)	14–17	11–13, 18–19
Infant (4–11 months)	12–15	10–11, 16–18
Toddler (1–2 years)	11–14	9–10, 15–16
Preschool (3–5 years)	10–13	8–9, 14
School age (6–13 years)	9–11	7–8, 12
Teen (14–17 years)	8–10	7, 11
Young adult (18–25 years)	7–9	6, 10–11
Adult (26–64 years)	7–9	6, 10
Older adult (65+ years)	7–8	5–6, 9

Source: National Sleep Foundation

deprivation, the accumulation of "sleep debt" is often hard to fight, and the drive to sleep can overcome the person's ability to remain awake. In the two-process model, the circadian system, centered in the suprachiasmatic nucleus (SCN) of the brain, will send signals to the pineal gland to secrete melatonin. Melatonin then signals the brain to move to a sleep state. Typically, levels are low during the day and increase in the evening to promote sleep (Carskadon and Dement 2005; Kryger et al. 2015; Luyster et al. 2012). The timing of this is dependent upon genetics as well as environmental cues (light exposure) and volitional cues (using an alarm clock). Light exposure serves as one of the most powerful stimulants to entrain the circadian clock. Lack of light/dark input, such as with an individual who is blind, can result in dysregulated sleep/wake cycle (Luyster et al. 2012; Sheldon et al. 2014).

Circadian Variability and Chronotypes

Chronotypes determine the optimal time of day for mental and physical performance as well as alertness and sleep. Morning chronotypes, or "larks," tend to prefer to rise earlier in the morning and go to bed earlier. These are the "morning people" who feel most alert at the start of the day. Evening chronotypes or "owls" tend to prefer going to bed later and rising later the following morning. This group tends to feel more productive and creative late at night and will often still stay up late and wake up early the next morning to go to school or work. This builds sleep debt over time and often they need to "catch up" on sleep over the weekend (Taillard et al. 2003). Most people exist somewhere on the spectrum between the two extremes, and one can determine natural tendencies with a sleep diary when the schedule is not driven by societal pressures of work or obligation. Hospital norms and practices tend to favor the morning chronotype with early OR times and morning rounds. Night owls may be labeled "lazy" for being a little less alert in the early morning, when in truth they are just functioning outside of their natural circadian rhythm.

Effects of Sleep Loss

With sleep playing a restorative role in overall health and learning, it is not surprising that inadequate sleep is associated with negative health and cognitive consequences (Besedovsky et al. 2012; Luyster et al. 2012). Studies with healthy young adults show that chronic sleep deprivation can have significant detrimental effects. People who are chronically sleep deprived (getting only 6 or less hours of sleep each night for 2 weeks) experience deterioration of performance, memory, and cognitive function. These detriments are similar to those seen in acute sleep loss or loss of one night of sleep (Van Dongen et al. 2003).

When considering the sleep-deprived human brain, scientists have identified the impact of sleep deprivation across various functional domains, including attention, working memory and memory consolidation, and negative and positive emotional processing. The sleep-deprived brain will suffer attention loss, manifesting as response failures or errors of omission. These are attributed to "microsleeps" which are brief moments when the brain will overwhelm even volitional attempts to remain awake, and sleep will inevitably occur (Krause et al. 2017; Kryger et al. 2015; Luyster et al. 2012; Poudel et al. 2014). Fatigue, engagement in a monotonous task, and times of natural circadian alertness dips (i.e., afternoon hours after lunch) may increase the risk of microsleeps, despite a person's best efforts to remain awake. Decreased working memory will often manifest as inability to recall a name or the reason one walked into a room. Neuroimaging research has shown that sleep-deprived individuals also have diminished hippocampal-dependent learning, important for neuroplasticity, and the ability to solidify learning of new concepts and procedures. Again, much of learning consolidation happens in slow-wave sleep, so loss of this type of sleep specifically exacerbates the problem (Krause et al. 2017). Sleep-deprived individuals have more difficulty distinguishing rewards/incentives appropriately. It becomes hard to appropriately determine the reward value of an item or action. For a sleep-deprived individual, low-effort rewards (e.g., grabbing a donut sitting at the nurses' station) bring more joy compared to high-effort rewards (e.g., walking over to the cafeteria for a more balanced meal). Sleep-deprived people not only show a decreased mood, they also demonstrate impairment in emotional discrimination. This can be why an intended neutral comment or facial expression by a colleague can be perceived as threatening by a sleep-deprived intern. There is an inaccurate perception of negative threat due to flattened and saturated responses to emotional stimuli by the amygdala, insula, and cingulate in the brain (Krause et al. 2017).

Sleep deprivation is associated with higher prevalence of medical errors, functional impairment, and burnout among physicians (Howard 2005; Olson et al. 2009). A study in 2012 focused on surgical residents, measuring their sleep/wake patterns and assessing their mental effectiveness over the course of 2 weeks. Residents were found to be fatigued 48% of the time and significantly impaired 27% of their time awake with the mean daily sleep time of 5.3 hours. Night-float residents were even more fatigued (McCormick et al. 2012). Another study found that surgeons and obstetricians who were allowed less than 6 hours of sleep opportunity had triple the complication rates when performing elective procedures the following day (Rothschild et al. 2009). It is important to note that not only sleep deprivation but also sleep fragmentation will result in similar negative cognitive effects (Bonnet and Arand 2003), and both are associated with depression and lower quality of life among physicians. Chronically sleep-deprived people underreport their impairment with reports of sleepiness levels (by the Epworth Sleepiness Scale) incongruent with the objectively observed sleepiness seen on a Multiple Sleep Latency Test (MSLT) or the Maintenance of Wakefulness Test (MWT) (Belayachi et al. 2013; Kalmbach et al. 2017).

The earlier discussions about trainee wellness revolved around duty hours, hoping that restricting work hours would have a positive effect on resident wellbeing, sleep-related impairment, and even patient safety. The first major duty-hour restrictions, including the 80-hour limit for weekly hours, were implemented in 2003. Analysis of resident work time and sleep time shows that when comparing data from 1999 to 2009, there was a significant decrease in weekly work hours and an increase in weekly sleep hours. While considered encouraging, residents still reported sleeping on average 40.8–46 hours per week, or 5.7–6.5 hours a night. This is well below recommended nightly sleep times as noted earlier. Residents may have less time at work; however, they are not spending all the extra time sleeping due to a variety of reasons (Baldwin et al. 2010). Further duty-hour restrictions in

2011 limited intern work hours to a maximum of 16 continuous hours. However, this seemed to have perceived negative consequences in resident education and clinical care, and these restrictions were lifted in 2017 (Bolster and Rourke 2015; Jamal et al. 2014; Parshuram et al. 2015). There are some studies that suggest improvement in quality of life and reduced burnout with hour limits; however, more data are needed.

Insomnia (Acute and Chronic)

There is an important distinction to be made between insomnia and sleep loss. Sleep loss, as discussed above, is when there is a drive to sleep but there is a lack of sleep opportunity. Insomnia differs in that there is plenty of opportunity to sleep but there is a decreased ability. The distinction is important as the effective intervention will be different. With acute insomnia, typically, adopting some healthy sleep habits may be sufficient to overcome insomnia. The American Academy of Sleep Medicine offers these sleep hygiene tips:

- Avoid alerting agents, such as caffeine, just before desired sleep time.
- Keep a consistent wake/sleep schedule (i.e., wake up around the same time each and every day, even on vacation or weekends)
- Plan for at least 7 hours of sleep.
- Use the bed only for sleep and sex.
- Go to bed only when sleepy. If unable to fall asleep within 20 minutes of lying in bed, get out of bed.
- Establish a "wind down" routine to facilitate relaxation before bed.
- Avoid bright light and screens/blue light (TV, phones, tablets) at least 30 minutes before bedtime.
- Maintain a quiet, cool, relaxing sleeping space
- Avoid large meals or alcohol right before bedtime
- Maintain a healthy diet and regular exercise schedule

Chronic insomnia is when symptoms of insomnia persist for at least 3 months. Characteristic symptoms of chronic insomnia include daytime cognitive impairment and foul mood. The etiology of chronic insomnia is typically multifactorial with psychophysiological contributors. The gold standard treatment for insomnia is Cognitive Behavioral Therapy for Insomnia (CBT-I). This treatment focuses on the behavioral and cognitive factors contributing to a person's inability to fall or stay asleep. This treatment is different from psychotherapy and goes beyond the abovementioned healthy sleep habits. It utilizes tools such as sleep restriction, bright light therapy, and even sleep aids to help reverse habits and negative associations that inhibit a person's ability to sleep. Studies have shown face-to-face therapy with a specialist is the most effective method of CBT-I; however, there are online resources available when time and money constraints make face-to-face therapy difficult.

Stress and Burnout

Stress is an often-cited cause for chronic insomnia, so treatments specific to helping physicians deal with stress, and symptoms of burnout may be important interventions to treat insomnia. Excessive stress is also associated with sleep disruption, excessive fatigue, depression, and burnout. Burnout is a work-related syndrome involving emotional exhaustion, depersonalization, and reduced personal accomplishment (Maslach and Jackson 1981). The literature shows rates of burnout that exceed 50% among physicians in training and physicians in practice. Burnout is associated with medical errors, decreased patient satisfaction, and increased healthcare costs. Excessive workloads, including long work hours and frequent overnight call or weekend duties, contribute to the occurrence of burnout, depression, and decreased professional satisfaction (Avidan 2013; Eddy 2005; Papp et al. 2004; Schrijver et al. 2016; Tucker et al. 2015; West et al. 2018; West et al. 2009). As described above, addressing duty hours has been in part to address high burnout rates in physicians in training. The results have been mixed when looking at reduced work hours and medical error rates, with the positive effects most obvious in junior physicians. Encouragingly, reducing physician work hours in intensive work areas (i.e., the critical care unit) has been associated with reduced burnout (Kalmbach et al. 2017; Landrigan et al. 2004; Regehr et al. 2014; West et al. 2016).

A recent meta-analysis of published controlled interventions demonstrated that physician-directed interventions focused on themes of mindfulness-based stress reduction, opportunities for self-care, and workshops on coping and reframing exercises, while organizational-directed interventions tended to focus on workload and scheduling while a few aimed to promote communication and a connectedness. Organization-directed approaches demonstrated the largest effect size; however, evidence-based, individually directed strategies still showed some benefits. These include mindfulness-based stress reduction, meditation, communication skills training, practices to increase resilience, self-compassion training, exercise programs, coaching programs, and participation in groups to promote connectedness and community (Panagioti et al. 2017; Regehr et al. 2014; West et al. 2018; West et al. 2016).

Causes of Excessive Daytime Sleepiness

Studies have shown that a significant proportion of physicians demonstrate levels of sleepiness similar to that of patients with sleep-disordered breathing or even narcolepsy (Avidan 2013). As discussed above, insufficient sleep and fragmented sleep due to environmental and intrinsic factors may play a role in excessive daytime sleepiness; however, it is important to consider additional primary sleep disorders. Treatable sleep disorders include sleep-disordered breathing (e.g., obstructive sleep apnea), circadian rhythm dysfunction, restless legs syndrome, and insomnia (discussed above), as well as narcolepsy, or idiopathic hypersomnia.

Sleep-Disordered Breathing

Sleep-disordered breathing is another known cause of fragmented sleep and is considered relatively common in the USA. Recent data suggest that up to 34% of men and 17% of women have obstructive sleep apnea (OSA) that can be seen on polysomnogram (Peppard et al. 2013). Sleep-disordered breathing refers to a wide spectrum of sleep-related breathing abnormalities. This can include upper airway obstruction leading to OSA (lack of airflow in spite of continuing breathing effort) as well as central disorders causing central sleep apnea (lack of airflow without a breathing effort), obesity hypoventilation syndrome, and hypoventilation secondary to muscle weakness or respiratory depression from medication. When humans fall asleep, the muscles that maintain the airway relax and can even completely collapse, causing an apnea. In the event of a closed airway, the brain will instinctually increase the breathing effort, hoping to overcome the obstruction. The increased breathing effort may overcome the obstruction, or the brain will cause an arousal to increase airway tone and open up the airway. These arousals can be brief; however, they bring a person out of deep sleep, reducing time in restorative sleep. In addition to excessive daytime sleepiness and fatigue, symptoms of sleep apnea can include restless sleep, morning headaches, snoring, dry mouth, or a sore throat. Obese patients and nonobese patients with craniofacial features consistent with a narrow upper airway (e.g., retrognathia, high arched palate, large tongue, chronic nasal congestion) are at increased risk for OSA. Comorbidities such as allergies and gastroesophageal reflux can exacerbate already existing issues. Untreated OSA is associated with significant negative health effects, including cardiovascular disease, poor diabetes control, and even long-term cognitive impairment. Anyone with possible OSA should be evaluated by a sleep specialist as soon as possible. A sleep study may reveal the diagnosis. Treatments include positive airway pressure therapy, oral appliances (such as those that hold the lower jaw and/or tongue forward), and surgical intervention to widen the airway or realign the anatomy and relieve upper airway obstruction.

Circadian Rhythm Dysfunction

Circadian rhythm dysfunction can be intrinsic due to neurological dysfunction, or it can be precipitated by exogenous factors, such as shift work. Shift work disorder occurs when a person is expected to stay awake and work at the time his brain would prefer to sleep and tries to sleep at a time that brain would rather be awake. This is commonly seen in physicians working night shifts or even in a natural "night owl" forced to adhere to an early morning operating schedule. Entraining the circadian clock to better fit the required work schedule is the best treatment for circadian rhythm dysfunction. The combined use of strategic bright light exposure (and avoidance) in addition to exogenous melatonin and a regular sleep/wake schedule can effectively shift the internal circadian clock to better match the work schedule. This can prove more challenging in those with a rotating or changing shift time (e.g., emergency medicine or ICU shifts); however, shifting schedules in a clockwise fashion (meaning the next shift will start later than the previous) will make the transition easier. Strategic use of caffeine (i.e., drinking coffee upon waking to overcome sleep inertia and avoiding caffeine within 5–7 hours of desired bedtime) and even pharmacologic therapy with modafinil or armodafinil have been used to help increase alertness and performance in people with shift work circadian rhythm disorder (see Table 15.2).

Table 15.2 Countermeasures for sleepiness and fatigue

Goal	Intervention	Details/recommendations	Barriers/considerations
Increasing alertness	Caffeine use	Strategic use of caffeine can be an effective way to increase alertness.	Side effects of gastrointestinal disturbance, increased need for urination, and feelings of anxiety/jitteriness can affect procedural tasks
	Available in coffee, tea, pills, energy drinks, soda, etc.	Coffee/tea (which also contain phytonutrients) are ideal sources over soda/pills	
	Effective dose range, 40–400 mg (depends on body composition/age)	Consider green tea over coffee for sustained alertness with reduced jitteriness. L-theanine and EGCG can have effects of improved mood	
	Tea/soda, 15–70 mg Coffee, 90–200 mg Doses > 600 mg are associated with anxiety/jitteriness	Caffeine typically takes 15–30 minutes to take effect and 60–90 minutes to reach peak effect. Half-life is 2.5–6 hours Increasing core body temp with caffeine and warm drinks/foods also reduces sleepiness	
	Power nap	Short 20-minute nap taken at times of sleepiness, ideally done before complete exhaustion Can drink caffeine just before ("caf-nap") for synergistic effect when you wake up	Work schedule limits time for naps. Sleep-deprived individuals may find it hard to keep the nap short. Long naps lead to sleep inertia, which causes drowsiness

Bright light exposure	Bright light can have immediate alerting effects. Bright light exposure is also important when entraining your circadian rhythm by signaling to your pineal gland to stop secreting melatonin	Avoid bright light 60 minutes to desired sleep time. For instance, when coming home from a night shift, block morning light with dark sunglasses
Prescription alerting agents (i.e., modafinil/armodafinil)	Approved for excessive sleepiness associated with circadian rhythm dysfunction, shift work type	Requires a prescription. May mask impaired cognitive performance caused by sleep deprivation. Effects of long-term use in physician population are unclear
Stay active	Using a standing desk or maintaining movement will help increase body temperature and increase alertness	Difficult during times when sustained sitting or standing still (e.g., long surgery or marathon charting) is needed
Music	Use upbeat/stimulating music to improve alertness	May be difficult in areas/times where listening to music is not professional or feasible

(continued)

TABLE 15.2 (continued)

Goal	Intervention	Details/recommendations	Barriers/considerations
Increasing sleep duration and reducing sleep disruption	Improved sleep hygiene habits	Keep a regular sleep/wake schedule, sleep in a cool, dark, quiet environment; avoid screen time 60 minutes before sleep time; maintain a regular exercise schedule each week; plan for 7 hours of sleep each night	
	Use of sleep aids (hypnotic medications, like Ambien)	Good for short-term acute insomnia	Potential side effects of daytime grogginess, abnormal sleep behaviors in some situations
	Cognitive Behavioral Therapy for Insomnia	Meet with behavioral sleep medicine specialist or consider online or self-directed courses	Time constraints for the busy physician may reduce ability to attend therapy sessions
	Evaluation and treatment of primary sleep disorders (e.g. sleep apnea, restless legs syndrome, narcolepsy, insomnia, etc.)	Meet with a sleep medicine specialist. You may need a sleep study to assess for sleep-disordered breathing or abnormal sleep architecture	Time constraints for the busy physician, unwillingness to be tested, or diagnosed with a sleep disorder. Unwillingness to undergo treatment (e.g, use a CPAP machine)

| *Entrainment of circadian clock to better match work schedule* | Strategic bright light exposure and bright light avoidance | Use bright light (natural or from a light box) within 15 minutes after desired wake time and intermittently for 20–30 minute intervals during desired wake time. Avoid bright light or screen time 60 minutes before desired sleep time. When leaving the hospital after a night shift, wear dark sunglasses to minimize exposure to morning light. Pair this with melatonin use | Variable availability of bright light in the hospital at desired time. Computer use (EHR) too close to the time of desired sleep |
| | Melatonin | Melatonin 3–5 mg at 1.5–2 hours before desired sleep time Pair this with bright light therapy noted above | |

(continued)

Table 15.2 (continued)

Goal	Intervention	Details/recommendations	Barriers/considerations
Overall wellbeing and safety	Regular exercise	Maintaining a regular exercise regimen at least 3x/week (not too close to sleep time) is good for overall health and energy	Time constraints and fatigue may discourage sticking to a regular schedule
	Healthful eating	Avoiding high fat/high carbs, especially in the middle of the night. Avoiding eating between 2 and 5 am during your natural circadian dip in metabolism Warm drinks/foods to increase core body temperature also reduce sleepiness	Sleep-deprived brain may crave unhealthful options. Decision to eat healthy may need to be made in advance to avoid impulse decisions
	Avoiding driving while drowsy	Physicians should avoid driving while under the influence of sleep deprivation. Consider carpooling, using public transportation or a ride-sharing/taxi service. Live close to work if possible. Take a power nap just before driving home. Use caffeine strategically (well before you need to drive) to avoid its peak effects when you make it home and are ready to sleep	May be difficult to live close to work. Expense of taxi/ride sharing

Restless Legs Syndrome and Periodic Limb Disorder

Restless legs syndrome (RLS) is a condition characterized by an uncomfortable or painful sensation in the legs/arms and an almost irresistible urge to move legs/arms to achieve relief. The uncomfortable sensation can prevent sleep, despite the patient's level of fatigue. This is different from periodic limb movement disorder (PLMD), which is a repetitive cramping or kicking of the legs while the patient is asleep. The movement or cramping can cause premature awakenings, leading to additional sleep disruption. The treatment for both RLS and PLMD can range from daily exercise, to iron supplementation, to use of dopamine agonists or opioids. The diagnosis of RLS is typically by clinical history, while PLMD can be confirmed by polysomnography, or sleep study that measures limb movements. If either of these conditions are suspected, evaluation by a trained sleep specialist is important.

Narcolepsy and Hypersomnia

Although less common, excessive daytime sleepiness may be a sign of narcolepsy. Narcolepsy is a long-term neurological disorder that involves a decreased ability to regulate sleep/wake cycles due to a deficiency of hypocretin (orexin), a neurotransmitter that regulates wakefulness. Narcolepsy can be accompanied by cataplexy, which is a sudden, brief loss of muscle tone triggered by strong emotion, usually mirth or laughter. It is lifelong; however, it can be managed by pharmacotherapy and strategic napping. Idiopathic hypersomnia can present clinically similar to narcolepsy, however, without the genetic marker or hypocretin/orexin deficiency.

Countermeasures to Excessive Sleepiness

With the importance of sleep well established, physicians should make a concerted effort to enact countermeasures to sleep deprivation and sleepiness. The most effective countermeasure for sleepiness is sleep (Avidan 2013; Buysse et al. 2003; Luyster et al. 2012; Papp et al. 2004; Shea et al. 2014). When possible, physicians should seek out opportunities to increase sleep opportunity and sleep ability. Table 15.2 outlines recommended countermeasures to sleepiness and fatigue. Countermeasures including strategic use of caffeine, bright light, and good sleep habits, as well as sleep and alertness aids which can help improve overall alertness, sleep quality, and performance at work.

A specific word on caffeine: Caffeine has been identified as the most popular or commonly used countermeasure to sleepiness and reduced alertness. It has been shown to improve alertness, reduce reaction time, and reduce error rates in night shift workers (Ker et al. 2010). Strategic use of caffeine is important to optimize the positive effects, while minimizing the side effects. Coffee/tea are considered superior sources over soda, energy drinks, or pills. Caffeine also increases your core body temperature, which reduces sleepiness. Green tea specifically can provide sustained alertness with less risk for jitteriness. L-theanine has synergistic effects with caffeine, so improved alertness can be achieved with a decreased caffeine dose. Green tea might be a better option over coffee for those more prone to feeling nervous or shaky with coffee.

Case Illustration 15.1

Brandon is an otherwise healthy 30-year-old internal medicine resident. He is 1 week into his night-float rotation and feels exhausted. He will start his shift around 6 pm and will stay up all night, sipping on an energy drink through the night. To remain alert during morning sign out of patients at 7 am, he drinks a cup of coffee at 6 am.

He leaves the hospital around 7:45 am and walks home, enjoying the sun's warmth on his face. Once he gets home, he is unable to fall asleep for several more hours, so he watches TV and checks email to relax. He finally falls asleep around 12:30 pm. When his alarm goes off at 5 pm, he feels exhausted. He quickly showers, eats, and gets ready for his night shift starting again at 6 pm.

Question: What countermeasures could Brandon incorporate into his daily routine to help him feel more rested at work?

Case Illustration 15.2
Mark is a 45-year-old nephrologist who is part of a busy practice at a local academic center. Now, with two children, he has less time to exercise and has noted a 30-pound weight gain since completing his fellowship a few years ago. His wife complains that he snores loudly at night; however, he doesn't believe that it is all that bad. He does wake up with a dry mouth and occasional headache. Despite getting 7–8 hours of sleep each night, he complains of feeling sleepy through the days and drinks 3–4 cups of coffee just to function. He has cut out alcohol from his diet, thinking he just "can't handle a beer like he used to," but he continues to feel tired each morning.

Question: What should be Mark's next steps? Is he at risk for any primary sleep disorder?

Conclusion

In summary, adequate sleep is important for the optimal functioning and performance of humans. Physicians face several intrinsic and extrinsic factors that threaten the optimization and enjoyment of sleep, and it is important for physicians to make purposeful and deliberate decisions to prioritize sleep and recovery, especially before and after times of unavoidable sleep deprivation. The countermeasures noted above can help mitigate the damaging effects of sleep loss.

References

Avidan AY (2013) Sleep and fatigue countermeasures for the neurology resident and physician. Continuum 19(1 Sleep Disorders):204–22.

Baldwin DC Jr, Daugherty SR, Ryan P, Yaghmour NA (2010). Changes in resident work and sleep hours 1999 to 2009: results from a survey of 4 specialties. J. Grad. Med. Educ 2(4):656–8.

Belayachi J, Benjelloun O, Madani N, Abidi K, Dendane T, Zeggwagh AA, et al. (2013) Self-perceived sleepiness in emergency training physicians: prevalence and relationship with quality of life. J. Occup. Med. Toxicol 8(1):24.

Besedovsky L, Lange T, Born J (2012) Sleep and immune function. Pflugers Arch. 463(1):121–37.

Bolster L, Rourke L (2015) The Effect of Restricting Residents' Duty Hours on Patient Safety, Resident Well-Being, and Resident Education: An Updated Systematic Review. J. Grad. Med. Educ. 7(3):349–63.

Bonnet MH, Arand DL (2003). Clinical effects of sleep fragmentation versus sleep deprivation. Sleep Med. Rev. 7(4):297–310.

Buysse DJ, Barzansky B, Dinges D, Hogan E, Hunt CE, Owens J, et al.(2003) Sleep, fatigue, and medical training: setting an agenda for optimal learning and patient care. Sleep 26(2):218–25.

Carskadon MA, Dement WC (2005) Normal human sleep: an overview. In: Kryger M, Roth T, Dement WC (eds.): Principles and practice of sleep medicine. Elsevier, Philadelphia, pp 13–23.

Centers for Disease Control and Prevention (CDC) (2011) Effect of short sleep duration on daily activitiesDOUBLEHYPHE-NUnited States, 2005-2008. MMWR Morb. Mortal. Wkly. Rep. 60(8):239–42.

Eddy R (2005) Sleep deprivation among physicians. BCMJ 47(4):176–180.

Fung MM, Peters K, Redline S, Ziegler MG, Ancoli-Israel S, Barrett-Connor E, et al. (2011) Decreased slow wave sleep increases risk of developing hypertension in elderly men. Hypertension 58(4):596–603.

Grandner MA (2017) Sleep, Health, and Society. Sleep Med Clin 12(1):1–22.

Hirshkowitz M, Whiton K, Albert SM, Alessi C, Bruni O, DonCarlos L, et al.(2015) National Sleep Foundation's sleep time duration recommendations: methodology and results summary. Sleep Health 1(1):40–3.

Howard SK (2005) Sleep deprivation and physician performance: why should I care? Proc (Bayl Univ Med Cent). 18(2):108–12; discussion 112–3.

Jamal MH, Wong S, Whalen TV (2014) Effects of the reduction of surgical residents' work hours and implications for surgical residency programs: a narrative review. BMC Med. Educ. 14 Suppl 1:S14.

Kalmbach DA, Arnedt JT, Song PX, Guille C, Sen S (2017) Sleep Disturbance and Short Sleep as Risk Factors for Depression and Perceived Medical Errors in First-Year Residents. Sleep [Internet]. Mar 23; Available from: https://doi.org/10.1093/sleep/zsw073.

Ker K, Edwards PJ, Felix LM, Blackhall K, Roberts I (2010) Caffeine for the prevention of injuries and errors in shift workers. Cochrane Database Syst. Rev (5):CD008508.

Krause AJ, Simon EB, Mander BA, Greer SM, Saletin JM, Goldstein-Piekarski AN, et al. (2017) The sleep-deprived human brain. Nat. Rev. Neurosci 18(7):404–18.

Kryger MH, Roth T, Dement WC (2015) Principles and Practice of Sleep Medicine. 5th ed. St. Louis: Elsevier Health Sciences

Landrigan CP, Rothschild JM, Cronin JW, Kaushal R, Burdick E, Katz JT, et al. (2004) Effect of reducing interns' work hours on serious medical errors in intensive care units. N. Engl. J. Med. 351(18):1838–48.

Luyster FS, Strollo PJ Jr, Zee PC, Walsh JK, Boards of Directors of the American Academy of Sleep Medicine and the Sleep Research Society (2012) Sleep: a health imperative. Sleep 35(6): 727–34.

Maslach C, Jackson SE (1981) The measurement of experienced burnout. J. Organ. Behav 2(2):99–113.

Mathur R, Douglas NJ (1995) Frequency of EEG arousals from nocturnal sleep in normal subjects. Sleep 18(5):330–3.

McCormick F, Kadzielski J, Landrigan CP, Evans B, Herndon JH, Rubash HE (2012) Surgeon fatigue: a prospective analysis of the incidence, risk, and intervals of predicted fatigue-related impairment in residents. Arch. Surg. 147(5):430–5.

Olson EJ, Drage LA, Auger RR (2009) Sleep deprivation, physician performance, and patient safety. Chest. 136(5):1389–96.

Panagioti M, Panagopoulou E, Bower P, Lewith G, Kontopantelis E, Chew-Graham C, et al. (2017) Controlled Interventions to Reduce Burnout in Physicians: A Systematic Review and Meta-analysis. JAMA Intern. Med 177(2):195–205.

Papp KK, Stoller EP, Sage P, Aikens JE, Owens J, Avidan A, et al. (2004) The Effects of Sleep Loss and Fatigue on Resident–Physicians: A Multi-Institutional, Mixed-Method Study. Acad. Med. 79(5):394.

Parshuram CS, Amaral ACKB, Ferguson ND, Baker GR, Etchells EE, Flintoft V, et al. (2015) Patient safety, resident well-being and continuity of care with different resident duty schedules in the intensive care unit: a randomized trial. CMAJ. 187(5):321–9.

Peppard PE, Young T, Barnet JH, Palta M, Hagen EW, Hla KM (2013) Increased Prevalence of Sleep-Disordered Breathing in Adults. Am. J. Epidemiol. 177(9):1006–14.

Poudel GR, Innes CRH, Bones PJ, Watts R, Jones RD (2014) Losing the struggle to stay awake: divergent thalamic and cortical activity during microsleeps. Hum. Brain Mapp 35(1):257–69.

Regehr C, Glancy D, Pitts A, LeBlanc VR (2014) Interventions to reduce the consequences of stress in physicians: a review and meta-analysis. J. Nerv. Ment. Dis. 202(5):353–9.

Rothschild JM, Keohane CA, Rogers S, Gardner R, Lipsitz SR, Salzberg CA, et al. (2009) Risks of complications by attending physicians after performing nighttime procedures. JAMA 302(14):1565–72.

Schrijver I, Brady KJS, Trockel M (2016) An exploration of key issues and potential solutions that impact physician wellbeing and professional fulfillment at an academic center. Peer J. 4:e1783.

Shea JA, Dinges DF, Small DS, Basner M, Zhu J, Norton L, et al. (2014) A Randomized Trial of a Three-Hour Protected Nap Period in a Medicine Training Program: Sleep, Alertness, and Patient Outcomes. Acad. Med. 89(3):452–9.

Sheldon SH, Kryger MH, Ferber R, Gozal D (2014) Principles and Practice of Pediatric Sleep Medicine E-Book. London/New York/Oxford/Philadelphia/St Louis/Sydney/Toronto: Elsevier Health Sciences

Taillard J, Philip P, Coste O, Sagaspe P, Bioulac B (2003) The circadian and homeostatic modulation of sleep pressure during wakefulness differs between morning and evening chronotypes. J. Sleep Res 12(4):275–82.

Tucker P, Bejerot E, Kecklund G, Aronsson G, Åkerstedt T (2015) The impact of work time control on physicians' sleep and well-being. Appl. Ergon 47:109–16.

Van Dongen HP, Maislin G, Mullington JM, Dinges DF (2003) The Cumulative Cost of Additional Wakefulness: Dose-Response Effects on Neurobehavioral Functions and Sleep Physiology From Chronic Sleep Restriction and Total Sleep Deprivation. Sleep 2:117–26.

West CP, Dyrbye LN, Erwin PJ, Shanafelt TD (2016) Interventions to prevent and reduce physician burnout: a systematic review and meta-analysis. Lancet 388(10057):2272–81.

West CP, Dyrbye LN, Shanafelt TD (2018) Physician Burnout: Contributors, Consequences, and Solutions. J. Intern. Med. [Internet]. 2018 Mar 5; Available from: https://doi.org/10.1111/joim.12752.

West CP, Tan AD, Habermann TM, Sloan JA, Shanafelt TD (2009) Association of resident fatigue and distress with perceived medical errors. JAMA 302(12):1294–300.

Index

© Springer Nature Switzerland AG 2019
L. Weiss Roberts, M. Trockel (eds.),
The Art and Science of Physician Wellbeing,
https://doi.org/10.1007/978-3-319-42135-3